INTERPERSONAL COMMUNICATION
Where Minds Meet

INTERPERSONAL COMMUNICATION
Where Minds Meet

Kathleen K. Reardon

UNIVERSITY OF SOUTHERN CALIFORNIA

HEALTH BEHAVIOR RESEARCH INSTITUTE

WADSWORTH PUBLISHING COMPANY

Belmont, California

A Division of Wadsworth, Inc.

Communications Editor: Kris Clerkin
Editorial Associate: Naomi Brown
Production Editor: Lisa Danchi
Print Buyer: Barbara Britton
Text and Cover Designer: Lisa Mirski
Copy Editor: Pat Tompkins
Compositor: Kachina Typesetting
Signing Representative: Patricia O'Hare

Cover painting: *Interlude* by Milton Avery, 1960, oil on canvas. Provided courtesy of The Philadelphia Museum of Art; given by The Woodward Foundation: Centennial Gifts.

Photographs: Tim Davis

Printed in the United States of America

1 2 3 4 5 6 7 8 9 10---91 90 89 88 87

ISBN 0-534-07182-1

Library of Congress Cataloging-in-Publication Data

Reardon, Kathleen Kelley,
    Interpersonal communication.

    Includes index.

    1. Interpersonal communication.
2. Communication.   I. Title.
BF637.C45R42   1987   153.6   86-19025
ISBN 0-534-07182-1

To my brother Kevin

Contents

CHAPTER THREE
The History of Interpersonal Communication / 19

CHAPTER FOUR
The Young Communicator / 49

CHAPTER FIVE
Interpersonal Communication Competence / 73

Foreword

I have a bookshelf or two in my office filled with textbooks on interpersonal communication. None of them tell me much about the history of this important subdiscipline. While each of these texts contains a great deal of conventional wisdom, much of it is not based on research findings. When research is cited in these books, it is usually psychological research that looks mainly at individual differences rather than communication research concerned with human relationships and information exchange. Further, many of the interpersonal communication textbooks in my office deal with specific subfields, such as persuasion, conversation analysis, and communication competence. There is little integration of theory and research across the specialities within interpersonal communication.

Interpersonal Communication: Where Minds Meet is a book that overcomes these shortcomings of past volumes on interpersonal communication. My colleague Kathy Reardon has written a comprehensive text that represents a unique approach to interpersonal communication. She tells us the history of this subdiscipline so that newcomer and veteran alike can better understand where we came from and how we got to where we are today. The present volume represents a relational approach to interpersonal communication, looking at the process of information exchange between two or more individuals. The overdependence of the subdiscipline in the past on psychology has been overcome here. A more appropriate way of understanding interpersonal communication is to focus on communication relationships as units of analysis, rather than just on individuals. The generalizations and principles stated here are based on evidence from communication research. Finally, this book in an integrative synthesis across the main subfields of study in interpersonal communication, like persuasion, communication competence, communication and conversation development, relationships, health, small groups, and so on.

I used earlier drafts of the chapters of *Interpersonal Communication: Where Minds Meet* with my students in the Annenberg School of Communications at the University of Southern California. They reacted very favorably, attracted by the review of theory and research for each of the subfields of interpersonal communication. Students will like the examples and illustrations that provide a vehicle for the concepts and theories that are the intellectual core of *Where Minds Meet*.

So welcome to the subdiscipline of interpersonal communication. You are about to depart on a most interesting tour of this important topic.

Everett M. Rogers

Annenberg School of Communications
University of Southern California

Preface

The field of communication has matured significantly since the early 1970s when I was a graduate student. The books from that period typically focused on psychological and social psychological theory and research. The style of presentation was less sophisticated than that of communication books of this decade, in part because the field was young. When I decided to write *Interpersonal Communication: Where Minds Meet*, my intention was to help students understand how the study of interpersonal communication emerged and to provide them with an overview of the current theory and research that define the field today.

I chose the title *Where Minds Meet* not because minds actually meet during communication in the sense of reaching identical perceptions, but because interpersonal communication is the means by which two or more people share information and affect each other's thoughts and behaviors. As we all know, the result of our communication with others is often not what we had hoped it would be. When minds meet they do not always agree, but they always have the potential to share and mutually shape each other's perspectives. It is in this sense that minds meet in the course of interpersonal communication.

It is difficult if not impossible for any one book to do justice to an entire field of study. Interpersonal communication has roads where we might have tarried longer. Nevertheless, I hope that you will gain a sense of what we've learned over the years and that you will explore in greater depth areas you find of interest.

There are several people to whom I am indebted for their comments on this book and for their support while I was writing it. First, Chris, my husband and dearest constructive critic, contributed more than he may even realize by listening to me talk about each chapter and by offering suggestions that were invariably useful. Second, Kris Clerkin deserves my appreciation for her abiding faith in this project and for her determination to persuade me to undertake it. To Everett Rogers I extend my gratitude for several good suggestions and for the opportunity to test an earlier draft of *Where Minds Meet* with his students, to whom I also offer my appreciation for useful comments.

To Lisa Danchi and Lisa Mirski, who labored over the text to make every line meet their admirable standards—my appreciation. My gratitude goes to Art Bochner, who lessened my anxiety over not covering all topics by saying, "A book should be judged not by what it covers so much as by what it covers well," and who wrote a thorough review of an earlier draft. Thanks go to Al Sillars, who contributed valuable suggestions and a thought-provoking review that I found most useful in writing the final draft, and to Gerry Miller, for once again in my career giving me some useful insights into the writing of books in this field. And finally my appreciation goes to the individual chapter reviewers who shared their expertise with me: Karen Tracy, Temple University; Mary John Smith, University of Wyoming; Claudia Hale, Iowa State University; Gail Fairhust, University of Cincinnati, Janis Anderson, San Diego State University; Marshall Scott Poole, University of Minnesota; Brian Spitzberg, North Texas State University; Rebecca Rubin, Kent State University; Brant Burleson, Purdue University; Gerald Miller, Michigan State University; Mary Anne Fitzpatrick, University of Wisconsin at Madison; and Michael Scott, Chico State University.

Kathleen K. Reardon

Health Behavior Research Institute
University of Southern California

INTERPERSONAL COMMUNICATION
Where Minds Meet

CHAPTER 1

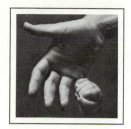

Introduction to the Study of Human Communication

Socrates insisted that words be defined carefully prior to their use in discussion. He believed this reduced ambiguity. Adhering to Socrates' dictum has proven one of the more challenging tasks facing scholars. People find it difficult—and sometimes impossible—to develop a shared definition of an important concept.

What Is Communication?

We often speak of **communication** as if we knew just what the term means. Journalists have described President Ronald Reagan as an "expert communicator," often neglecting to tell their audience what they meant by "communicator." To avoid this error of omission, this text begins with a discussion of six characteristics of human communication.

1. *People communicate for a variety of reasons.* We communicate to entertain, to impress, to be cordial, to gain information, to show interest, to persuade, and so on. We do not speak to others merely to hear the sound of our voices. For example, if you were alone in the elevator of a dark parking garage in a crime-ridden neighborhood, you might feel uncomfortable if a stranger entered the elevator. You might carefully observe his appearance and movements or speak to him in the hope of eliciting evidence of his nature and intentions. Or, when people ask,

"How are you?", they may be demonstrating their interest in you and seeking information. Should you respond, "Fine, and yourself?", you would provide information about your well-being and demonstrate a degree of social sensitivity.

Most people do not speak with others merely to hear the sound of their voices. They speak for many reasons. One reason is to gain information. If you were alone on an elevator in a dark parking garage in a crime-ridden neighborhood, the entrance of other people could either be comforting or unsettling. You might interpret their movements and appearance with a feeling of relief. You might greet them in the hope of eliciting further evidence of their intentions. In such a circumstance, communication would help you gain information necessary to self-protection.

Sometimes people talk just to lessen the discomfort caused by protracted silences. They communicate to develop and maintain relationships, to teach, to learn, or just to be sociable. Whatever the reason, communication enables us to convey information about the personal, intellectual, emotional, and social aspects of our selves.

2. *Communication may have intentional or unintentional effects.* What we say and do is not always interpreted as we intend. Sometimes absence of a particular action is interpreted in ways not intended by the person who failed to act in the expected manner. For example, the husband who forgets his wife's birthday may not intend to hurt her feelings, but his neglect demonstrates that her birthday is not sufficiently important for him to remember it.

3. *Communication is often reciprocal.* While one person is speaking, the other may display nonverbal cues of disinterest or deep interest. These cues communicate, even as the first person speaks. People may take turns speaking, but in most interpersonal situations, they communicate simultaneously. Even when one person is monopolizing a conversation, the expressions, vocalizations, and gestures of the other provide reciprocal information. Mass communication and some interpersonal communication such as letters and telephone conversations are often less reciprocal than face-to-face interaction.

4. *Communication involves at least two people who, to varying degrees, influence each other's actions.* People communicate with, rather than to, each other. In the 1960s a commonly accepted perspective of communication was a source conveying a message via a channel—memo, record, or television, for example—*to* some receiver. With sufficient message clarity and little interference, the receiver was considered likely to interpret the source's message with a reasonable degree of accuracy. Recently, communication scholars have altered their perspective. Communication is now considered an activity in which no action or utterance is meaningful except as it is interpreted by the people involved. Together, com-

municators create meaning, rather than merely transfer it intact to each other.

Could human communication be otherwise? No doubt you have had the uncomfortable experience of having your words completely misinterpreted. Meaning is not solely dependent on accurate word choice and lack of interference. It is the product of at least two persons' responses to each other's verbal and nonverbal behavior.

5. *Communication need not be successful to have occurred.* In this sense it resembles many other activities. You may win or lose a tennis game, but in either case you have played tennis. In like fashion, even when you cry in frustration, "We're not communicating!", you are indeed communicating. Whether or not communicators accomplish their goals, they are engaged in communication. Communication is what we do when we express our thoughts and feelings verbally or nonverbally to others. Whether we do so effectively is another matter.

6. *Communication involves the use of symbols.* Words and many gestures are symbols. They refer to thoughts and feelings. To the extent that communicators share similar meanings for the symbols they use, communication is facilitated. One of the major challenges of human communication, however, is that people often have different meanings for the same symbols.

What Do We Communicate?

If people do not communicate intact meanings, what do they communicate? They communicate messages that are potentially meaningful and informative. The meaning of these messages is influenced by the denotation and connotation of words.

Messages

All **messages** consist of sets of symbols. **Symbols** are words, gestures, figures, sounds, or movements that are useful because the persons using them more or less agree about the objects, events, and feelings to which they refer. The word *house,* for example, means nothing to people who do not know the English language. The word itself is merely a symbol used by English-speaking people to refer to a structure built for human occupancy. The word *home* may refer to a house but need not be a house. For many people, home means much more than a structure for human occupancy. It may mean one's birthplace or where one's family dwells.

We often use words as if everyone with whom we interact shares exactly the same meaning as we do. In reality, we can consider ourselves fortunate if the person with whom we are conversing understands a large proportion of our meanings. Even so, words and gestures are the best vehicles we have for most types of communication. Mozart preferred musical notes, Picasso chose paint on canvas. Most of us, however, must rely on words and nonverbal expressions that do not serve us well unless the people with whom we communicate understand our meanings for at least some of the words and gestures we employ.

Information and Meaning

Messages can be informative and meaningful. The arrangement of symbols in "That dog bites" is likely to be informative if the person approaching the dog is unaware of the dog's aggressive tendencies. If this person already knows that the dog bites, the message has meaning but is uninformative.

According to information theory, which quantifies information by determining its value based on what it contributes to prior knowledge, messages must reduce uncertainty in order to constitute information. Messages that convey information are those that make the choice among alternative actions easier (Krippendorff, 1975). The person who receives the warning "That dog bites" receives information if she was unaware of the dog's aggressiveness and if the newly acquired knowledge assists her in deciding how to respond. The warning "That dog bites, so don't take another step" is even more informative because it renders one behavioral option, continuing to walk toward the dog, ineffective.

Early models of communication treated information as an object passed from one person to another via a channel—for example, face-to-face or via mass media. According to these models, given few distractions and reasonable communication skills, the receiver of information could understand the source's meaning. More recent models of communication view communicators as "in the business of prediction" (Kelly, 1955) or "sense makers" (Dervin, 1983). People attend to information relevant to their needs and desires. The meaning they derive from the information depends on how they integrate it with their past experiences. They shape it to fit their own needs and expectations.

An analogy may be useful here. Models of communication that treat information as an object passed between people create an image of information similar to that of a brick. If nothing happens to interfere with the passing of the brick from one person to the other, the interaction is successful. More recent models reject this image in favor of one that treats information as easily reshaped by the person receiving it. Information is more like clay than brick (Dervin, 1983). Clay can be shaped and molded, while a brick, which began as flexible clay, has a set form. The information passed from one person to another is transformed into a shape that suits the needs and desires of the receiver.

In the course of communication, people share and shape information.

Each person's contribution to the shape of the shared message affects the contribution the other may make. In terms of our clay analogy, the shape one person gives the clay limits the types of shaping the other might perform. If Person A shapes the clay into a four-legged creature, Person B will likely use that form as a base from which to add his contribution. Person B may add a long tail, thereby limiting the type of four-legged animal they will create together. Of course, one person may totally reject the other's contribution. In terms of our example, Person A may remove part of the tail and insist that the animal have a short tail. Should Person B accept this revision, the interaction may continue in a cooperative manner. Should he reject A's revision, the interaction is threatened. They will either renegotiate their course of action or cease to interact.

Denotation and Connotation

One major obstacle to the sharing of information is that people often derive different meanings from the same words and actions. Meanings are in people, not in words. Some people heed warnings while others do not because they interpret what they see or hear differently. Meaning, like beauty, is in the eye of the beholder. This is one of the primary reasons why people experience difficulty communicating. In 1984, when Vice President George Bush told a crowd of people, "We kicked a little ass yesterday," referring to his televised debate with Democratic opponent Geraldine Ferraro, some people considered that remark crude and unbecoming for a vice president. Others thought Bush was just being "one of the guys." Bush opted for the latter interpretation and refused to apologize to Ferraro. Meanings are not in words; they are in the people who use and interpret them.

Two types of meaning involved in communication are denotative and connotative. **Denotative meanings** are shared descriptive meanings. In the dictionary, we can find the denotative meanings of *love,* for example. **Connotative meanings** are personal meanings, not so easily identified and not necessarily shared with others. The word *love* is subject to numerous personal interpretations; it is fraught with connotations: from affection to obsession, from brotherly to marital, from platonic to sexual. Therefore, *love* is often a difficult word to use with confidence. It may elicit very different meanings for different people and in different situations. Similarly, the words *slender* and *skinny* may share the same denotation but have quite different connotations. *Slender* is a more positive description of underweight people.

The variety of meanings for most words makes communication a challenge and an interesting phenomenon of study. Try to imagine a world in which there were only denotative meanings. People would understand each other perfectly, but there would be no personal expression. Conversation would be very dull indeed.

How Do We Construct Messages?

The construction of a message requires certain types of knowledge. From childhood people are taught how to use their language, how to read situations and people, and when it is appropriate to deliver messages.

Grammar

To elicit some semblance of shared meaning when we communicate with others, we must know how to arrange our symbols in the most effective manner. To accomplish this difficult task, we use our knowledge of grammar, of other persons, and of the situation. Grammar is a set of rules for language usage. Without an awareness of the rules for constructing coherent sentences, human communication, as we know it, would be impossible. Consider this string of words: "ran store Bill me to the for." Your knowledge of grammar allows you to convert this incoherent jumble of words into the meaningful sentence "Bill ran to the store for me." Without grammatical construction, the use of verbal symbols is severely restricted.

Knowledge About the Other Person

Knowledge of grammar is only one asset in the successful construction and sharing of meaning. Knowledge about the person or persons for whom the message is intended is usually indispensable. Communication scholars as far back as Aristotle have been aware of the need to adjust the message to the audience. Imagine the response of dentists to a colleague who addresses them in the same style she uses with young patients: "Fellow dentists, I want to tell you today about a really neat new way to fight mean old Mr. Tooth Decay and avoid big nasty holes in your little teeth." The knowledge we have about other people and our relationships with them influence the way we construct our messages.

Knowledge About the Situation

Finally, knowledge about the situation influences message construction. For example, people who lecture others at informal parties rather than participating in casual conversation often find themselves sitting alone. Situations also indicate which types of messages are appropriate. A classroom lecture is not the place to ask a friend to help you wash your car. Churches are not usually proper places for outbursts of raucous laughter.

Messages are the result of accumulated knowledge about how to arrange symbols grammatically as well as when and with whom to use them. We know what to say and how to say it because of our past experiences. Of course, we make mistakes. You've no doubt heard people say, "I should have known better than to say that to him." As we come to know people, we learn how volatile they are and how much to monitor what we say to them.

Often our knowledge of grammar, people, and situations is incomplete. We sometimes phrase our ideas incorrectly or talk when we should listen. "Putting one's foot in one's mouth" aptly describes formulating messages on the basis of inadequate knowledge about the person or situation.

Fortunately, we repeatedly face many of the same types of events and situations. We know how to greet people and how to depart without offending them because we have learned to do so over the years. We take turns speaking in conversations, we whisper in libraries, we stand an appropriate distance from others, and we usually know how much talk is too much. We may not share exactly the same understanding of these rules of communication, but we are often "in the same ballpark" if the others involved are from our culture.

How Do We Study Communication?

Science is but one means of studying human communication. The painter, playwright, photographer, dancer, poet, and musician are all students of communication. Their work can inform and enlighten us about human behavior in ways as valid as those of science.

Interpersonal communication research is currently undergoing what has been called a "crisis in confidence" concerning methods of study (Bochner, 1985). Scholars are discovering that the subject of interpersonal communication may be approached in several different ways. It has been primarily studied from an objective science approach where the researcher is an independent observer of human interaction. Such a researcher attempts to discover the truth or reality of interaction patterns by generating hypotheses from theory and testing them by experimental methods (see Poole & McPhee, 1985). Recently a number of social scientists have begun to claim that researchers can never be truly objective in their study of human behavior since they are human beings themselves. Moreover, some research questions about human communication do not lend themselves to "objective" methods of study.

This crisis in confidence over research methods has encouraged interpersonal communication scholars to be somewhat more accepting of less objective methods of research. Some researchers immerse themselves in their subject of study. For example, in an attempt to understand the rules of communication in a small town in Mexico, the researcher might live in that town and become what researchers call a participant-observer.

There are many ways to study interpersonal communication. The choice of method depends on the research goal. This does not excuse researchers from rigor in their investigations. Good research blends rigor and creativity. As Bateson (1972, p. 75) explained, "As I see it, the advances in scientific thought come from a combination of loose and strict thinking and this combination is the most precious tool of science."

Summary

To the extent that you find human behavior intriguing, you are likely to be interested in the study of interpersonal communication. You will probably find yourself impressed with some theoretical perspectives and skeptical about others. Since no single text can do complete justice to any perspective that has taken years to develop and test, you might want to read further. We recommend that you refer to the reference section at the end of the book to guide you in your own exploration of interpersonal communication.

Each of the perspectives introduced in this text was selected because it has made an important contribution to the development of interpersonal communication study. Several of the perspectives were advanced by sociologists, psychologists, and social psychologists. More recent ones have been advanced by communication researchers. As Gerald Miller (1981) pointed out in a review of the communication field, there is a growing trend toward original theorizing by communication scholars. In this text we will focus on recent original theories and relevant research support. You will notice that there are often conflicting theories to explain the same phenomenon. As Karl Popper (1982) tells us, some events are like clouds and others like clocks. Clocks are predictable in part because they follow a mechanical routine; most clocks are similar. Clouds, on the other hand, take any number of unpredictable shapes. Some scientists might argue that the lack of cloud predictability reflects the complexity of weather conditions about which we currently know little; one day we may know as much about clouds as we do about clocks—then we will be able to predict their formations. Whether the behavior of clouds will ever be predictable at the same level of accuracy now achieved with clocks is something we are not likely to know for a long time. Similarly, whether human communication behavior will ever be as predictable as clocks is not to be answered soon. If you approach interpersonal communication with a healthy tolerance for the disagreement among researchers characteristic of a young field, you are likely to come away with a positive view of its future. After all, the subject is one of the most complex and fascinating on earth: human interaction.

CHAPTER 2

Characteristics of
Interpersonal Communication

Until quite recently, interpersonal communication was defined in terms of the characteristics of a situation—the number of people involved, their physical distance from each other, and the potential for feedback, for example. Interpersonal communication, from a situational perspective, is face-to-face interaction between two or several persons with the potential for immediate rather than delayed feedback, as in the case of letters.

New definitions have attempted to free the concept of interpersonal communication from purely situational descriptions. Miller and Steinberg (1975) argue that situational definitions treat interpersonal communication as a static phenomenon, one that does not develop. According to Miller and Steinberg, communication becomes more interpersonal as communicators become more familiar; they see interpersonal communication as a matter of degree. In other words, communication between strangers is less interpersonal than communication between friends. Friends know each other well. Each friend knows a fair amount about the way the other tends to think and feel about a variety of topics. Thus friends' interactions are more interpersonal than those of strangers. Interpersonal communication *develops* as people get to know each other better.

However, a purely developmental definition of interpersonal communication is not without its drawbacks (Bochner, 1978). After all, how do we, as observers, know when two or more persons know each other personally rather than superficially? At what point can we confidently say that a particular interaction is interpersonal? At what point does interpersonal communication begin? Despite the static nature of situational descriptions of interpersonal communication, they do tell us what is and is not interpersonal communication.

Perhaps what we need is an integration of situational and developmental perspectives. While recognizing that interpersonal communication is developmental—that communication between strangers is not the same as communication between friends—we can also specify characteristics that separate interpersonal communication from other forms of communication. Here are seven key attributes that distinguish interpersonal communication:

1. Interpersonal communication involves verbal and nonverbal behaviors.
2. Interpersonal communication involves spontaneous, scripted, or contrived behaviors or some combination of them.
3. Interpersonal communication is not static but developmental.
4. Interpersonal communication involves personal feedback, interaction, and coherence.
5. Interpersonal communication is guided by intrinsic and extrinsic rules.
6. Interpersonal communication is an activity.
7. Interpersonal communication may involve persuasion.

Nonverbal and Verbal Communication

Most interpersonal communication involves verbal and nonverbal behaviors. Human communication is not merely a function of words. Communication has both content and relational components. The **content component** consists of what is said or done. The **relational component** consists of how it is said or done (see Watzlawick, Beavin, & Jackson, 1967).

Imagine for a moment how you might tell someone that you love him or her. How would your face look as you said the words "I love you"? Would you have a broad grin on your face? Would your body be slouched in a chair? Would your voice be loud or soft? You know the answers to these questions because you know how to use your body and voice to complement or contradict what you say. The way you say something is at least as important as what you say. It conveys a relational message indicating how the content "I love you" should be interpreted.

Interpersonal communication usually gives participants ample opportunities to observe each other's nonverbal behaviors while also listening to each other's words. Nonverbal communication is important to interpersonal communication because it can complement, contradict, exaggerate, regulate, or dismiss the verbal content of a message. Verbal content can do the same to the content of a nonverbal message. As with verbal behavior, nonverbal behavior can signal interpersonal closeness or repulsion. It can convey warmth, enthusiasm, friendliness, and other dispositions. Both nonverbal and verbal behaviors are fundamental to interpersonal communication.

Spontaneous, Scripted, and Contrived Behavior

When we communicate with others, we may consciously consider our every action, we may say whatever comes to mind, or we may combine conscious consideration with spontaneity. The method we choose depends, among other things, upon the importance of the interaction to our goals, how familiar we are with the person(s) and situation, and our mood. In other words, the amount of conscious thought we put into a verbal or nonverbal behavior determines whether it is spontaneous, scripted, or contrived.

Most of us prefer to consider ourselves primarily rational rather than emotional beings. We like to think that our actions are the result of reason rather than emotion. Social scientists are no exception. They have historically preferred to view communication as a primarily cognitive, rather than an emotional, activity. Most current models of interpersonal communication focus on people's conscious choices and ignore their spontaneous, emotional behaviors (see Buck, 1984).

Yet no conclusive evidence supports the contention that people are more rational than emotional in their interpersonal interactions. Since we are relatively advanced beings, we are capable of monitoring much of our emotional behavior to make it appear rational. We can often suppress emotions like anger, sadness, jealousy, and joy. But this does not mean we are more rational than emotional. As adept as we might sometimes be at controlling our emotions, few of us are capable of constant control. Occasionally we act before we have a chance to think. When we attempt to suppress an emotional reaction, our tone of voice, posture, or facial expression may reveal our true feelings.

Behavior that is elicited by emotion and is free of cognitive revision is spontaneous communication. It can be verbal or nonverbal. Have you ever suddenly shouted, "Shut up!"? Have you ever tilted your head when you were confused or jumped into the air with joy? These are examples of spontaneous behavior. They occur without cognitive meddling. They bypass the mind's scrutiny and result from unbridled emotion.

A second type of interpersonal behavior is scripted behavior. Abelson (1976, p. 33) defines a script as a "highly stylized sequence of typical events in a well understood situation." Behaviors that you have learned so well that they are elicited without conscious thought are scripted. Greetings such as "Hi. How are you?" are often said automatically—without conscious consideration of the meaning and without concern for the answer.

According to Langer (1978), people conduct much of their daily lives in a "mindless" state. Thinking and reasoning can be exhausting. Thus people consciously consider their behavior only when the situation requires it. Of course, some people are more aware and critical of their behaviors than others. These people are high self-monitors. These highly self-conscious people rely less on scripts than other people do (see Snyder, 1974; Roloff, 1980).

The major difference between spontaneous and scripted behavior is that scripted behaviors are learned and practiced until they become automatic. They are culture specific. Spontaneous behaviors, on the other hand, are reactions to emotions that can be observed in the communication of human beings across cultures. Sadness, joy, and anger are a few of the primary emotions that elicit spontaneous behavior. Even attempts to suppress these behaviors can fail if the emotion is sufficiently strong. By contrast, scripted behaviors are learned behaviors that through repetition become automatic responses to specific environmental cues. "Hello, how are you?" is an environmental cue for the scripted response, "Fine, and you?"

The third type of interpersonal behavior is contrived. These are behaviors chosen because they seem appropriate to the situation at hand. Contrived behaviors involve greater amounts of cognitive effort than scripted and spontaneous behaviors. They are reasoned behaviors.

Because human beings have relatively advanced mental capacities, we are able to contrive responses to others' comments even as they speak. We are able to think ahead to how the other person might respond to the behavior we plan to enact. For example, if someone asks your opinion on nuclear weapons, you may consider the purpose of his question before you respond. If this person is interviewing you for a job in the weapons industry, you may decide to downplay any negative thoughts you have about nuclear weapons. Instead, you might emphasize your positive thoughts about national security.

During any interpersonal encounter, we can observe spontaneous, scripted, or contrived behaviors or some combination of the three types. If the topic of discussion is an emotional one, the participants are likely to engage in much spontaneous behavior. If the encounter is brief and very familiar, it may be characterized by predominantly scripted behavior. If the situation is not familiar to the participants, they are likely to use much contrived behavior. Novel situations, such as meeting future in-laws for the first time, tend to require much conscious monitoring of actions—much contrived behavior.

Interpersonal Communication as a Developmental Process

The third attribute of interpersonal communication is its developmental rather than static nature. Here we borrow from Miller and Steinberg's (1975) perspective. By **developmental** we mean that interpersonal encounters vary according to the nature of the relationship between or among the parties involved. Miller and Steinberg explain that people meeting for the first time have only descriptive (superficial) knowledge about each other. Each of them knows little about the other aside from observable attributes. After they have gotten to know one another better, their interpersonal encounters are likely to be increasingly based on **predictive knowledge—** that is, each person has some knowledge of the other's beliefs and behavioral preferences. As the relationship progresses, they become privy to each other's reasons for believing and acting as they do. This is known as **explanatory knowledge.**

The point is that interpersonal communication differs according to familiarity between the participants. As people get to know each other, they can more accurately predict one another's actions. People can use accumulated knowledge about others to determine how they should express their thoughts and feelings to achieve their communication goals. For example, knowing that a particular friend is easily distracted, you might decide to tell him important information in private to ensure his attention.

Personal Feedback, Interaction, and Coherence

For interpersonal communication to occur and succeed, participants must respond to each other, using nonverbal and verbal behaviors which are logically related to (a) prior events in the interaction and (b) the overall purpose of the interaction. They must employ at least minimal amounts of feedback, interaction, and coherence.

Personal feedback refers to one communicator's verbal and nonverbal responses to the verbal and nonverbal actions of another. By including feedback in our definition, we exclude unanswered letters from interpersonal communication. Such letters may be personal communication, but they are not interpersonal communication. The latter requires at least two people—one who initiates communication and one who responds. *Personal* feedback, unlike much mass media communication, is directed at some particular person or persons rather than an aggregate of unidentified people.

Interpersonal communication also involves some level of *inter*action between the participants. (Remember that the prefix *inter-* means between or among.) **Interaction** refers to communication in which the action of one person influences the actions of the other(s). When two people interact, the behavior of the second depends, to some extent, on the behavior of the first. In the following example, Mary's remarks were influenced by Jim's question.

Jim: What's new, Mary?
Mary: Not much. How about you?

Mary might have said, "Where were you?" That would be feedback but not interaction because "Where were you?" does not address Jim's question. Interaction requires the interdependence of verbal and nonverbal behavior.

Let's look at two ways that Jim and Mary's conversation might proceed if Mary were to respond to Jim with "Where were you?" Example A represents the absence of interaction; Example B represents interaction:

Example A *(No interaction)*	*Example B* *(Interaction)*
Jim: What's new, Mary?	*Jim:* What's new, Mary?
Mary: Where were you?	*Mary:* Where were you?
Jim: Nothing new, huh?	*Jim:* Oh no! I forgot! I'm really sorry.
Mary: I said, where were you?	*Mary:* You should be. I waited for an hour.
Jim: Nothing new with me either.	*Jim:* I'll make it up to you. I promise.
Mary: I waited for an hour.	

In Example A, Mary and Jim are talking past each other. They might as well be miles apart. Occasionally people do talk past each other. However, most conversations are characterized by some level of interaction. Example B has a considerable amount of interaction.

Conversations vary in amount of interaction. To the extent that each person's comments are related to the comments of the other, interaction occurs. To the extent that the people involved say what they wish without regard for the comments of others, interaction is lacking.

Interpersonal communication also involves **coherence.** While interaction depends on immediately prior actions, coherence is largely a matter of the fit of a remark with the whole of the conversation, both in terms of an immediately prior utterance and to the conversation to date (McLaughlin, 1984). In other words, conversations have goals to which the individual comments of each participant should be related. The following conversation demonstrates how coherence may be achieved even if the topic is constantly shifting:

Mike: I went to the beach yesterday.
Fred: Great! I went there with Joan last week.
Mike: How is Joan?
Fred: She's doing well. She's taking a lot of courses though.
Mike: That can be miserable. I'm overloaded myself this semester.
Fred: Speaking of misery, did you see that awful movie on TV last night?
Mike: No. I went out with Ben.
Fred: Talk about misery!

Notice that Mike and Fred are interacting. Even though the topic shifts frequently, each comment is related to something said earlier. For example, when Fred introduced Joan into the conversation, Mike dropped the topic of his beach trip to find out how Joan was doing. And when Fred introduced the topic of work overload, Mike picked up on it. Fred commented on Mike's work overload by calling it miserable. The topic then shifted to the misery of watching an awful movie. Mike indicated that he did not see the movie because he was out with Ben. Fred linked Ben to the topic of misery.

The remarks in this conversation are coherent because they fit with immediately prior comments and fit the conversation to date. Had Mike responded to Fred's mention of Joan with the comment, "You went with Joan? How could you do that? Joan is my girlfriend," the tone of the conversation would have shifted from idle banter to serious talk about dating the girlfriend of a friend. Had Fred responded to Mike's serious remark with the comment, "Joan really liked the beach," coherence would have been threatened. Mike might have then responded by saying, "This is not a joking matter, Fred." If Fred then said, "Okay, okay, let's decide whose girlfriend Joan is," coherence would be evident again. Coherence involves both interaction—relatedness of proximate verbal and nonverbal behaviors—and **global relatedness**—the ways verbal and nonverbal behaviors relate to the overall goal of the conversation to date (see Jacobs & Jackson, 1983).

Coherence devices, or strategies, are available to communicators. For example, the phrase "What you just said reminded me of . . ." is often used to change topics in a coherent fashion. Such phrases can be used to direct the course of conversation. As such, they are coherence devices (Sanders, 1983). They are used to create meaningful relations between otherwise disparate utterances.

When a conversation goes off the track because of misinterpretation or an inappropriate shift of topic, communicators can realign their comments with **accounts** or **disclaimers.** Accounts are excuses or justifications for inappropriate behavior. "I'm sorry, I thought you'd finished speaking" is an account. Communicators can use accounts to save conversations threatened by inappropriate actions (see Scott & Lyman, 1968). Disclaimers rectify or reinterpret potential problems in conversations. "I don't want you to think I'm rude, but I must change the topic" is an example of a disclaimer. It disclaims the negative attribute that would normally be associated with someone performing the behavior in question (Hewitt & Stokes, 1975).

Intrinsic and Extrinsic Rules in Communication

The fifth attribute of interpersonal communication is its dependence on rules that are intrinsic and extrinsic to relationships. **Intrinsic rules** are standards of behavior developed by people to guide how they communicate with each other. They are peculiar to a particular relationship. For example, two friends may avoid certain topics of discussion because their positions on those topics are at odds. These two friends have a relationship-intrinsic rule about acceptable and unacceptable topics of discussion. **Extrinsic rules** are imposed on the relationship by other people or by the situation. They are often social constraints. For example, two people who have only known each other briefly are not likely to discuss highly personal matters. This would be inappropriate given the early stage of their relationship.

Miller and Steinberg (1975) explain that as relationships develop, the communicators may negotiate and define many of the rules themselves. Thus the proportion of intrinsic to extrinsic rules increases as relationships develop. Close relationships are characterized by idiosyncratic rule structures. For example, a married couple might bring two cars to a party so one of them can stay later than the other. Another couple may take one car but have an agreement concerning how late they will stay. Both have intrinsic rules for time spent at parties.

Every relationship is a blend of intrinsic and extrinsic rules. The newer the relationship, the more dependence there is on extrinsic rules such as social norms and role expectations. According to Miller (1978), relationship development involves concern for perceiving and responding to the other as an individual.

Interpersonal Communication as an Activity

The sixth characteristic of interpersonal communication is that it is something people do *with* each other, not *to* each other. It is an activity.

Prior to the latter half of the 1970s, communication scholars typically focused their studies on communication outcomes—for example, on whether a message was correctly interpreted by the receiver. They wrote of "communication breakdowns," occasions when communication stopped

because the people involved were unable to effectively convey their meanings. Theorists described communication as starting with a source and
ending with a receiver. This perspective was a product of the behaviorist,
stimulus-response view of communication behavior. This cause-effect
orientation led communication scientists to view communication in terms
of a series of now's and then's. More recent views (Millar & Rogers, 1976;
Berlo, 1977; Reardon, 1981; Parks, 1985) suggest that communication is an
activity. That is, communication, whether interpersonal or mass, is much
like a game in which the moves of each player affect the moves of the other
players. They do not do something to each other, but rather with each
other.

Football provides a useful analogy here. Football is an activity people
play with each other, not at or to each other. In football, the moves of each
player may be guided by some team-determined decision, but one or more
players on the other team may behave in a manner that renders the
decision useless. If the quarterback is tackled before he has a chance to pass
the ball, the team's play plan becomes useless. Similarly, communicators
may have some idea of how they will approach a topic, but the actions of
others can render their plans useless. Interpersonal communication is an
activity in which each participant may shape the outcome. Communication
can occur whether the outcome is expected or unexpected. Communication need not break down or stop when unexpected events occur. It may
continue on another course. Thus communication is an activity, not an
outcome.

Viewing interpersonal communication as an activity in which the participants shape the outcome of each interaction has come to be known as the
relational view of interpersonal communication (see Watzlawick, Beavin, &
Jackson, 1967; Millar & Rogers, 1976; Parks, 1985). From this perspective,
the unit of analysis for communication research is the relationship rather
than the individual source or receiver of a message. The focus is on what
people do with, not to, each other during interaction.

Interpersonal Persuasion in Communication

The last of the seven characteristics of interpersonal communication listed
at the start of this chapter concerns persuasion, a form of communication.
Interpersonal persuasion occurs when the interactants encourage each
other to change their thoughts, feelings, or behaviors relevant to some
topic of discussion.

Until quite recently, communication scholars tended to view persuasion
as something one person does *to* another rather than *with* another. From
this perspective, effective persuaders change passive persuadees. Only the
persuaded person changes. Today communication scholars realize that

when one person attempts to change the thoughts, feelings, or behaviors of another, that person often ends up changing her own thoughts, feelings, or behaviors. Remember, interpersonal communication involves interaction. The persuadee typically responds to the persuader. His response may be an attempt to change the thoughts, feelings, or behaviors of the persuader. In this way the persuadee becomes the persuader. In interpersonal persuasion, the roles of persuader and persuadee may alternate or occur for each person simultaneously. Interactants typically play both roles. Frequently, one person begins a conversation with the intention of persuading another to change, only to discover that the other person's perspective has considerable merit. In this sense, persuasion is a product of interaction.

Summary

Interpersonal communication involves verbal and nonverbal behaviors done with others, not to others. Such communication allows us to share our thoughts and feelings with others. Interpersonal communication involves spontaneous, scripted, and contrived behaviors. It is not static, but developmental. As people come to know each other, their interpersonal communication is increasingly characterized by intrinsic rules rather than extrinsic rules. Unlike much mass communication, interpersonal communication involves varying degrees of personal feedback, interaction, and coherence. It need not be successful to have occurred, and it may involve persuasion.

This view of interpersonal communication departs significantly from early twentieth-century models that treated communication as an outcome achieved when a source conveys a message to a receiver face to face. Current perspectives on interpersonal communication are relational, treating it as an activity, the outcome of which is jointly determined by the participants.

The relational view is affecting the way we talk about and study interpersonal communication. Instead of focusing on what goes on inside the mind of each communicator, relational communication theorists and researchers focus on communication patterns that emerge during interpersonal communication. They see interpersonal communication as an activity during which participants negotiate their relationships. You will discover, as you read subsequent chapters, that the relational view has exerted considerable influence on the way communication scholars think about and conduct research in interpersonal communication.

CHAPTER 3

The History of Interpersonal Communication

It is difficult, if not impossible, to know oneself without some sense of history. In *Orator*, Cicero commented, "To be ignorant of what occurred before you were born is to remain always a child." In this chapter, an historical overview of interpersonal communication study, we chart a course through time to follow the development of this field. The course passes through several fields of study and ends with the emergence of a separate field: the study of human communication, of which interpersonal communication is an important part.

The Classical Period: Roots of Rhetoric

The earliest recorded treatises on human communication date back to the classical period (500 BC to AD 400). The study of human communication during the classical period was actually the study of rhetoric. Although the term *rhetoric* rightly belongs to a body of theory about human communication, it has been used often throughout history to refer to the skills involved in public speaking.

Public speaking was an important skill for the Greek citizen around 400 BC. The democracy of that era required that citizens be capable of defending themselves in court if need be. Moreover, public speaking was important to success in public life. To facilitate such success, many Greek citizens sought assistance from teachers of public speaking.

Plato (circa 427–347 BC), a student of Socrates and a teacher, credited persuasion—interpersonal and public—with a paramount position in guiding societies toward truth. Plato believed that persuasion between two people is as important as persuasion of the masses. He believed the highest duty of philosophers like himself was to guide society by persuasion rather than brute force.

One of Plato's works, the *Phaedrus,* a dialogue in which Socrates plays the major role, establishes a place for interpersonal persuasion in the study of rhetoric:

> Is not rhetoric, taken generally, a universal art of enchanting the mind by arguments; which is practised not only in courts and public assemblies, but in private houses also, having to do with all matters great as well as small, good and bad alike [1956, p. 261].

Plato, and Aristotle after him, recognized that much of what is valuable to the orator is also important in private discourse.

Aristotle (384–322 BC), a student of Plato's, paid a good deal of attention to rhetoric, which he defined as "the faculty of observing in any given case the available means of persuasion" (1967). The *Rhetoric,* one of Aristotle's most famous works, is a treatise on persuasion in public situations. In this work, Aristotle converted rhetoric into a unified theory of human communication rather than a set of skills.

Aristotle did not develop a theory of interpersonal communication or interpersonal persuasion. He believed that rhetoric embraced what we might call the interpersonal situation and that many of the tenets of public speaking could be useful outside of public interactions.

Cicero (106–43 BC), a great Roman orator, did much to advance the study of styles of communication. Cicero defined the good communicator as one who, whatever the topic, "will speak thereon with knowledge, method, charm, and retentive memory, combining these qualifications with a certain distinction of bearing" (*DeOratore,* 1942, I. xv. 64).

Quintilian (circa AD 35–100), also a Roman, was especially interested in the study of style. Quintilian believed that clarity is the foundation of style. He identified figures of speech (tropes) such as metaphor, synecdoche, and metonomy. These figures were important to style because they "move the feelings" and "steal their way secretly" into the minds of the audience (1888).

The Theological Impasse

After Quintilian, the sphere of rhetoric shifted. Harper (1979, p. 69) explains, "The content of medieval and Renaissance human communication theory, though maintaining a surface resemblance to that of the classical, seems by comparison superficial and academic rather than philosophical and pragmatic." Letter writing and preaching became the focus of rhetoric. The ascendancy of Christianity and the Christian church moved rhetoric into a theological sphere.

The medieval emphasis on theology was generally a stumbling block in the development of human communication theory, especially scientific theory (La Piere & Farnsworth, 1936). Religion and rhetoric were inseparable. People's actions were interpreted in terms of their tendency to adhere to the forces of God or Satan. The "free will" theory of mankind that developed during this period essentially described people as free to choose between two competing forces—good or bad.

It became impossible to consider the elements of good communication and persuasion without considering whether the purpose of the communicator or persuader was good or bad. "Goodness" and "badness" were inextricably entwined with rhetoric, a condition that was instrumental in the scientist's tendency to reject rhetoric as a means of obtaining an objective view of communication.

The Rise of Modern Science

While the medieval period witnessed what seemed an inexorable connection between theology and philosophy, the Renaissance witnessed the beginnings of science as we know it today. The Renaissance was marked by the revival of classical learning, the invention of the printing press, the improvement of the compass for navigation, the discovery of the New World by Columbus and his successors, and the discovery of an all-water route to India and the Far East. These events and the growth of the Protestant Reformation begun by Martin Luther weakened the Roman Catholic Church's hold on philosophy.

During the Renaissance, a shift in the perception of truth occurred. In place of the belief that human truth is subordinate to divine, supernatural, and transcendent reality that is inaccessible to human reason came the view that human reason is a way of knowing the truth of reality. Nicolaus Copernicus (1473–1543) introduced the heliocentric theory of the universe, which held that the sun was the center around which the earth and other planets rotated. Galileo (1564–1642) provided strong evidence for Copernicus's theory by developing a telescope through which he observed other planets. Scientific discovery directly contradicted theological belief.

From the Renaissance emerged two conflicting theories of scientific method: empirical and rational. **Empiricists** such as Francis Bacon of England believed that people can know reliably only what their senses convey and that this knowledge must be tested by experimentation. **Rationalists** such as René Descartes (1596–1650) of France believed that reason is the most important element in human nature and the only way to determine what is morally right and good (Lavine, 1984).

The rationalists and empiricists shared the belief that everything that exists has a cause. From this premise a perspective called **determinism** developed. According to a deterministic view, everything in existence has resulted necessarily from one or more prior conditions. Descartes, to avoid offending the Church, stated that determinist science concerns itself solely with the physical world, which is predictable and subject to causal laws. The mind, Descartes said, is immune from determinism, capable of spontaneity, and divinely imprinted and is neither quantifiable nor predictable. This compromise of science and theology has been termed the "Cartesian compromise." But Bacon, Locke, Hume, and other empiricists encouraged secularization, and eventually theology lost its hold on science.

Is truth knowable? Does it even exist? Are cause-effect explanations of reality the most accurate? And are these cause-effect relations actually creations of the mind or do they exist apart from the human mind, which knows them by reason? Must scholars turn to empiricism to escape the entrapment of their own sensory impressions? Can human behavior be understood by introspection, the mainstay of philosophy? These are the questions that Bacon, Locke, Hume, Kant, Hegel, and others struggled to answer. They are questions that still generate debates today. Each student of human behavior must choose a world view. During the modern period, rhetoricians, scientists, and philosophers did so, and their choices affected the development of human communication science.

The Modern Period: Development of Theories

Eighteenth-century conflicts between the rationalists and empiricists influenced the course of communication study. Many rhetoricians found faculty psychology and associational psychology appealing areas of study. **Faculty psychology** posited the existence of five powers of the mind: understanding, memory, imagination, passion, and the will. **Associational psychology** focused on the connections among these faculties.

George Campbell, a clergyman of the Church of Scotland, was one of the major proponents of blending rhetoric with psychology. In 1776, Campbell published *The Philosophy of Rhetoric*, in which he integrated the works of Aristotle, Cicero, and Quintilian with those of Locke, Berkeley, and Hume in the creation of Campbell's own perspective on rhetoric.

Campbell's philosophy was based on the premise that rhetoric is dynamic: its development as an area of study did not cease after the classical period. The inclusion of scientific findings in his definition of rhetoric was one way to "avoid the sterility that results from undue reliance upon the Greek and Roman rhetoricians" (Golden, Berquist, & Coleman, 1976, p. 93).

Borrowing from Locke's conceptualization of the mind, Campbell argued that persuasion results from a four-step process involving understanding, imagination, emotion (or, as Campbell termed it, "the passions"), and will. He believed that persuasion requires imagery, which excites the imagination, which inevitably stirs emotion. This excitation of emotion motivates the will. Thus Campbell saw both reason and emotion as important factors in persuasion.

Campbell encouraged emphasis on the receiver in the study of human communication. He believed that successful communication requires an understanding of the purposes or goals of the audience. He urged communicators to consider the ways in which the receivers of their messages interpret reality. Campbell's attention to the issue of adjusting messages to audiences is especially evident in his discussions of the types of evidence appropriate for different situations.

Richard Whately, another rhetorician of the modern period, extended Campbell's psychological-philosophical view to the study of argument, the invention and arrangement of arguments by an orator. In *Elements of Rhetoric*, written in 1828, Whately elaborated a system of logic that is both a revival and extension of Aristotle's views within the context of modern psychology. He considered human communication a science that relies very much on the ability to know one's audience. Whately's emphasis on order of arguments influenced scientific studies of message organization that became prevalent in the early twentieth century. Moreover, his views on presumption, burden of proof, a priori argument, sign argument, and progressive argument strategy contributed significantly to modern treatments of argument and debate.

Thomas De Quincey was not the most famous theorist of his time, but he contributed directly to the study of interpersonal communication. In his 1847 essay "Conversation," De Quincey (1877) distinguished between talking *to* and talking *with* someone. He considered the former a "violent interruption" of the "silent contract" of conversation, because it destroys the sympathy between interactants necessary to the sharing of ideas and feelings. He believed that conversation requires some control of movements by each party so that it may proceed properly. De Quincey claimed that conversation lacks rules to keep people from talking too long about topics that are of little interest to others. He pointed to interruptions and digressions from the topics as examples of the "diseases" that plague conversation.

De Quincey's interest in conversation was, from his perspective, a function of the times. He believed that certain poets, philosophers, and others who spoke endlessly of their own interest without regard for the contributions of others would someday meet with disdain from their audiences. De Quincey predicted that modern times would encourage great-er use of conversation for learning. He observed the trend of greater dependence on conversation emerging in western Europe even as he wrote his essay on conversation. This led him to further predict:

> A corresponding change will gradually take place in the usages which regu-late conversation. It will come to be considered an infringement of the general rights for any man to detain the conversation, or arrest its move-ment, for more than a short space of time, which gradually will be more defined. This one curtailment of arrogant pretensions will lead to others. Egotism will no longer freeze the openings to intellectual discussions; and conversation will then become, what it never has been before, a powerful ally of education, and generally of self-culture [1877, pp. 350–351].

De Quincey did not develop a theory of conversation. He did, however, anticipate the growing importance of conversation in daily life and its emergence as a field of study.

Herbert Spencer contributed to the development of human communica-tion theory with his perspective on style. He studied language and its meaning. In his *The Philosophy of Style* (1953), Spencer articulated a perspec-tive that was to become a central premise of modern communication theory: the meaning of a message is created by the receiver through his or her own categorization and conceptualization of symbols. As noted later in this chapter, Spencer's perspective of persons as symbol-using beings, whose messages are often interpreted differently than intended, was later elaborated upon by symbolic interaction theorists in the late nineteenth and early twentieth centuries. And in 1960, when Berlo popularized the perspective that "meanings are in people, not in words" his view of communication harkened back to the ideas expressed by Spencer.

The modern period was an age of impressive communication theory development. Not since the classical era had communication theory en-joyed such attention and progress. It was also a time when the seeds of communication science, as we know it today, were planted. The identifica-tion by rhetoricians of a complementarity between psychology and philosophy was one important step. Another was the developing interest in society's impact on human behavior and vice versa, territory that was beginning to be claimed by social psychologists.

Behaviorism Versus Cognitivism

By the turn of the century, scientific method had gained considerable esteem among scholars. The preference for objectivity over subjectivity caused a schism between those who studied human communication by introspection (observing one's own and others' behaviors and drawing "reasonable" conclusions) and those who relied on scientific experiment.

Eventually rhetoricians were faced with the choice of becoming social scientists or continuing to study human communication by nonquantitative means. Most chose to let the interest in science expressed by George Campbell and other modern-era rhetoricians wane in favor of critical methods of human communication analysis. Only a few rhetoricians ventured into the field of interpersonal relations, which was dominated by social scientists (see Oliver, 1961a; 1961b; Ewbank, 1964). This is one of the major reasons why rhetoric had little influence on the development of interpersonal study during the contemporary period.

Interpersonal relations became fertile ground for social scientists during the twentieth century. Approaches to the topic varied widely. Instinct theorists believed that all behaviors, including social behaviors, result from inherited instincts. Taking their lead from the works of Darwin, instinct theorists believed that good and bad traits are transmitted from generation to generation. Evidence for the existence of instincts came from observations of ant behavior that seemed predetermined. For instance, ants rebuild hills in the same spots despite repeated damage by animals or humans. Such observations and the nurturant behavior of human and nonhuman mothers toward their offspring provided enough evidence for the instinct theorists to feel comfortable for some time.

Around 1920, behaviorism began to gain popularity. **Behaviorists** believed the study of human behavior should focus solely on observable behavior; from observations, hypotheses could be developed and tested, and laws of human behavior could be discovered. **Cognition**—the mental activity involving considerations of alternative behaviors—was considered an unobservable phenomenon and therefore unimportant (see Watson, 1925). Behaviorists explained human behavior in terms of the bonds between stimuli and responses (S-R theory). **Cognitivists,** on the other hand, believed that thought, rather than an external stimulus, is the motivating factor of human behavior.

The cognitivists and S-R theorists were joined by the gestalt theorists, who believed that many events cannot be explained in terms of their separate pieces but only in terms of their whole structure. Unlike behaviorists, **gestaltists** did not reject cognition, but refused to study it as a set of faculties, as did most nongestalt psychologists of the early twentieth century. Several later theories (some discussed in Chapter 7) were influenced by gestalt psychology: Heider's balance theory, Festinger's cognitive dissonance, and Osgood and Tannenbaum's congruity principle.

The conflict between behaviorism and cognitivism exists today. However, a cognitivist-behaviorist compromise seems possible. Some theorists claim that human behavior is the result of S-C-R (stimulus-cognition-response) rather than S-R (stimulus-response) linkages. As we discussed in Chapter 2, a modern perspective is that some behaviors are spontaneous, involving little if any cognition, whereas other behaviors result from thoughtful consideration of alternatives.

The Individual in Society: Social Influence Perspectives

A group of scholars refused to accept explanations of individual behavior that neglected the social environment of the individual. Charles Horton Cooley, George Herbert Mead, John Dewey, and Harry Stack Sullivan were a few of the many early twentieth-century scholars who argued that much human behavior can be explained in terms of social process or human communication. They believed that people come to know themselves through social experience: other people tell them who they are and what is expected of them. People differ, they claimed, because each person receives different responses from others.

Charles Horton Cooley, born in 1864, was a professor of economics and later of sociology at the University of Michigan. Cooley believed that people learn mainly through their experiences with others. He argued that thought is actually communication with another person who might be real or imaginary. The self, he asserted, exists only in relationship to others (1909, 1918).

Cooley's concept of the "looking-glass self" was a major contribution to the development of social psychology. He used a looking glass, or mirror, as an analogy to the way people come to know themselves. An understanding of self develops only from observing the reactions of others to oneself. No self exists apart from other people, since it is only through interaction with others that a perception of self emerges. Cooley believed that social relationships can cause emotional normalcy or disturbance. A satisfactory life, he claimed, depends on satisfactory relationships.

George Herbert Mead, a professor of philosophy at the University of Chicago, also had a major impact on social psychology and sociology. Like Cooley, he believed that others are the means by which we come to know ourselves.

At the heart of what later became known as the symbolic interactionist perspective was the emerging concept of interpersonal communication. Even thinking, according to Mead, is a conversation between the "I" and the "me." The "I" is the impulsive, unpredictable part of a person. The "me" is the "generalized other"—a person's perspective of the way others see him or her. According to Mead, neither component of the self can exist without the other.

The generalized other, "me," develops through role playing. We are able to think as others think by mentally putting ourselves in the positions of others. This ability allows individuals to see themselves as others see them. It also allows them to make predictions about the actions of others. The ability to imagine the thoughts of others makes interpersonal communication possible. Human beings do not merely react to past events; they anticipate future ones as well. They use these anticipations to determine their own actions.

Mead did much to advance the understanding of symbolic communication. He explained how symbols allow human beings to convey complex messages. Symbols are the stuff of which interpersonal communication, and all human communication, is made. According to Mead:

> Symbolization constitutes objects not constituted before, objects which would not exist except for the context of social relationships wherein symbolization occurs. Language does not simply symbolize a situation or object which is already there in advance; it makes possible the existence or the appearance of that situation or object, for it is a part of the mechanism whereby that situation or object is created. . . . Meaning is thus not to be conceived, fundamentally, as a state of consciousness, or as a set of organized relations existing or subsisting mentally outside the field of experience into which they enter; on the contrary it should be conceived objectively, as having its existence entirely within the field itself [1934, p. 78].

Mead argued that symbols are used to *create* meaning. They do not have meaning outside the context of experience to which they refer. Language does not report what is the case in reality; it functions to create a social reality. This was an important contribution to communication study. Meaning came to be viewed as something cocreated by interactants rather than something that exists apart from them or something belonging to the person, object, or event described.

When communicators describe objects, persons, or events, they use words to refer to (1) characteristics of them; (2) relations between them and other persons, objects, and events; or (3) opinions about characteristics and relations. In so doing, communicators create meanings for objects, persons, and events that other communicators may understand, misunderstand, accept, reject, or revise.

One reason why two persons' meanings for the same object, person, or event are rarely, if ever, exactly the same is that people attend and perceive differently. Each person, object, and event has many characteristics and many possible relationships with other objects, persons, and events. People attend to those characteristics relevant to them and perceive them from their particular vantage points or perspectives. Should they wish to communicate their perceptions, they select words and gestures that they consider likely to accurately convey their meaning. Though two people may observe the same object, person, or event, they are likely to attend differently, to interpret it differently, and to select different words and gestures to convey their meanings. Thus it is a wonder that we can communicate effectively at all.

Fortunately people from the same culture tend to share the same language and can therefore create shared meanings. From Mead's perspective, the meanings of words are not fixed but open. To have a language, symbols must have common or shared meanings. In order to have communication, symbol users must be able to adopt the perspectives of others to understand how they are likely to interpret particular symbols.

Mead encouraged movement away from the typical psychological notion of the human mind as an isolated entity serving a variety of functions. Instead, he encouraged students of human behavior to view the individual as a part of an influential social environment. Mead and many of his contemporaries shifted the focus from the individual outward to the social environment. This shift in perspective credited interpersonal communication with an important role in the formation of human thought and behavior.

Harry Stack Sullivan, a psychiatrist, was influenced by the works of Cooley and Mead. Sullivan developed what he called an interpersonal theory of psychiatry. He believed that other people affect our minds much more than do other sources of information. He considered faulty interpersonal relations the primary cause of schizophrenia and contended that anxiety results from anticipated disapproval from others.

Sullivan saw a need for a discipline to study not only the individual human organism (psychology) or the social heritage (sociology) but also the interpersonal situations through which people manifest mental health or mental disorder. He wrote:

> Psychiatry seeks to discover and formulate the laws of human personality. It is only indirectly concerned with the study of abstractions less or more inclusive than the person. Its peculiar field is the study of *interpersonal phenomena*. Personality is made manifest in interpersonal situations, and not otherwise. It is to the elucidation of interpersonal relations, therefore, that psychiatry applies itself [1938, p. 121].

Before and during World War II, Sullivan applied his views to topics that typically had been studied by social psychologists. These topics included propaganda, anti-Semitism, leadership, and morale. In his studies, he emphasized the importance of interpersonal relations. He believed that some of our interpersonal relations involve imaginary persons and that these relations are at least as important as those with real persons. Like Cooley and Mead, Sullivan considered the self-concept a product of communication with others.

The Meaning of Meaning: Symbols, Referents, and Context

While Mead, Cooley, and Sullivan advanced their theories of human interaction, other scholars focused attention on the concept of meaning. C. K. Ogden and I. A. Richards, two early twentieth-century scholars, collaborated in the study of language's influence upon thought. The resultant book, *The Meaning of Meaning* (1923), elaborated a scientific perspective of meaning. Like their contemporaries just mentioned, these two British researchers took an interest in interpersonal relations. In this regard, they wrote:

> There is no doubt an Art in saying something when there is nothing to be said, but it is equally certain that there is an Art no less important of saying clearly what one wishes to say when there is an abundance of material; and conversation will seldom attain even the level of an intellectual pastime if adequate methods of Interpretation are not also available [Ogden & Richards, 1923, p. 9].

Ogden and Richards believed that symbols are the tools used by humans to direct, organize, record, and communicate thought. Words or symbols mean nothing by themselves, but are only related to **referents**— the objects, persons, or events to which they refer through thought. The primary reason for difficulties encountered in the study of language and thought was the faulty belief that symbols and referents are directly related. Ogden and Richards argued that the only real relationship between symbols and referents is an indirect one. Symbols and referents, they wrote, are connected by thought. For example, the word *bark* is connected by thought processes to the sound made by dogs and to the outer layers of trees. Thought determines which referent the word *bark* pertains to at any given time. The way symbols are interpreted depends on the thought processes of their users.

Ogden and Richards also noted that the intention of the speaker may complicate the interpretation of meaning. Language, they claimed, is not merely a means of symbolizing references but also "an instrument for the promotion of purposes." People, they said, often attempt to deceive others with words—a "technique of deliberate misdirection."

Another important contribution by Ogden and Richards was their concept of **"psychological context"**—sets of past experiences associated with particular signs. They explained that it is only through evoking past experiences that a dog knows to come when its owner rings a bell. If the bell has been associated with past rewards, the dog will respond as the owner wishes. Similarly, when people see the word *hot*, they may back away because of past experiences with that word.

The use of symbols, Ogden and Richards argued, is not as simply explained as the use of signs. Symbols can have mixed references. For example, the combination of "strong" with "hold" gives stronghold. Symbols often contain references subject to emotional interpretation. *Mother earth* has a different connotation than the word *earth*. Ogden and Richards saw these emotional effects as important to the study of language. Any disagreement over whether emotion should be considered in the study of language they compared to a dispute over whether one's mouth should be used for speaking or eating. Nevertheless, the study of emotional communication has received little attention from social scientists until very recently.

The Emergence of a Focus on Groups

In the first decade of the twentieth century, the term **social psychology** began to be used to describe a discipline that combined the individual focus of psychology with the societal focus of sociology (see McDougall, 1908; and Ross, 1908). The social psychologists of the early twentieth century were interested in the relationship of individuals to groups and the role of society in the life of the individual.

Kurt Lewin (1947a, 1947b) was among the most influential early social psychologists. Lewin believed that each person sees the world from her "psychological field." Within this field are goals that the person wishes to obtain and events or people she wishes to avoid. Each action a person takes is based on the tensions in that field.

An important aspect of Lewin's perspective was his belief that people's life spaces include groups with which they identify. Each group, like each person, has a life space of its own. It also has goals that influence the behaviors of each group member. According to Lewin, people typically belong to several groups. Each group creates tension in the individual's life space, thereby influencing her actions. Since group values never coincide completely with a person's needs, the individual must continually adjust to group demands.

While the individuality of its members is what allows a group to change, the group's cohesiveness—the degree of mutual interest among members (Littlejohn, 1983)—keeps it intact even as it evolves. Cohesiveness requires interdependence among group members in their quest for certain goals. Cohesive groups exert more influence on their members than do noncohesive groups.

Lewin's group dynamics view is a systems perspective. In a system, each element is affected by and affects every other element. In a group, each individual member is both affected by and affects every other member. Each individual is constantly adjusting to group demands or seeking to alter the group to meet her needs. In Lewin's terms, the group affects the members' life spaces and the members affect the life space of the group.

J. L. Moreno, a Romanian-born psychologist educated in Vienna, was also interested in group relations. However, his focus was on relations among group members. He developed a procedure for assessing intragroup relations called **sociometry.**

Sociometry, a term derived from the Latin *socius* (companion) and *metrum* (measure), refers to a means of measuring the relationships among members of groups. Questionnaires are administered to group members asking them who they prefer to work with, who they like most, or some other questions of relationship preferences. On the basis of the respondents' choices, the researcher develops a sociogram, which depicts relationships among group members in terms of the questions asked. A sample sociogram appears in Figure 3.1.

The sociogram allows the researcher to see whether the group is cohesive or whether cliques have formed. It enables tracking of the potential flow of influence within the group and identification of cliques that may affect group progress. This procedure has been used extensively by medical researchers and education researchers. For example, Coleman, Katz, and Menzel (1966) used the technique to assess the sources doctors turn to for information concerning new drugs.

Sociometry attracted the interest of many social scientists from 1934, when it was formally introduced, through the 1960s. The sociometric movement spawned the journal *Sociometry: A Journal of Inter-Personal Relations* in 1934 and the *Sociometry Reader* in 1960. The greatest contribution of Moreno's sociometry to interpersonal communication study was the interest it generated in measuring the structure of interpersonal relationships within groups.

Muzafer Sherif, a social psychologist, began studying groups during the 1930s. While interest in the effects of groups on the emergence of self (Cooley, Mead, Sullivan) and in intragroup relationships (sociometry) was developing, Sherif investigated the influence of group norms on human decisions. He was the first to study norms experimentally.

To study group norms, Sherif used the autokinetic illusion, which is the illusion of movement by a stationary pinpoint of light reported by viewers when the light is continuously viewed in darkness. Sherif found that if others disagree with them, people will change their minds about the distance they consider the light to have moved. Each participant changes his mind in the direction of a group standard or group norm.

Sherif's early work culminated in a book entitled *The Psychology of Social Norms* (1936). From his study of prestige norms (the tendency for people to raise their assessment of works attributed to prestigious persons) and other work, he concluded that stereotypes, fads, fashions, customs, traditions, and attitudes are highly influenced by socially determined norms. Sherif's

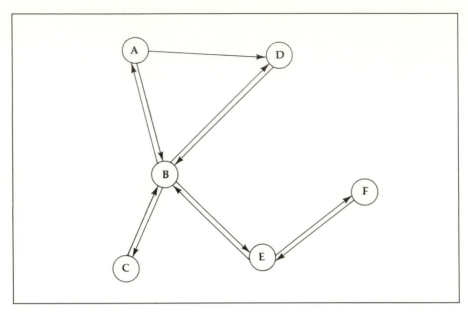

Figure 3.1.   Sociogram of reports by persons A through F of group members with
whom they were acquainted prior to the first group meeting.

work encouraged further experimentation in the study of social relations.

Robert Freed Bales, a contemporary of Sherif and a Harvard researcher, developed a method for studying groups, which he labeled "interaction process analysis." Its basic premise is that people act and react in groups. Bales attempted to explain the pattern of responses people make to each other during small group interaction. From 1942 to 1950, he developed twelve major interaction categories for scoring purposes (Bales, 1950). He used these categories to classify interpersonal behaviors of group members. Figure 3.2 depicts the twelve interaction categories.

Observers used these categories to score the behavior of group members. A 1970 revision altered the names and content of the categories, but methods of scoring remained similar.

Bales's contribution to interpersonal study was extensive. His interaction process analysis is still used by small group researchers in their assessments of interpersonal group behavior.

The Development of an International
Communication Association

While Bales developed his interaction process analysis, Elwood Murray and others worked to establish an organization that would welcome communication scholars from several disciplines. Murray is credited as the

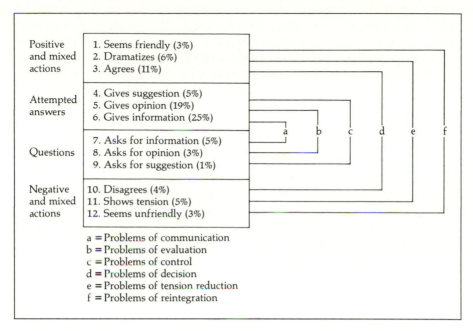

Positive and mixed actions	1. Seems friendly (3%) 2. Dramatizes (6%) 3. Agrees (11%)
Attempted answers	4. Gives suggestion (5%) 5. Gives opinion (19%) 6. Gives information (25%)
Questions	7. Asks for information (5%) 8. Asks for opinion (3%) 9. Asks for suggestion (1%)
Negative and mixed actions	10. Disagrees (4%) 11. Shows tension (5%) 12. Seems unfriendly (3%)

a = Problems of communication
b = Problems of evaluation
c = Problems of control
d = Problems of decision
e = Problems of tension reduction
f = Problems of reintegration

Figure 3.2.   Bales's twelve interaction categories.
Source: Littlejohn (1983, p. 228). Used by permission of Wadsworth, Inc.

father of the International Communication Association (Brownell, 1983). In 1949 when the Speech Society of America seemed to focus almost exclusively on public speaking, Murray called for a broadening of the field of communication. He recognized that it was becoming an interdisciplinary field in need of interdisciplinary organization. The International Communication Association is today a society of communication scholars interested in interpersonal, mass, organizational, and health communication, to name just a few of its areas of study.

Murray also helped establish a place for interpersonal study in the field of speech communication. In a 1948 article entitled "Personality, Communications, and Interpersonal Relations," he posited an important connection between personality and interpersonal relationships:

> The relationship of communicating to personality to interpersonal relations may have special importance for the social sciences. The breakdowns of enterprise and society have their parallel breakdowns in the breakdowns in communications and interpersonal relations incidental thereto. In fact, if history were written in terms of the "successes" and "failures" of communication and if enterprises were studied through experiences in a communication laboratory the teaching of both the social sciences and speech might become much more functional and valuable in the lives of our students [Murray, 1948, p. 83].

At that time, interpersonal communication and persuasion were of interest because they contributed to an understanding of human personality, self-image, and other concepts of concern to psychologists. Interpersonal study was not yet of interest in and of itself. But Murray's work helped to move interpersonal communication to a more visible position among the interests of mid-twentieth-century social scientists.

The Influence of Information Theory

About the time that Elwood Murray was laying the foundations for the International Communication Association, Claude E. Shannon (1948) of the Bell Systems Laboratories published his mathematical theory of communication. He set down a unified theory of signal transmission based on the idea that transmitted information may be considered statistically and its probabilities figured. At first, Shannon's theory was used solely by communication engineers, but within a few years his theory was applied to psychology, physics, linguistics, biology, sociology, statistics, and journalism (Dahling, 1962).

Shannon and Weaver (1949) published a book on their mathematical theory of communication based on their own model, which helped to integrate the field of communication. (See Figure 3.3.) It gave communication scholars an image of communication previously absent. It provided a badly needed theory, and it enabled the development of a common language about communication.

Shannon and Weaver's model had far-reaching effects on communication theory and research. For decades the terminology they developed was used by communication scholars to describe the steps involved in both mass media and interpersonal communication.

Emergence of a Focus on Relations Between Two People

In 1958, psychologist Fritz Heider published *The Psychology of Interpersonal Relations*. "The study of interpersonal relations," Heider wrote, "has been treated only tangentially in the field of personality and social psychology. Personality investigators have been largely concerned with the isolation of personality traits and their patterning in personality structure. . . . Social psychologists have been mainly interested in the relations between people when larger groups play a role." Heider added, "One might ask whether a study of the relations between two people might throw new light on group problems" (1958, p. 3).

Heider was one of the first cognitive social psychologists to develop an interest in how persons perceive others in the course of interaction. For

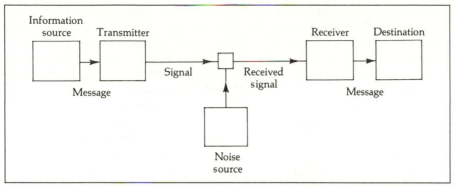

Figure 3.3.   Schematic diagram of a general communication system.

this reason, some scholars believe that his book should have been titled "The Psychology of Interpersonal Perceptions" (Sahakian, 1982).

Heider's book was intended to stimulate development of a language to help scholars represent interpersonal relations. Heider saw interpersonal relations as usually **dyadic relations**—that is, relations between two people—involving thoughts, feelings, perceptions, expectations, and reactions. According to Heider, people look for information that will help them understand why others act as they do. They operate as "naive psychologists" gaining information about people and attributing causes to those people's actions. This perspective is known as **attribution theory** (see Jones & Davis, 1965; Kelley, 1973).

Despite its emphasis on how people perceive each other rather than on the structure of interaction between people, Heider's book helped move interpersonal study to a vital position in the social sciences and encouraged an interest in dyadic interactions (see also Argyle, 1967).

John Thibaut and Harold Kelley developed another dyadic perspective important to the development of interpersonal study. Influenced by their studies with Kurt Lewin, they became interested in social perception. Later, after publication of Heider's *The Psychology of Interpersonal Relations,* Thibaut and Kelley developed a theory of interaction outcomes that focused on dyadic interactions. They addressed the problems of why and how people initiate, maintain, and terminate relationships. The result of their work was *The Social Psychology of Groups* (Thibaut & Kelley, 1959).

The fundamental premise of Thibaut and Kelley's theory is that persons tend to repeat those interactions for which they are suitably reinforced. Their theory explains social interactions in terms of rewards and costs. Dyadic relationships are formed, maintained, and ended on the basis of reward-cost forecasts. If a person feels that a relationship is unlikely to be rewarding, he is likely to find a way to end that relationship or maintain it without commitment.

One way people determine the nature of their relationship outcomes is through "comparison levels." Thibaut and Kelley explained that persons compare the outcomes of their current relationships to a standard norm. They may also use the "comparison level for alternatives," the lowest outcomes a person will accept given the available alternatives to the relationship in question. For example, a person may decide to end a romantic relationship because the rewards obtained compare unfavorably with those expected from another available relationship.

Thibaut and Kelley advanced the study of dyadic interpersonal communication by exploring how persons start, keep, and end relationships. They examined interpersonal interactions and resultant patterns more closely than their predecessors did. More than simply who talks to whom, or who likes whom, they were intrigued by the actual give and take of interpersonal interaction. In this sense, their work constitutes another important step toward the development of interpersonal study as we know it today. We will look further at Thibaut and Kelley's perspectives, including their more recent work on interpersonal relations, in Chapter Eight.

While Thibaut and Kelley were investigating the cost-reward structure in interpersonal interactions, Sidney Jourard, a psychologist, was taking an interest in self-disclosure. Jourard observed that people with emotional problems are usually closed to others. They do not have someone with whom they can discuss their "real selves." Jourard believed that **self-disclosure**—the revealing of one's private needs, thoughts, and feelings— is necessary to mental health. In *The Transparent Self*, Jourard (1964, p. 15) wrote that too much or too little self-disclosure "betokens disturbance in self and in interpersonal relations."

Jourard's perspective initiated a strong interest by scholars of interpersonal communication in the effects of self-disclosure on relationships. The topic was alluring and hypotheses about self-disclosure were usually subject to experimental validation. The influence of self-disclosure study on definitions of interpersonal communication continues to be influential today.

The Attitude-Behavior Link

As we have seen, the works of many scholars from diverse fields of study contributed to the development of interpersonal communication and persuasion study. We should, however, give special attention to an era that began in the 1920s. This is the attitude era—a time when many of the best minds in social science turned their attention to the study of how attitudes influence behavior and how, through persuasion, attitudes and behaviors are changed.

In 1925, social psychologist Emory S. Bogardus conducted one of the first scientific studies of attitudes by measuring **social distance**—the degree of understanding and intimacy characterizing personal and social relationships. Essentially, social distance reflects a person's approach and avoidance tendencies toward specified racial, religious, or other groups (see Bogardus, 1925a, 1925b).

In 1928, Louis Thurstone encouraged the developing interest in attitude with his paper "Attitudes Can Be Measured," and in 1929 he and E. J. Chave developed a scale to measure attitudes. An attitude scale would reflect varying degrees of favorableness or unfavorableness (from least to most) toward an object, person, or event. Other scales were developed in 1932 by Renis Likert and in the 1940s by Louis Guttman.

The attitude research era was underway. Most communication researchers focused their efforts on the study of attitude change. Leonard Doob (1947), for example, applied behaviorism to attitude study. He defined attitudes as implicit, drive-producing responses that are socially significant to the individual's society. Other definitions followed as theorists struggled to define **attitude**—a hypothetical construct that could not be seen, heard, or touched. Basically attitudes were believed to predispose people to act in certain positive or negative ways toward objects, people, and events. Despite difficulties faced by those scholars who attempted in vain to create an enduring definition of attitude, attitude research claimed the attention of numerous social scientists.

Influenced by the gestalt perspective, several theorists became interested in how the human mind deals with inconsistent cognitions. These theorists, beginning with Fritz Heider, developed a series of cognitive consistency theories: balance, dissonance, congruity, and symmetry theories.

Consistency theorists argued that persons tend to behave in ways most likely to produce internal consistency of their cognitions. According to Leon Festinger's (1957) theory of cognitive dissonance, people experience tension when they recognize that a decision they have made is inconsistent with one or more of their current attitudes or behaviors. The research based on cognitive dissonance theory examined the conditions that create dissonance and the means people use to reduce it. Festinger (1954) applied his theory to social relations and developed **social comparison theory,** which is based on the premise that people are driven to self-evaluation through comparisons with others, especially when they lack confidence in their own actions.

Cognitive dissonance theory also served as the cornerstone of a body of research on **counterattitudinal advocacy,** a form of persuasion accomplished by encouraging people to temporarily act in a way that contradicts their attitudes. An example is convincing someone who is in favor of legalizing marijuana to prepare and present a speech about the reasons why marijuana should not be legalized, in order to change her opinions on the subject. According to counterattitudinal advocacy theory, seeing or hearing oneself behave in a manner inconsistent with one's attitudes causes dissonance. To reduce dissonance, the individual is likely to change her original attitude. We will discuss the viability of this and other theories based on consistency at greater length in Chapter Seven.

While consistency theorists studied how people reduce the discomfort associated with inconsistent cognitions, the Yale Communication Research Program was also becoming involved in the study of attitude change. Directed by Carl I. Hovland, this group of researchers focused their studies on learning and persuasion. Hovland and his colleagues, including Irving Janis, Harold Kelley, and William McGuire, made significant advances in studying the relationships of personality to persuasibility, attitude organization, attitude change, propaganda, and persuasive message organization. They also discovered a phenomenon called "the sleeper effect" where persons who were initially unswayed by the arguments of a low-credibility source showed signs of influence later. Over time, information initially conveyed by a low-credibility source may become disassociated from that source and remembered favorably.

By today's standards, only a modest amount of research was triggered by the Yale Communication Research Program, and its members have been criticized for not developing a systematic theory of persuasion (Deutsch & Krauss, 1965; Kiesler, Collins, & Miller, 1969). Nevertheless, their work had a considerable impact on persuasion study during the middle of this century.

William J. McGuire was affiliated with the Yale Communication Research Program before going to Columbia and to the University of California at San Diego. He is now at Yale again. Influenced by Lumsdaine and Janis (1953) and Hovland, Janis, and Kelley's (1953) interest in resistence to persuasion, McGuire studied the concept of **inoculation,** which involves forewarning persuadees of possible counterarguments so they will be prepared to resist them. If a child is told how he might respond if someone tells him that other children will like him more if he takes drugs, he may be better prepared to resist the offer than a child whose parents have not provided such information. Inoculation theory is relevant to both interpersonal study and to mass communication research. Just as someone may be inoculated against possible disease, a person may be inoculated against possible counterpersuasion.

Another line of study during the attitude era was Solomon Asch's research on group pressure. Asch's (1951) experiments involved asking a group of subjects to match a line with one of three other lines of unequal lengths. However, prior to the meeting, all but one member of the group had received directions to select the wrong line. Asch wanted to know whether the uninformed subject would change his judgment to match that of the group. Asch found that subjects were only 67 percent accurate when faced with group opposition to their judgment; without group pressure they were 93 percent accurate.

Asch's work instigated much research on the influence groups exert on individual decisions. Group size, situational variations (for example, face to face versus anonymous), amount of group pressure, and gender were some of the variables manipulated in group pressure studies. These studies indicated that group pressure can exert considerable influence on individual judgments.

Many other social scientists, whose work will be discussed in Chapter Seven, devoted much effort to the study of attitude-behavior relationships. Rokeach's (1968) work on beliefs and values, Fishbein's (1963; 1967) models of attitude, Bem's (1967) interpersonal theory of self-perception, and Bandura's (1977) social learning theory are a few of the many contributions made during the attitude era that continue to influence communication and persuasion study.

The Process View of Communication

While communication researchers focused their efforts on attitude change, David Berlo (1960) introduced a perspective on human communication that had a tremendous impact on the emerging field. His *The Process of Communication* defined communication as a continuous, ongoing process with no real beginning or end. He identified the elements of this process as source, message, channel, and receiver. Berlo introduced a definition of human communication from a scientific standpoint.

Although the model proved to be somewhat limited, it provided a vocabulary and a dynamic view of human communication. For many years communication scientists spoke of "process" when they discussed mass and interpersonal communication. Berlo's model did not adequately capture the relational, reciprocal nature of interpersonal communication. Nevertheless, *The Process of Communication* helped communication researchers take a major step toward answering the difficult question: What is human communication?

Emergence of Departments of Communication

Despite all of the research activity focused on communication during the early twentieth century, universities did not yet have departments of communication. Communication was not considered a discipline; social scientists studied communication and then returned to their own fields. Wilbur Schramm (1959) called communication research "one of the greatest crossroads where many pass but few tarry."

According to Everett Rogers, "This in-and-out venturing was related to a lack of institutionalized structure for communication research. The founders provided a rich diversity of intellectual backgrounds for communication research. But their temporary commitment didn't contribute toward the integration of theories and methods for attacking communication problems" (Rogers & Chaffee, 1983, p. 21).

In the 1950s, programs such as those at Illinois, Stanford, Minnesota, and Wisconsin began offering doctorates to students who were committed to communication research. A few years later, Michigan State initiated a program of communication study headed by David Berlo that attracted scholars interested in defining the field of communication. By the mid 1960s and early 1970s, communication departments were being formed by merging rhetoric and communication science or by merging journalism with mass communication.

The relationship between communication scientists and rhetoricians was not always a comfortable one. Because of emphasis on science since the late nineteenth century, rhetoric had come to be associated with the less popular form of study—introspection. Many scientists felt uncomfortable with their nonempirical associates. Herbert Simons explains, "Because 'rhetoric' tends to be a 'devil' term in our culture—often preceded by 'mere,' 'only,' and 'empty' or worse—scientists understandably recoiled from it, insisting instead that their discourse is purely 'objective'" (1980, p. 127). Interpersonal and mass communication scientists were already feeling inferior to natural scientists, whose subject matter leant itself to higher levels of prediction and control. Association with rhetoric merely exacerbated the condition.

Rhetoricians were not generally happy about their new situation either. They had experienced a setback when disciplined thought took a backseat to science. Also, scientists succeeded in converting many young would-be rhetoricians to science.

While the science versus rhetoric controversy divided communication scholars, so too did the distinction between interpersonal and mass communication studies. At the time, this division made some sense. There was a need to define one's niche. Moreover, political decisions such as hiring required some convenient distinctions. The result, however, was divisiveness among persons developing potentially complementary theory (see Reardon & Rogers, 1986).

The Mass Communication Connection

In 1966, Elihu Katz and Paul Lazarsfeld published *Personal Influence*, which explained the connection between interpersonal and mass communication. They described interpersonal communication as an intervening variable between mass media and behavior change. They reported research indicat-

ing that group television viewing is often more effective at shaping attitudes and behaviors than is individual viewing. And Katz and Lazarsfeld
introduced the two-step model of mass media effects, which depicted
interpersonal interactions as channels of mass media information.

Another connection between mass and interpersonal communication
was established when Everett Rogers first published *Diffusion of Innovations*
in 1962. Rogers explained the complementary roles mass and interpersonal channels play in the decision to adopt or reject an innovation: "Mass
media channels are relatively more important at the knowledge stage
and interpersonal channels are relatively more important at the persuasion stage in the innovation-decision process" (1983, p. 199). In short, mass
media are particularly useful in making people aware of new products
or ideas, but when it comes to a decision to buy a product or adopt an
idea, people often seek the opinions of friends, relatives, and acquaintances.

A third connection between interpersonal and mass communication is
found in the socialization effects in mass communication literature. The
main question addressed by socialization researchers is, To what extent do
mass media influence the way people, particularly young people, behave
in and view their social world?

Socialization refers to "the process by which people learn the fundamental parameters of their culture" (Roberts & Maccoby, 1984, p. 34).
Mass media is one source from which people learn about the society in
which they live. Research indicates that the media serve as important
socializing agents for children and that they influence the antisocial and
prosocial behaviors of adults. In this way, mass media influence the way
people relate to each other on the interpersonal level.

Gerbner and Gross argue that television "cultivates" basic assumptions
about the nature of social reality. These assumptions also affect the way
people relate to each other (Gerbner & Gross, 1976a; 1976b; 1980).

Study of Nonverbal Communication

While departments of communication were emerging at universities
around the United States, several anthropologists and psychologists took
an interest in nonverbal communication. Anthropologist Ray Birdwhistell,
(1952, 1970) coined the term *kinesics* to describe his study of body language.
Birdwhistell developed a theory of kinesics that helped to establish a place
for nonverbal behavior in interpersonal study. He argued that body movements are systematic and subject to systematic analyses, that they are
influenced by the social system of the communicator, and that they influence the behavior of those with whom the actor communicates.

Anthropologist Edward Hall established a place for *proxemics* in interpersonal study. Proxemics refers to the use of space in communication

and persuasion. Hall reasoned that when people engage in conversation, the distance between them is influenced by their sex, culture, nature of the relationship, and other factors. Hall's *The Silent Language* (1959) and *The Hidden Dimension* (1966) have had a considerable impact on the development of nonverbal study.

A third contribution to nonverbal communication comes from the work of Paul Ekman and Wallace Friesen (1969; Ekman, Friesen, & Ellsworth, 1972). They divided nonverbal behaviors into five types: emblems, illustrators, adaptors, regulators, and affect-displays. They also developed a three-part approach to the analysis of nonverbal behavior: (1) origin (the source of the act), (2) coding (the relationship of the act to its meaning), and (3) usage (how a behavior is used by the actor). Their theory and research constitute a significant contribution to the advancement of nonverbal theory within the field of interpersonal study.

The study of nonverbal communication has received less attention by interpersonal theorists and researchers than has verbal communication. Only recently, through the efforts of these and other researchers, has nonverbal study received recognition as a fundamental part of most interpersonal interactions.

Dramaturgical Perspectives on Communication

The final entry in our historical overview is focused on a man who is a theorist rather than a researcher. Erving Goffman, a symbolic interactionist of the dramaturgical tradition, used a stage metaphor to analyze human interaction. Goffman saw interpersonal communication as presentation through which aspects of the self are projected (1961; 1963; 1967; 1971). Goffman's work, spanning more than twenty years, has been criticized for its lack of integration. Each book presents a new theory with little or no reference to past perspectives. Moreover, Goffman's approach is interpretive and humanistic rather than scientific.

Despite these criticisms of Goffman's work, his perspectives have influenced the thinking of interpersonal communication theorists of the current era. His focus on self-presentation during interpersonal interactions has been an important contribution to both verbal and nonverbal study.

Relational Perspectives on Communication

During the 1950s and 1960s, anthropologist Gregory Bateson gathered a group of researchers at the Mental Research Institute in Palo Alto, California, to study relational communication. This group of scholars came to be known informally as the "Palo Alto Group."

Bateson and his colleagues applied what has been termed the *interactional view* to the study of mental health and pathologies of communication. Although they were originally interested in developing a general theory of communication, monetary support for clinical work was available. Their clinical orientation limited the exposure of interpersonal communication theorists to the Palo Alto Group's theoretical perspective until the 1967 publication of *Pragmatics of Human Communication.*

Paul Watzlawick, Janice Beavin, and Donald Jackson (1967), the authors of *Pragmatics of Human Communication,* took an interactional approach to communication. They analyzed the individual in terms of her important relationships, most typically the interactional system of the family. They were not interested in the causes of behavior as much as in the current process: what is going on in the relationship at the time of observation, rather than why it is happening or how it got to be that way (Wilder, 1979).

The major contribution of the Palo Alto Group to interpersonal study development has been its emphasis on the relational or interactional view of human communication. In contrast to prior linear views of source, message, channel, and receiver, the members of the Palo Alto Group study the communication patterns that emerge in human relationships. Rejecting the experimental paradigm, they do not look for independent and dependent variable relationships. They argue that relationships are systems guided by rules. In the course of relationship development, recurring patterns of interaction emerge, and dysfunctional patterns, or problems, can often be identified and altered.

For a time, their rejection of cause-effect relationships as a model for interactional research did not endear the Palo Alto Group to interpersonal communication researchers, despite the relevance of their work. However, their ideas about human communication are compelling. It is likely that their influence will continue to be felt as we enter an age of relational theories of human communication.

Another theorist who influenced the relational view of interpersonal communication is R. D. Laing (Laing, Phillipson, & Lee, 1966; Laing, 1967, 1969), who wrote several books on the process of perception in communication. His primary thesis was that communicative behavior is largely shaped by the experience or perception of the relationship one has with another communicator. A communicator interacting with another communicator has two levels of experience or perspectives: **direct perspective** and **metaperspective.** Direct perspective is the actual perceptions of another's behavior. Metaperspective is imagining the perceptions of the other.

People often misperceive the perspectives of others. This can threaten their relationships. For example, if Jack thinks that Jill loves him when in actuality she merely likes him, Jack's metaperspective is inaccurate. This situation might be remedied by Jill recognizing Jack's erroneous metaperspective and attempting to revise it.

Laing's work helped advance current relational views of interpersonal communication. He recognized that communicators' actions are based on more than one perspective. Moreover, he saw each communicator's actions as a result of his perceptions of the other person's actions. Together communicators shape each other's perceptions.

Summary

The development of interpersonal communication study has involved many side roads through fields of rhetoric, psychology, sociology, linguistics, anthropology, and social psychology. Methods of study—qualitative and quantitative—have varied according to the preferences of major theorists of each era.

The roots of interpersonal study can be traced to the classical period, when public speaking was of greater interest to communication scholars than interpersonal interaction was. Rhetorical theories were considered relevant to private communication, but such encounters received little direct attention.

The medieval period, when theology was the dominant interest, was a time of minimal development of communication theory. Communication was defined as good or bad according to the speaker's purposes. During the Renaissance, a time of discovery and interest in science, Locke, Bacon, Hume, and others lessened the influence of theology. Their interest in scientific method influenced the work of such rhetoricians as George Campbell and encouraged a blending of psychology and communication study.

At the turn of the century, scholars Charles Cooley, Herbert Mead, and Harry Stack Sullivan gave the study of interpersonal communication an important place in the development of the self. Their assumption that the self develops through interaction with others facilitated the growth of interpersonal theory.

The twentieth century has been a period of rapid advance for interpersonal communication theory. Group study gained credibility through the work of Lewin, Moreno, Bales, and others. Heider, Argyle, and Thibaut and Kelley developed theories of dyadic communication. Persuasion became the primary focus of much psychology and social psychology research. Rhetoricians left the study of interpersonal communication and persuasion to the social scientists, and a division, based on methodological differences, emerged among scholars of communication. As departments of communication developed throughout American universities, interpersonal study became a fundamental area of study in most of them.

Our historical overview stops at 1970 because the work conducted since then is contemporary. The remainder of this book will be devoted to discussions of current interpersonal theory and research.

During the past fifteen years, many communication books have been published and courses in interpersonal study have become common at universities and colleges. Interpersonal researchers have begun to move away from the study of attitude change toward research that examines the structure of interpersonal interaction. The person perception approach introduced by Heider in his *The Psychology of Interpersonal Relations* has given way to a new relational focus—considerations of how interactants define and respond to each other's behaviors.

It has become obvious that the study of human communication is a field in its own right. Its researchers study family or child interaction, health communication, organizational communication, cross-cultural communication or some other topic, but they share one primary focus of study: "symbolic exchanges within the context of developing relationships" (Miller, 1983, p. 35).

Conflicts over definitions of major concepts and over methodology have been characteristic of the past ten years of interpersonal study. The present era has been described as a time of "ferment in the field" of communication (*Journal of Communication*, 1983). It is a time of disagreement and a time of theoretical growth, an exciting time to be a student of interpersonal communication. Ironically, in an era of mass communication proliferation, there is increased recognition of the importance of interpersonal communication to mass communication effects (Chaffee, 1982). Computers have created a new context of interpersonal interaction—machine attenuated interpersonal communication. Communication theory and research have expanded dramatically over the past decade. The future of interpersonal study is very promising.

Classical Period	Medieval Period	Renaissance	Modern Period
Early roots of the study of human communication	Theological influence on the study of communication	The rise of science	First studies of the inter-relationship of psychology and communication
Early studies of rhetoric	Focus on letter writing and preaching	Rationalists vs. Empiricists	
First theories of public speaking	Religion and rhetoric linked	Deterministic (cause-effect) approach	The study of argument, style, and conversation
Some Major Players	Elements of good communication and persuasion associated with "Goodness" and "Badness"	Greater trust in human reasoning	Persuasion seen as a process involving understanding, imagination, emotion, and will
Socrates		Early studies of link between emotion and reason	
Plato			
Aristotle			
Cicero	*Some Major Players*	*Some Major Players*	*Some Major Players*
Quintilian			
	St. Augustine	*Bacon*	*Campbell*
	St. Thomas	*Descartes*	*Whately*
		Locke	*De Quincey*
		Hume	*Spencer*
		Kant	
		Hegel	

Figure 3.4.   The history of interpersonal communication.

Early Twentieth Century	Mid-Twentieth Century	The 1960s and Early 1970s
Behaviorism vs. Cognitivism	Group dynamics view	Emergence of departments of communication
Gestalt psychology	Sociometry	
Focus on self	Group norms	The process view of communication
Social influence perspectives	Interaction process analysis	Science vs. rhetoric
The looking-glass self	Development of an international communication association	Mass communication linked to interpersonal communication
Symbolic interactionism		
An interpersonal theory of psychiatry		Attention to nonverbal communication
Focus on meaning	A mathematical theory of communication	
	Emerging interest in dyads	Self-presentation or dramaturgical perspective
Some Major Players	Attribution theory	Interactional views and relational perspectives
Cooley	The study of the effects of self-disclosure on relationships	
Mead		***Some Major Players***
Sullivan	Attitude study	
Ogden & Richards		*Berlo, Katz & Lazarsfeld, Rogers, Birdwhistell, Hall, Ekman & Friesen, Goffman, Batesen, Laing, Palo Alto group, Woalowick, Beavin & Jackson*
Lewin	***Some Major Players***	
Moreno		
Sherif	*Lewin, Moreno, Sherif, Bales, Murray, Shannon & Weaver, Heider, Argyle, Thibaut & Kelley, Jourard, Bogardus, Thurstone, Chave, Likert, Guttman, Doob, Festinger, Osgood & Tannenbaum, Houland, Janis, McGuire, Asch, Rokeach, Fishbein, Bem, Bandura*	

C H A P T E R   4

The Young Communicator

In this chapter we will look at the ways children learn to participate in interpersonal communication and persuasion. Despite decades of studying children's communication, much of the way children learn to communicate remains a fascinating mystery. Research has increased our understanding of the process of children's communication development. Yet there remains much controversy among experts concerning how children learn language and how they learn to use language differently in different social contexts. In this chapter, we will introduce you to some of the topics and issues that interest those who study children's communication and to some relevant theory and research.

Why Do Children Learn to Talk?

Those who adopt a behaviorist perspective believe that children learn to talk because they are rewarded for it (see Skinner, 1957). Cognitivists, on the other hand, typically believe that children are predisposed to learn language (see Chomsky, 1969, 1975). The latter view has often been referred to as "the innateness hypothesis" because adherents believe that certain innate structures of the human mind account for the ability to learn language. These structures are "prerequisites" to learning.

The cognitivist's answer to the question "Why do children learn language?" is that they are cognitively predisposed to do so, just as they are physiologically predisposed to walk on two legs. The behaviorist's answer to the same question is that children are rewarded for learning language or punished for failing to learn it. In the 1980s, as we begin to recognize the hazards of slavish adherence to purely cognitive or purely behaviorist learning theory perspectives, we are starting to see that "there is no reason why a final theory should deny the importance of either kind of influence" (Elliot, 1981, p. 29). Human beings may have an innate capacity for language acquisition. They also learn language, at least in part, by operant conditioning—in which comments are rewarded or punished according to some criteria of appropriateness. Just as the robin is biologically predisposed to fly, humans may be biologically predisposed to talk. And just as the robin learns from reward and punishment that there are various modes of flight for different purposes, so too does the human child learn to use language to help attain goals.

How Do Children Learn to Communicate?

You have probably witnessed the parents of an infant swell with pride at their offspring's utterances. They may smile and hug the child. In this way they reward him for using verbal language. As children mature, their parents become critical of inappropriate remarks while still rewarding appropriate ones. This is one means by which children learn to communicate.

Communication development is both a learning and training experience. Learning can occur without someone who consciously plays the role of teacher. Much learning is incidental. It occurs as the result of observation. Training, on the other hand, requires instruction. At least one person sets out to teach another to acquire a skill. If children could acquire the ability to communicate only by training, parents would be very busy preparing their children for kindergarten. Fortunately, children can learn much about communication without training. They learn by observation of naturally occurring communication, for example. In this section, we will consider three aspects of learning a language without training: imitation, expansion and correction, and categorization.

Young children are like "busy little scientists" (Wood, 1981). They search for the rules or schemas underlying the speech they hear and then they practice applying those rules. When they misapply a rule, parents, peers, or teachers may show them how to apply it properly. Let's look now at some of the ways that adults and children work together in the development of children's communication.

Imitation

Any parent who has witnessed her young child reprimand a doll in the same fashion as the child has been reprimanded knows that **imitation**— mimicking of observed behavior—is one means by which children learn to communicate. They not only learn what to say, but how to say it to people of different status, age, and gender.

McNeil (1966) studied child language imitation and discovered that imitations often fall short of being accurate. The following dialogue, recorded by McNeil, demonstrates that children do not imitate with high degrees of accuracy until their stage of language development allows it.

Child: Nobody don't like me.
Mother: No, say, "Nobody likes me."
Child: Nobody don't like me. *(Eight repetitions of this dialogue follow)*
Mother: No, now listen carefully. Say, "Nobody likes me."
Child: Oh! Nobody don't likes me.

While this child's imitation may not be an exact copy of the mother's words, Wood (1981) explains, it may approximate what the child sees and hears. In other words, children can only imitate language to the extent that their current stage of grammatical development affords that imitation. Wood writes:

> It is important to note that children's imitations are very much affected by their perceptions of the communication patterns to be imitated. In other words, children's imitations are a product of their particular stage of development in verbal and nonverbal language. It makes little sense to view the imitating child from an adult's eyes and ears. Instead we have to "get inside" the child's eyes and ears to see and hear as he does [1981, p. 51].

Imitation also provides opportunities for language rehearsal. Ruth Anne Clark (1977) explains that young children imitate out loud as a means of rehearsing language because they are as yet unable to rehearse silently. At very young ages, children's ability to think language rather than utter it is underdeveloped. Vygotsky (1962) believed that children's early speech is often cognitive self-guidance. In other words, the child muttering as she plays with blocks is talking through the task because of an inability to think it through silently. Similarly, the child who imitates an adult's remarks is practicing aloud what he is as yet unable to practice silently.

Imitation of adult communication behavior occurs early in life (Elliot, 1984). It is not uncommon for mothers to report "conversations" with their newborns. These conversations are, of course, quite different from adult conversations. Parent-infant interactions are brief and sporadic and characterized by mutual attention, responsivity (amount and level of reactions to each other), taking turns, and synchrony of signals. In short, newborns learn much about conversation before they are able to talk. They engage in what Trevarthen (1979) called a "dance of expressions and excitements" with their parents.

Expansion and Correction

One way that parents can facilitate their children's communication development is by engaging in what psycholinguists call **expansion.** This involves imitating the child's speech and expanding on it. For example:

> *Child:* Daddy car.
> *Mother:* Yes, Daddy is in the car.

This expansion provides a verb, a preposition, and an article. Such expansions can facilitate a child's language development, especially if the child attempts to imitate the adult's expanded version of his less-developed speech. Not all parents expand their children's speech. Many continuously speak "baby talk" to their children or merely respond to the meaning implied in the child's utterance. This may hinder language development.

The following conversation between a father and his five-year-old son suggests that children's understanding of past, present, and future may be facilitated by adult expansions and corrections of children's talk.

> *Joshua:* I like Disneyland too. Wanna talk about Disneyland too?
> *Father:* Yeah.
> *Joshua:* Okay. Remember the roller coaster that go this fast?
> *Father:* Oh, when we *went* to Disneyland you mean.
> *Joshua:* Yeah. That one *went* too fast.

Notice that Joshua was able to move his conversation into the past tense after his father's correction of "go" to "went." Had his father not corrected him, Joshua might have used "go too fast" to describe the roller coaster the second time.

Categorization

Another way that parents can facilitate communication development is through **categorization,** which involves subsuming several objects under the same category. For example, a parent can point out that apples and oranges are fruits.

The following conversation from Reardon-Boynton and Henke (1978, pp. 209–210) demonstrates how parents can help children learn to categorize information to avoid excessive talk. Notice that Lisa Beth expends a great deal of effort describing her play with objects "that go." Her father's description of these items teaches Lisa Beth to categorize similar objects. To the extent that she learns this, she can economize on talk. Reardon-Boynton and Henke (1978) suggest that while younger children (approximately ages three to four) apparently provide insufficient information and are encouraged to elaborate, older children (approximately ages five to six) may provide too much information and may be encouraged to formulate categories.

Lisa Beth: I liked school.

Father: Yeah, what did you do today?

Lisa Beth: Yeah, cause today we made a little um picture. We glued on, um, little airplanes and things and I put the helicopter in the water because it had water skis—the kind that land in the water.

Father: Oh.

Mother: What else was in the picture? (*Request for elaboration—invitation to converse*)

Lisa Beth: Um, a car, someone walking, a train, boats, and every kind of airplane and boat and air balloon, helicopter.

Father: That's a lot of stuff. All things that go. (*Categorization and verification*)

Lisa Beth: Yep. And also I got to write the number of wheels and attach them to that picture they go on. And and ah too the tables I made something that fell apart when you had rubber cement. And one of the others I made really good as car, train, and camper.

Father: Ah hah. Was this a whole day of things that go? (*Second verification of categorization*)

Mother: Yes. I think they've been studying transportation all week. (*Label for category*)

Lisa Beth: Yep.

Father: I see.

Imitation, expansion, and categorization are only three of many ways that children learn to communicate without being trained. To the extent that parents or guardians use these means to advance their children's communication ability, their children are likely to be effective at interpersonal communication.

Four Stages of Communication Development

Jean Piaget (1959) developed what is perhaps the most noteworthy theory of child cognitive development. Piaget's goal was to understand the nature of knowledge, and his work has provided many insights into the stages of communication and conversation development.

Piaget believed that thought precedes language. He distrusted language as a means of determining what children truly know. He argued that children's language often conceals rather than reveals what they know about an object. In other words, children often know more than they are capable of expressing. Therefore, verbal expression is often a poor indicator of a child's level of intelligence.

Sensorimotor Stage

The first of Piaget's stages is the sensorimotor intelligence stage (from birth to two years). During this time, children attempt to understand their environment by acting upon things physically. They suck things, bite things, and push and squeeze things. By doing so, children come to perceive the world as made up of separate objects, people, and activities rather than the kaleidoscope of sensations characteristic of their early perceptions.

According to Piaget, sensorimotor children "act on" the environment. They grab, kick, sock, poke, and so on, in an attempt to understand. During this time, children begin to speak. They learn that objects, people, and events have names. "Daddy car" may mean that Daddy is in the car or that he has gone to work in the car. "Mama shoe" may mean that the shoe is lost or that Mama should tie the shoe. Early child utterances depend highly on the situation at hand for interpretation.

To name objects and persons, a child must understand that these objects and people are separate entities and, despite any slight changes in them, they remain the same. For example, even if Mommy changes clothes, she is still Mommy. It may not seem a difficult task to recognize that a change of clothes does not change a person. For the young child, however, it is quite an accomplishment.

When children begin to place items in categories, they are also accomplishing a feat of significance. Vygotsky ([1934] 1962) refers to this ability as "associative complex," a process in which the child relates features of one situation to features of another. Wood (1981) tells us that these associations may not be clear to adults, but they seem to be clear from the child's point of view. For example, the child who says "giddyap" while bouncing in the tub as she does when bouncing on her toy horse is formulating an association.

Another process involved in the child's development of meaning is what Vygotsky (1962) calls the "chain complex." Here the child formulates a series of associations between referent situations and a word. He may say "wawa" to refer to bath water, water from the hose, and gas from the pump. According to Wood, calling gas from the pump "wawa" is an example of "overextension." Here the child is applying the word erroneously because the referents share certain features. Eve Clark (1978) contends that these overextensions occur because children want to communicate, despite their limited vocabulary. In order to communicate, they stretch the usage of words even if they are wrong. They do the best they can given what they have to work with.

Preoperational Stage

Piaget's second stage of child development is called the preoperational stage (from two to seven years). During these years, the child begins to deal with symbols but shows many contradictions and errors of logic. Children begin to adapt their language to the needs of other persons. However, during preconceptual thought (two to four years) the child's concepts are incomplete and appear illogical. During what Piaget called intuitive thought (four to seven years), thinking is more logical but still is dominated more by perception than by reasoning.

It is during the stage of preoperational development that children learn to ask questions. Much to the chagrin of many parents, "who, what, where, when" and, of course, "why" become very frequent aspects of a child's communication. Much like a "little scientist" the child seeks to understand her environment by asking seemingly endless questions.

Prior to age five, children tend to talk without really addressing other children in their vicinity. They talk to themselves in front of others. The following are two examples of this type of talk from Piaget (1959); he called it "collective monologue":

Pie: Where could me make another tunnel? Ah, here Eun?
Eun: Look at my pretty frock.

Cat: Have you finished, Bur?
Bur: Now it goes that way again.

Piaget states that talk of this type clearly anticipates future conversation. The speaker expects an answer from his hearer. Since the hearer is not listening, these two exchanges are collective monologues. The fact that Pie and Cat are both six-year-olds, whereas Eun and Bur are four-year-olds, probably accounts for the former being interested in cooperative interaction. Children of approximately three years of age tend to engage in collective monologues in which neither participant expects an answer from the other. At approximately five years of age, children begin to converse rather than merely speak in the presence of others.

According to Dale (1972), children in the sensorimotor stage do not produce "wh" questions. They also fail to understand them. However, many two- and most three-year-old children are capable of formulating questions, even if they depend initially upon intonation. For example, a two-year-old may ask if Billy is home by saying "Billy home?" and raising the pitch of his voice when saying "home."

Questions allow children to explore their environment more aggressively. Once they are able to ask questions, they no longer have to wait for events to occur before they can act upon them. As bothersome as continuous "whys" may be, they are one important means by which the little scientist advances her understanding.

During the preoperational stage, children are saturated with rules. They learn that there are right and wrong ways to do things. Children imitate the rule-following behavior of older children and adults. Their focus is on learning the rules verbatim. They are not yet ready to alter rules to suit the situation, but merely treat them as if they were laws.

Concrete Operations Stage

Piaget's third child development stage is called the concrete operations stage (from seven to eleven years). During this stage, the child acquires conceptions of time, space, number, logic, and the ability to conserve. **Conservation,** as Piaget uses the term, refers to the ability to recognize that transferring marbles or candies from a short jar to a tall jar does not change the number of marbles or candies. Children at this stage are not yet able to deal well with abstractions or with events that are not visible.

Children in the concrete operations stage are able to collaborate with others. Their chief interest is social. At approximately seven years of age, children begin to collaborate in abstract thought. These conversations involve explanations of things, discussion of the motives of actions, and the reality of events. According to Piaget, prior to this stage, children do not really converse. They are egocentric in that they are not truly social. Piaget places the beginnings of the socialization of thought between the ages of seven and eight.

During the concrete operations stage, discussions of right and wrong are frequent. Children seek to cooperate rather than to play for themselves as younger children do. To accomplish this cooperation in play they agree, usually only briefly, on the rules and are generally hostile to any innovation once the rules have been laid down. Not yet able to reason effectively, children, especially early in this stage, know that rules can be changed by consensus, but they also believe in the absolute and intrinsic truth of consensual rules (Piaget, 1960).

Formal Operations Stage

Stage four, the formal operations stage, is characterized by the ability to deal with the hypothetical and the abstract (eleven to fifteen years old). Children in this stage can reason in terms of cause-effect relationships. They can draw inferences based on accumulated data.

At this age children begin to realize that rules of play are not etched in stone. Rules are seen as the outcome of free decision worthy of respect only insofar as they enlist mutual consent. Children begin to alter rules as long as others approve. Piaget wrote of this period, "There are no more crimes of opinion, but only breaches in procedure" (1960, p. 57). Innovations are welcome if they increase the interest of the game. Children at this stage believe in the value of experiment insofar as it is sanctioned by others.

According to Piaget, this change in ideas about the rigidity of rules has profound effects on social conduct. The consciousness of autonomy—freedom to question social rules—emerges around the age of eleven. Unlike the young egocentric child, the older child is able to separate the ego (self) and the social environment. This ability allows the child to discuss issues and consider alternatives. By contrasting his views with others, the older child discovers the boundaries that separate him from others and also learns to understand others. Through this process the potential for cooperation develops. Piaget (1960, p. 90) wrote, "Cooperation is really a factor in the creation of personality, if by personality we mean, not the unconscious self of childish egocentrism, nor the anarchical self of egoism in general, but the self that takes up its stand on the norms of reciprocity and objective discussion, and knows how to submit to these in order to make itself respected."

It is by recognizing that rules are not firm external constraints but rather creations of their users that the child learns that many topics are open to discussion. The self begins to criticize rules and act as a guide, along with social norms, in the development of reasoned thought and reasoned argument.

Although Piaget's stages have been very useful to the study of children's communication, the ages associated with each of his stages should be viewed as ranges rather than as definitive boundaries. Also, Piaget's idea that children are egocentric in their communication until approximately the age of seven has been the subject of criticism (Vygotsky, 1962). Many researchers believe that from birth children have a strong motivation to communicate with others (Schaeffer, 1979). A fortunate child is one whose parents are willing to collaborate with her in conversation, even as a newborn child. Having the motivation to communicate with others is only one ingredient in the development of communication. Parents and other adults affect the child's communication skill development through their attention to conversation (see Haslett, 1984).

Restricted and Elaborated Language Codes

As children pass through stages of language development, they do so within a variety of contexts. British sociologist Basil Bernstein (1958, 1959, 1960, 1971) developed the concept of restricted and elaborated language codes to describe the way language is used in particular contexts. A **restricted code** is one that employs language in a relatively context-bound manner. The child who employs a restricted code assumes that the listener shares her perceptions of the context. The following story told by a child exemplifies a restricted code:

> They're playing football and he kicks it and it goes through there it breaks the window and they're looking at it and he comes out and shouts at them because they've broken it so they run away and then she tells them off. [Bernstein, 1971, p. 145].

This child does not tell us who is playing football, where "there" is, who is doing the shouting, or who "tells them off." The child assumes that the listener shares her view of the context.

An **elaborated code** does not tie the meaning to a particular context. When children use an elaborated code, they create a context with language. They make the meaning of their stories universal rather than particular to the context. The following story demonstrates an elaborated code:

> Three boys are playing football and one boy kicks the ball and it goes through a window the ball breaks the window and the boys are looking at it and a man comes out and shouts at them and then that lady looks out of her window and she tells the boys off. [Bernstein, 1971, p. 145]

This child provides the listener with more detailed information. It is not necessary for the listener to have had the experience the child is describing in order to understand the child's meaning.

As you might imagine, there are some advantages to being able to communicate with others in a manner that does not require a shared context. Telling jokes well depends on the teller's ability to create a context in the mind of the receiver, as does describing an experience to someone who was not there when it occurred.

Bernstein contends that the ability to use both restricted and elaborated codes is linked to social class. He suggests that middle-class people use both restricted and elaborated codes, whereas working-class people use mainly the restricted code. Other research has supported Bernstein's observation (Cook-Gumpertz, 1973; Robinson & Rackstraw, 1978). This research indicates that middle-class mothers communicate differently to their children than do working-class mothers. Middle-class mothers tend to ask more questions of their children, and they give answers related to their children's experiences (Robinson, 1981).

Basil Bernstein's work has contributed to our understanding of children's communication. However, one word of caution may be in order. Even Bernstein realized that social class is a crude index for the study of communication differences. There is considerable variation in codes among social classes.

Influence of Family on Communication Development

The early years of child communication development are typically spent mainly with family members. Therefore, the communication patterns in a family can have a profound effect on children's communication development.

Wood explains that strict guidelines based on status relationships within the family can lead to closed communication patterns with little room for discussion or dispute. Here are a few examples of strict status-dependent rules:

1. In matters of money, your father always decides.
2. Never speak angrily with your mother.
3. Male children deserve more (money or possessions) than female children.
4. The female children must take care of the younger ones.
5. Never argue with your father.
6. You must always do as your mother says [Wood, 1981, p. 67].

Some of these rules may be familiar to you. This does not necessarily mean that you were brought up in a closed communication environment. There are always rules of family behavior. However, when there are too many rules or if the rules are too rigid, the child's reasoning ability and communication development may be threatened.

In a closed communication family, rules for appropriate and effective behavior are strictly enforced. There is little self-autonomy—freedom to behave as you prefer—unless it does not conflict with the established rules. This type of environment stifles creativity of thought and action. It teaches children that there are only two categories of action: proper and improper. There is little room for imagination or discussion. Right and wrong are not subject to interpretation, and problems are not presented for consideration by family members.

Open communication patterns allow greater rule flexibility. Doing as father says may still be important, but there may be exceptions. The child living in an open communication environment can say, "Dad, I think there may be a better way to do this." Disrespect toward the father may be as prohibited in an open communication family as it is in a closed communication family. However, in the open communication family, disagreement is not a clear sign of disrespect.

Open communication helps the child learn to reason. It also teaches the child that there is usually more than one way to solve a problem. Communication competence requires the ability to deal constructively with people who do not share the same rules. Closed communication environments foster communication myopia—the belief that there is one way to solve a problem, and if it fails to work, nothing will.

A second problem associated with closed communication families is severe limitations on the expression of feelings. Children need to experiment with emotions. This does not mean that they should be encouraged to throw tantrums. It means that emotions are a fundamental aspect of human existence. We must learn to use them to facilitate communication. In many families, male children are expected to thwart emotional expression. In families where communication is closed, discussions of emotional reactions are discouraged. Junior is told, "Act your age" or "Don't be a wimp." The reasons behind his emotions are ignored, and he is deprived of the chance to express what may be legitimate feelings.

In an open communication environment, decisions are derived through discussion rather than handed down. Feelings are not suppressed without regard for their reasons. It may be impossible for any family to be completely open in their communication. Sometimes authority rule must abide. The key is to avoid excessively stringent rules so children can learn that there are a variety of ways to accomplish the same goal.

An alternative and more complex model of family communication patterns was developed by McLeod and Chaffee (1971). They proposed a model consisting of four family communication patterns: Laissez-faire, protective, pluralistic, and consensual families. (See Figure 4.1.)

The family communication patterns in Figure 4.1 differ according to their social versus concept orientation. **Socio-oriented families** place considerable emphasis on harmony and pleasant social relationships within the family. **Concept-oriented families** encourage children to develop their own views on issues and to consider more than one side of those issues.

Laissez-faire families are characterized by a lack of either socio- or concept-oriented relations. There is simply little parent-child communication. In **protective families,** obedience and harmony are very important. There is little concern with conceptual matters. Children from such homes are typically easy to persuade since they have not learned to defend their

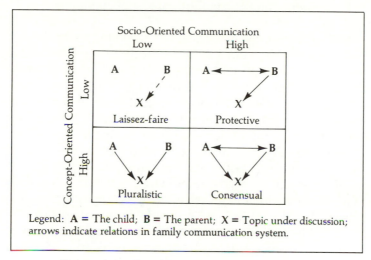

Figure 4.1.   Family communication patterns.
Source: McLeod and Chaffee (1971, p. 85).

own opinions. In **pluralistic families,** open communication and discussion of ideas are encouraged; family members have respect for each other's interests. The **consensual family** is characterized by pressure toward agreement. Children in consensual families are encouraged to take an interest in issues but to do so without disturbing the family power structure.

McLeod and Chaffee's model is a provocative addition to current perspectives on the effects of family patterns on children's communication styles. It has the added advantage of being free of class bias; it does not divide children's communication on the basis of socioeconomic status. McLeod and Chaffee's model suggests that children from different types of families likely approach communication situations within and outside the home in very different ways. For example, while the child raised in a pluralistic family is likely to feel comfortable exploring and discussing many sides of an issue, a child raised in a consensual home may shy away from expressing views that might contradict those of authority figures. Educators could certainly benefit from understanding how family communication patterns influence children's willingness to speak up in class, express opposing views, and defend their perspectives.

Influence of Peers on Communication Development

Families are not the only source of influence on the communication development of young children. Through day care, school, and other activities, children are exposed to others their own age. Peers can have considerable influence on the communication development of children (see Burleson, 1986).

Early childhood peer communication is most often part of play activity. Piaget has described the young child's speech during play as egocentric. The term **egocentrism** has sometimes been misinterpreted to mean that young children are selfish and inconsiderate. This is not Piaget's meaning. Egocentrism refers to the child's perception of experience being limited to his own. As children mature, egocentric communication gives way to more socialized communication. Children come to recognize that a situation may be seen from various perspectives and that often there is more than one way to solve a problem. With maturity, children learn to take the perspectives of others into consideration before selecting a behavior.

As we mentioned earlier in this chapter, Vygotsky (1962) disagreed with Piaget's claim that young children's speech during play is egocentric. He argued that children's communication is always social in interest. Vygotsky explained that egocentric speech provides cognitive self-guidance. He believed that thought and speech have different roots and that egocentric speech facilitates the development of logical thought. Young children who appear to be talking to themselves and ignoring others are, according to Vygotsky, guiding their inner thoughts as they formulate responses to others. Eventually, children are able to think without talking themselves through problems. Thought, as adults know it, becomes possible.

From Vygotsky's perspective, the young child is not unsocial but rather "parasocial"—a novice communicator. Although preschool children do not appear to differentiate between speaking to oneself and speaking to others, they are not antisocial. They are merely unable to recognize the perspectives of those with whom they communicate and are generally unaware that talking to oneself is not communication in the adult sense.

Both Piaget and Vygotsky would agree, however, that children's play becomes increasingly social with age. Irwin (1975, p. 16–17) has summarized the developmental stages of play as follows:

1. From birth to eighteen months or two years, the child plays in relation to his or her own body and the mother's. The child explores body parts, investigates environment, and begins to interact with significant others.
2. From age two to age seven or eight, the child engages in dramatic play or symbolic play. The child plays at make-believe alone, with peers, or with toys, and uses words to symbolize inner fantasies, images, thoughts, and feelings. Play is egocentric, and reality is distorted initially, but as the child becomes more socially adapted, play becomes more reality oriented.
3. From age eight to age eleven or twelve, the child's symbols and beliefs become modified through cooperation with others. The child plays games with carefully prescribed rules and regulations.

Allen and Brown (1976) explain that the early phase of the second stage of play is accomplished by mimicry of others' behavior. It does not involve taking the perspective of another person until the child has a self-concept. Only after children have a sense of who they are can they imagine themselves in the position of another person. Around age five to six, children become capable of going beyond mimicry to imagining how a mommy, doctor, or teacher might act.

Sachs, Goldman, and Chaille (1983) studied planning in pretend play among children two years to five and one-half years of age. The children were brought in pairs into a small playroom. They were told that they had a long time to play and were left alone together. The playroom contained numerous objects, many of which suggested a doctor theme. The play sessions lasted up to thirty minutes and were videotaped through a one-way mirror.

The researchers defined planning as the child was negotiating, organizing, and managing the play (1983). They differentiated between types of planning using the following schema:

Role:	"I'll be the doctor"; "You be the doctor."
Role Characteristic:	"I have a fever"; "Pretend you have a broken leg."
Object Description:	"That's a shot thing."
Object Transformation:	"This is the waiting room"; "Let's use this for a microphone" (holding up a block).
Action:	"I put it on"; "You put it on"; "Let's put it on."

Coders were asked to analyze the children's remarks using this schema. Analysis of the data indicated that two-year-olds did little pretending. When they did pretend, they never talked about roles. Seventy-one percent of the two-year-olds' utterances were in the action category. Object descriptions made up 16 percent of the two-year-olds' planning comments and object transformations constituted 13 percent.

The three-and-one-half-year-olds' play had a higher percentage of planning utterances about roles (18 percent) than did the play of two-year-olds and five-year-olds. Sachs, Goldman, and Chaille reason that the three-and-one-half-year-olds focused on roles more than other age groups in part because often both children wanted to be the doctor. The five-year-olds apparently were much better than the three-year-olds at politely negotiating role assignments. Action utterances made up 50 percent of the three-year-olds' remarks. Just 5 percent of their comments were object descriptions, while 15 percent were object transformations. The action utterances were characterized by simplicity. The researchers explain that "they most often consisted of talking about using the various objects on the other child who was (unwillingly) being a 'patient'" (1983, p. 123).

The five-year-olds were better able than the three-year-olds to compromise on role disagreements by calling on the notions of taking turns and fairness, as in "Your turn to be doctor maybe," or "And then next time you're the doctor for each of the babies, right?" They also used role characteristics. They said things like, "I have a sore throat," "Are you sick?," and "I steal things, right?" Such comments encouraged the other child to respond with role-appropriate action. For example, if one child said, "I have a fever," the other child might have given her a thermometer, reflecting knowledge about behavior appropriate to the role of the doctor. Such comments enrich play activities because they provide motivations for the other child's subsequent actions but do not tell the other child precisely what he should do, for example, "Give me a thermometer."

Object descriptions made up 13 percent of five-year-olds' planning utterances; 17 percent were object transformations. Sachs, Goldman, and Chaille explained that while object transformations were not greater for five-year-olds than for three-year-olds, there were qualitative differences. For example, five-year-olds are able to recognize the influence of time. Statements such as "Pretend it's tomorrow morning" are more characteristic of five-year-olds' play than of three-year-olds' play. Environmental variations are also more characteristic of five-year-old talk. They say such things as, "Pretend it's cold outside" more often than three-year-olds do.

Action utterances made up 49 percent of five-year-olds' planning. Their planning differed from that of younger children in that they were able to use "pretend" action utterances, as in "Pretend you put two blankets on me, right?" Five-year-olds were also capable of using the past tense, as in "Pretend I was driving in a car and I had an accident, okay?"

Five-year-olds' plots were more complex than those of three-year-olds, but the organization of the plots was not ordered correctly. When one child picked up a new object, a treatment or diagnosis or symptom would simply be invented to accompany the ensuing activity. Often that comment was not related to past utterances or actions.

Finally, five-year-olds were much more likely to talk about the theme: "Let's play doctor." Three-year-olds were guided more by the object in hand than by any explicit agreement on the theme of play.

The Sachs, Goldman, and Chaille (1983) study demonstrates how peer communication develops within the context of play. It is fascinating to witness how children enrich their play as they mature. While we tend to think of play as idle pastime, children's play is one means by which they move away from egocentrism. By taking the roles of others, they come to the realization that their own way of viewing the world is only one of many possible ways. As Flavell (1963, p. 279) explains, in resolving childish egocentrism the crucial factor is receiving information from other persons that forces the child to reexamine his own ideas in light of those of others.

Influence of Role-Taking Ability on Communication Development

One way that a child reexamines his own views is by taking the role of others. "Walk a mile in my shoes" as the saying goes, and you will see the world in a different light. **Role taking** is "the ability to understand the perceptual, cognitive, and emotional perspectives of others while at the same time maintaining one's own perceptual, cognitive, and emotional perspectives" (Johnson, 1977, p. 135). Children develop this ability as they mature.

Research suggests that role taking may enhance communication competence. Delia and O'Keefe (1976) argue that to be a fully competent communicator the child must be able to recognize and sustain another's perspective on the situation. Reardon (1982) found that this ability improves with age and the cognitive development of the child. However, she found that the ability to take the perspective of another child does not influence the ability to explain the other child's behavior. In other words, children can account for the actions of other children from their own perspective rather than from the perspective of others. This finding suggests that there are different levels of role-taking ability. Lower levels of role taking involve thinking about how "I" would feel in your situation. Higher levels of role taking involve thinking about how "I would feel if I were you." The young child thinks about how she would feel and assumes that the other child feels the same. With age, children learn to think in terms of how the other child, given his unique personality, might view the situation.

Although role-taking abilities improve with age, some people reach the age of eighty having developed little sensitivity to the perspectives of others. How does this happen? One likely reason is that these insensitive people were not rewarded for taking the perspective of others. While it is true that role taking requires cognitive ability, it also requires practice and reward. If parents encourage their children to see the world as others do and reward them for it, then they can expect their children to develop empathy. A parent might say, "I know you are angry with me, Johnny, but I want you to think for a minute. Why didn't I buy you that candy bar? Was it because I'm a mean mommy?" Such discussions can teach a child to consider the perspective of others. The parent who just says, "No, Johnny," without ever explaining why is not helping the child develop role-taking skills.

Parents do not need to explain every action, but children learn from adults. If parents do not attempt to take the perspectives of their children, how can they expect their children to do differently?

Influence of Gender Differences on Communication Development

One very interesting area of research is that of gender differences in verbal and nonverbal behavior. While sex is inborn, gender may be learned. In other words, a child is born either male or female but he or she must learn to act in ways consistent with societal expectations for his or her sex.

Gender training begins very early. Infant girls are dressed in pink more frequently than male infants are. Very early in life, little boys are discouraged from crying, shyness, and coyness. Little girls are rewarded for coyness and their shyness and crying meet with greater parental tolerance.

Although today's American society is characterized by less gender differentiation than in the past, female and male children still learn gender-specific roles. "Act like a lady" and "Big boys don't cry" are not antiquated phrases. The challenge for today's young people is to find creative ways to blend aspects of male and female gender roles. This may mean encouraging emotional sensitivity in male children and encouraging assertiveness in female children. No one has any final answers to the question, How can parents avoid trapping their children in gender stereotypes? A first step, however, is to sensitize oneself to one's own gender biases.

By the age of five or six, children are well aware of gender differences. They know what Ekman, Friesen, and Ellsworth (1972) call "display rules." These rules tell them which expressions are appropriate in a given situation for someone of their age and gender. Children learn these rules from adults and peers.

Children's Nonverbal Communication

For very young children, movement is the primary form of communication. Children use their entire bodies to communicate their needs and wants. Pointing and grunting is how many toddlers convey their desire for a ball or cookie.

Much early childhood nonverbal communication is spontaneous. As we discussed in Chapter Two, spontaneous communication occurs without cognitive intervention. For example, if an infant is frightened by an unfamiliar object, he may cry. This crying may communicate to the parent that the child is frightened, but, in all likelihood, the child did not consciously consider the parent's reaction prior to the outburst. Other nonverbal actions are contrived. The child intentionally uses them to communicate with someone. Pouting until the parent responds is an example of contrived nonverbal communication.

Children use nonverbal communication from birth. By the age of four months, infants are responsive to pictures of faces. By the age of six months, the child smiles in response to another's smile and responds to differences in the mother's posture and facial expressions. At approximately eight months, fear reactions to strangers occur. According to Allen and Brown (1976), these reactions of fear occur somewhat earlier in female infants than in male infants.

At approximately one year, learning of language and gesture begins. Much research indicates that as children become more efficient at verbal language, they rely less on gestures. Wood (1981) explains that more recent studies indicate that while some gestures decrease in frequency as the child matures, others increase. Wood describes three categories of gestures that vary with age. The first is what Wood calls "deictic gestures," which children use when they point to objects or places to refer to "this," "that," or "over there." A second category involves "pantomimic gestures" used to mimic something or someone children see or feel. Wood offers the example of a child showing the surprised look of a friend when he found a dollar bill. The third category covers arm or hand movements that add what wood calls "semantic or relational information." According to Wood (1981, p. 174), "When children use gestures to illustrate size or shape or to show emphasis, contrast, or amendment of the content, they are using gestures semantically." Wood explains relational gestures as those children use to communicate how they feel about people they talk to: "Relational gestures can convey feelings such as affection, hostility, and cautiousness" (p. 174).

Nonverbal communication is as important to the study of human interaction as the study of verbal communication. Remember that we are emotional as well as cognitive beings. To the extent that children's nonverbal communication training is lax, they are likely to become poor communicators. Much of who we are is conveyed via nonverbal cues.

Influence of Emotion on
Communication Development

For years communication scientists have treated emotion as secondary to cognition. Recent theory and research indicate that emotion is as important to interpersonal communication and persuasion as cognition (see Zajonc, 1980; Buck, 1984).

Ross Buck (1984) proposes that people vary in **emotional education**—the acquisition of knowledge of emotion via experience and instruction. Buck explains that the child is confronted by a host of subjective feelings, expressive behaviors, and reports of feelings in others, as well as feedback from his or her own behavior. He suggests that the ways in which children interpret these events depend on their stage of development. For example, the concrete operational child should be superior to the preoperational child in understanding that others have feelings different from his own.

Buck argues that children learn how to attend to emotional experience. To the extent that parents, peers, and acquaintances teach young children to experience and interpret emotions, emotional education is promoted. To the extent that children are taught to suppress emotions rather than to understand them, emotional education is hindered.

Although research on children's emotional development is sparse, there is evidence for increased control over emotional expression with age. As mentioned earlier in this chapter, children learn display rules—personal, situational, and cultural norms—that govern their emotional expressions. Ekman (1978) described three major types of display rules:

1. Simulation: showing feelings when you have none.
2. Inhibition: giving the appearance of having no feeling when you in fact do.
3. Masking: covering a feeling with the expression of one you are not experiencing.

To participate effectively in society, children must learn to engage in simulation, inhibition, and masking. The whole truth is often inappropriate to the situation at hand. If, for example, your best friend asks you if you like her new dress, could you reply, "It's the ugliest thing I've ever seen"? Of course, you could tell her that, but you might hurt her feelings and damage your relationship with her. Moreover, perhaps your first impression of her dress is negative, but you know that it is the latest style and in time you may even come to like it. Under such circumstances, it might be advantageous to withhold judgment.

To withhold judgment or refrain from telling the uncomfortable whole truth, children must learn how to control their emotional expressions. It appears that the nonverbal channel easiest to control is the face. In a study of student nurses' abilities to deceive, Ekman and Friesen (1974) found that the body reveals true feelings during deception whereas facial cues do not do so. Other research indicates that higher voice pitch is associated with deception and that voice is one of the least controllable emotional channels.

In a study of children's deception, Shennum and Bugental (1982) found that with age both boys and girls improved in their ability to manage facial expressions when attempting to mask negative feelings, but boys improved more than girls in their ability to inhibit negative feelings. These findings are consistent with social norms that encourage boys to avoid emotional expression more than girls. Shennum and Bugental found that both girls and boys were unable to control conveying negative feelings via the voice. They also found no developmental trends for the acquisition of control over positive feelings. Children ranging in age from six to twelve years were equally able to control expressions of positive feelings.

Another interesting finding from this study involved the relationship between role-taking ability and expressive control. It appears that to the extent that children are sensitive to the perspective of others, they are better able to manage their facial expressions.

Aside from better control of expression, older children also appear to be better than younger children at detecting deception from others. While this may seem a good thing, recent research indicates that superior deception detection may be socially undesirable. Rosenthal and DePaulo (1979) conducted a study of high school children's skills in detecting deception. They found that especially skilled males and females were rated by their teachers as less popular and less socially sensitive than other students. Moreover, these skillfull detectors of deception reported less satisfaction with the quality of their interpersonal relationships.

It seems that being too skillful at detecting deceit is not good if you wish to be popular and satisfied with your relationships. Seeing more than others want you to see can be socially hazardous. DePaulo and Jordan (1982) report that superior deception detection may be beneficial to people pursuing careers in such fields as psychiatry and medicine, although such an ability enables us to know some of the feelings of others that we might be happier not knowing.

The Young Persuader

In Chapter 2, we explained that persuasion involves the intention by at least one participant to change the thoughts, feelings, or behavior of another. To participate effectively in persuasion both in terms of attempting to change others or attempting to resist change, children must learn persuasion strategies.

Studies show a consistent development in children's persuasive strategies during elementary school years. Delia and Clark (1977) studied children's persuasive strategy development using picture pairs developed by Alvy (1973). Two similar picture pairs appear in Figure 4.2. Children were asked to tell the experimenters how they would ask the angry boy versus the happy boy if they could play with his trucks. Similarly, the children were asked how they would ask for a puppy from the girl with one puppy versus the girl with five puppies.

Delia and Clark (1977) and Reardon (1982) found that children's ability to adapt their strategies to the situation improved with age and cognitive complexity. Older, more complex children used elaborated strategies to persuade. Such children might say, "Can I use your truck for just a few

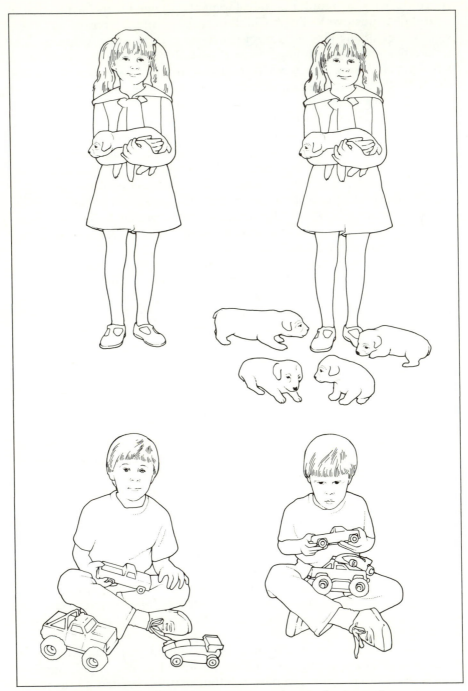

Figure 4.2.   Two picture pairs used to study persuasion.
Source: Alvy 1973.

minutes?" or "If you let me use your truck for a while, I'll let you play with my car."

These findings are consistent with our previous discussion of role taking. To the extent that a child is able to take the perspective of another, her attempts to persuade that person are likely to reflect attention to the listener's needs, wants, or concerns.

One of the earliest strategies employed by children is intentional crying. As children mature they realize that crying is not as effective as a simple request. Later they realize that simple requests are not as useful as strategic requests such as, "If I'm good today, can I stay up late tonight?" It is likely that strategies used by the young child are learned by imitation. With age and cognitive development, the child is able to create strategies.

Rodnick and Wood (1973) studied the communication strategies of fifteen children from one to eleven years of age in three situations: eating, sleeping, and playing. They found that the one- to two-year-olds used nonverbal strategies—crying, pulling, throwing, banging, and affectionate behavior. Three- and four-year-olds relied more on language accompanied by nonverbal communication. They also used more psychological tactics such as withdrawing affection, expressing loneliness, appealing to fear, expressing desire to be kissed and held, and using father to get around mother.

It appears that persuasion is learned very early in life. As children mature, they learn that certain strategies are inappropriate, inconsistent, or ineffective. They develop repertoires of strategies that they test in various situations. To the extent that a child is cognitively complex, he will be able to create elaborate strategies.

Children also vary in persuasibility, the ease with which they are persuaded. Some studies suggest that children may learn through parent-child interactions whether to focus their attention more on the source or the message. Stone and Chaffee (1970) explain that source and message orientations result from family communication patterns. Children from families where conflict is avoided tend to be more persuasible because they have not learned to refute arguments, they have only learned to avoid them. Children from families that stress the importance of considering various opinions are better prepared to resist persuasive arguments.

Obviously family interaction patterns have a considerable influence on communication and persuasion abilities. To the extent that a child is encouraged to reason, she may be better prepared to persuade effectively and to avoid being persuaded without good reason.

Summary

In this chapter we have examined how children acquire language within the contexts of interpersonal communication and persuasion. The rate of their progress depends not only on their own cognitive abilities but also on the language usage of those with whom they have the most contact.

In the next chapter we will look at communication competence, including the skills adults need to communicate effectively. The acquisition of many communication skills begins early in childhood. As we have discussed in this chapter, children whose conversation development is encouraged by adults are likely to come to adulthood with many of the skills that facilitate communication competence. They have a distinct communication advantage.

CHAPTER 5

Interpersonal Communication Competence

When you stop to think that communication is the means by which we make friends, acquire jobs, express love, obtain help, and explain our behavior, the importance of doing it well is apparent. Moreover, the mobility of modern society exposes people to a greater number of novel situations than ever before, so the ability to communicate effectively is important. Those who cannot communicate well may find themselves settling for relationships, careers, and self-images that fall short of those they might otherwise attain.

In this chapter we will define communication competence and look at what it takes to be a competent communicator. We will explore some of the skills that separate the more and less competent among us. Many of the skills are ones you have already acquired; others may need your attention. Keep these skills in mind as you read this chapter. Focusing on the skills that need your attention should help you increase your own level of communication competence.

What Is Interpersonal Communication Competence?

Communication scholars have been working toward an understanding of public speaking competence for centuries. It is only during the past few decades, however, that competence in interpersonal communication has received attention. We are at an early stage in our process of discovering how interpersonal communication competence should be defined. Little consensus exists. The definition we will use in this chapter is a synthesis of the contributions of several communication competence theorists: *Your level of interpersonal communication competence is the degree to which your behaviors are appropriate to the situation and help you attain personal and relational goals.* Let's take a few moments to discuss several aspects of this definition.

Competence: A Matter of Degree

Our definition describes competence in terms of degree. This means that competence is not something that is either present or absent in interpersonal interactions, but rather present at some level. Communication behaviors are more or less competent given the relationship, situation, and participants.

For example, laughter is usually an appropriate response to a joke. However, the amount of laughter appropriate after a joke depends on the situation. No matter how good the joke, raucous laughter in a church or synagogue is usually inappropriate. Should the minister, priest, or rabbi tell an amusing story, modest laughter might be acceptable.

There are levels of communication competence. Some people just get by, some do quite well, and others excel in terms of behaving in a manner that is appropriate, consistent, and effective given the relationship and situation.

Competence: An Individual and Relational Construct

Communication competence is, in large part, the degree to which both personal and relational goals are attained during an interaction. This means that achieving one's personal goals while neglecting to help other participants meet some level of goal achievement is not as competent as achieving one's goals while also ensuring that other participants reach some level of satisfaction.

Wiemann (1977) proposed a definition of communication competence that emphasizes the individual communicator's goals but also includes the need for relational consideration. He described the competent communicator as "the person who can have his or her way in the relationship while maintaining a mutually acceptable definition of that relationship" (p. 198). Unlike definitions that focus on individual goal achievement or mutual goal achievement exclusively, Wiemann's definition focuses on both the individual and the relationship. To the extent that communicators do achieve their personal goals while ensuring some level of goal achievement satisfactory to the other participants, their communication is competent.

Imagine consistently achieving your own goals during interpersonal interactions without regard for the goals of other participants. Eventually you would be without friends. We are social beings who need to maintain relationships with others. There may be times when maintaining a relationship is not as important as achieving a personal goal. However, in conversations with people important to us, keeping the relationship is often as important, and sometimes more important, than achieving one's own immediate goals.

Competence: Appropriate and Effective Behaviors

Spitzberg and Cupach (1984) argue that interpersonal communication competence is concerned with the quality of communication and therefore involves both appropriateness and effectiveness: to behave in a competent manner, a communicator must say or do what is appropriate to the situation and effective given personal and relational goals.

Appropriateness refers to the extent to which communication behavior is the right thing to do according to the social rules impinging on the interaction. For example, the appropriate response to "Thank you" is usually "You're welcome." Failing to respond to "Thank you" with "You're welcome" or some other appropriate phrase might be viewed as rude or inconsiderate.

Effectiveness refers to the degree to which communication behavior aids reaching personal and relational goals. Sometimes the effective thing to do is not the appropriate thing to do. For example, if your goal is to get the attention of someone who is talking to another person, an effective but perhaps inappropriate behavior is to interrupt.

Cultural differences can lead to confusion over what is appropriate and effective behavior. When conducting business in Saudi Arabia, much time is spent sipping tea and socializing before business discussions begin. Many American business executives find this social chitchat annoying because it takes time away from business negotiations. The experienced business traveler, however, knows that this socializing is imperative to successful negotiations. In short, he realizes that it is important to be appropriate in order to be effective—that is, convince them to sign a contract.

Another competence obstacle is the possible conflict between appropriateness and effectiveness. An employee faced with the choice of telling a supervisor that she did most of the work on a successful project or sharing the credit equally with a friend who had contributed to the success is experiencing conflict between effectiveness (in this case, getting ahead) and appropriateness (doing what a friend should do).

How might you resolve this conflict? Your answer depends on your priorities, your mood, the current state of your relationship with the friend in question, and a host of other factors.

Competence: Differences Across Situations

Is competence a trait individuals have that facilitates communication success across situations, or is it a different set of behaviors for each situation? This question reflects the trait versus state issue in the study of communication competence.

The **trait perspective** implies that research on interpersonal communication competence should eventually provide a list of skills possessed by effective communicators. The **state perspective,** or situation-specific view, implies that it is impossible to list skills that characterize interpersonal communication competence across situations. Instead, types of situations must be studied to determine the behavioral responses that lead to success in each.

State theorists also believe that the type of relationship influences competence. Are the communicators strangers, acquaintances, friends, or intimates? As you might expect, research indicates that we talk to acquaintances differently than we talk to intimates (Berger, 1982). Relationships among communicators affect the appropriateness and effectiveness of behaviors as much as the situation does.

The definition we have proposed in this chapter treats competence as both situation specific and relationship specific. Behavior that is appropriate and effective in one situation for one type of relationship may not be so in another situation or relationship. For example, you might effectively persuade a friend that what he's wearing is ugly and likely to make people laugh, but it might be considered inappropriate to criticize a friend's choice of clothes. Here an effective means of reaching your goal of persuading a friend to dress differently is inappropriate to the relationship.

The situational-relational perspective does not deny that some behaviors ease communication across situations. For example, listening is a valuable skill in most interpersonal interactions. However, certain other behaviors are valuable to specific types of situations and relationships. For example, Miller, Boster, Roloff, and Seibold (1977) found that people use different strategies when trying to persuade people with whom they expect to have long-term relationships than people who they do not expect to see again.

Competence: Spontaneous, Scripted, and Contrived Behaviors

In Chapter 2, we divided interpersonal communication behaviors into three types: spontaneous, scripted, and contrived. Spontaneous behaviors occur without any conscious planning or monitoring. They are elicited by emotional reactions to objects, people, or events. Both scripted and contrived behaviors, however, involve planning and monitoring. In the case of scripted behavior, the planning and monitoring occurs at the time the behavior is learned; with practice it becomes automatic. Scripted behaviors do not require any immediate planning or monitoring when they occur because they have been enacted many times before. Contrived behaviors involve conscious planning and monitoring. They are the most conscious acts of communication.

Can each of these types of behavior contribute to competence judgments? If someone bursts into tears and thereby effectively conveys his despair, can we then say that crying was the competent thing to do in this situation? The answer depends on your willingness to include within the realm of interpersonal communication competence those behaviors that are neither planned nor monitored. If by competent behavior we mean behavior that works given the goal of the communicator and situational constraints, then even spontaneous behaviors can be considered competent if they "work." If, however, by competent behavior we mean behaviors that communicators consciously use to reach a communication goal, then spontaneous behavior may have to be excluded from competence considerations.

The position taken by theorists and researchers on the consciousness issue influences their definitions of competence in interpersonal communication. Spitzberg and Cupach (1984, p. 77) state, "It is simply becoming unrealistic to develop theories of human interaction that are based on the presumption that people always or typically are highly conscious of their communicative behavior and strategic decisions. Likewise, there may be little reason to endow models of competence with an exceedingly high level of awareness." They cite research indicating that people vary in the degree to which they consciously consider their communication behavior (Snyder, 1974, 1979; Fenigstein, 1979; Cegala, Savage, Brunner, & Conrad, 1982).

People often behave without conscious consideration of the possible effects of their actions. From the results of these spontaneous expressions, they often learn new ways to act purposively. For example, a child might cry when he falls without any thought of being reassured by his parents. However, should his parents cuddle him and "kiss the boo boo," he might consciously decide to cry the next time he falls to bring about the same effect. People learn from the effects of their spontaneous behavior as well as from the effects of their scripted and contrived behaviors. To leave any of these types out of the interpersonal communication competence equation would distort the reality of human interaction.

In this section, we have introduced a definition of interpersonal communication competence that integrates a number of perspectives. This definition implies that interpersonal communication competence is not simply a list of social skills. Competence does require social skills, but the situation and the relationship between or among communicators influences which social skills are important. This definition also treats competence as a matter of degree. In other words, people are more or less competent in their interactions, rather than simply competent or incompetent. Appropriateness and effectiveness in terms of situation and relationship are the criteria by which degree of competence may be determined.

Social Skills: Cognitive and Behavioral

Two types of social skills are involved in communication competence: cognitive and behavioral. **Cognitive skills** facilitate the communicator's understanding of how personal and relational goals might be satisfied. **Behavioral skills** help carry out goal-directed behavior. Both types of skills are important. It is not enough to know how to achieve your communication goals. You also need the behavioral skills essential to do so.

Cognitive Skills

None of the skills to be described in this section guarantees competence. The importance of each cognitive skill depends on the situation at hand. For example, while empathy is a cognitive skill, it is not always needed to achieve personal and relational goals; it may occasionally be an obstacle. Perhaps you know someone who gets so involved in the problems of others that she becomes exhausted and of little help.

Consider each of the following skills as potential contributors to competence rather than necessary components of competence across situations. Competence, after all, depends on the situation. It is not a fixed quality that one carries around. It is a function of many factors, of which the cognitive skill of any single communicator is only one (Parks, 1985).

Empathy

The first cognitive skill we will discuss involves sensitivity to the thoughts and feelings of another person. Since each of us has different views of the same situation, we must understand each other's perspectives if we wish to communicate effectively.

There are numerous definitions of empathy (see Deutsch & Madle, 1975). Some describe empathy as understanding another's emotions or feelings (Kohler, 1929, 1947; Aronfreed, 1968; Stotland, Sherman, & Shaver, 1971). Other definitions describe it as imagining oneself in the place of another—role playing (Mead, 1934; Flavell, Botkin, Fry, Wright, & Jarvis, 1968; Kalisch, 1973).

There appears to be some recent consensus that empathy requires self-other differentiation and that it is a response to another's emotional state

(Deutsch & Madle, 1975). In other words, empathy is the ability to imagine the feelings of another person without abandoning one's own perspective on the situation. For example, being able to comprehend how another person feels about the death of a parent, without being overcome by the emotion oneself, is empathy.

Empathy can have important effects on social interaction. Research suggests that popular children are more adept at empathizing than are unpopular children (Deutsch, 1974; Rubin, 1972). The ability to sense the feelings of others seems to allow one to respond in socially sensitive ways (Rothenberg, 1970).

Empathy is important to interpersonal communication partly because there is often a shortage of information available from which to draw conclusions about others' feelings. Words can be weak vehicles for the expression of complicated feelings. Moreover, people are often unwilling to express their true feelings for fear of embarrassment or rejection. Empathy is a means by which we visit the minds of others to derive otherwise unavailable information.

Engaging in empathy poses the risk of becoming involved in the experiences of another person. But it affords the opportunity to know more than is obvious. Empathy involves experimenting with different roles in the imagination—seeing an issue from more than one vantage point. Robert Katz (1963) describes empathy as a worthwhile risk that requires both the ability to experiment with different roles in the imagination and the ability to detach oneself for the purpose of objective assessment.

Although empathy may not be necessary for successful participation in all interpersonal communication, it can enhance competence. It allows communicators to derive information about others that they may use in their choice of words, style of presentation, and strategies.

Social Perspective-Taking

While empathy is a sensitivity to the feelings of others, social perspective-taking is the ability to understand the options available to other persons involved in the interaction. To the extent that we comprehend how others see a given situation and their choices of behavior, we are in a better position to predict their actions. Such prediction aids our own attempts to respond in appropriate and effective ways.

People highly adept at social perspective-taking are more capable than others of seeing a situation from the perspective of another person, determining what options are available to that person, and selecting the option the other is likely to use.

Delia and O'Keefe (1974) describe social perspective-taking as a prerequisite to becoming a fully competent member of one's social environment. Research indicates that social perspective-taking influences communicators' choices of persuasion strategies (Clark & Delia, 1976; Delia & Clark, 1977; Delia, Kline, & Burleson, 1979). For example, a person with social perspective-taking skills is likely to consider carefully how the person to be persuaded views the situation before selecting a strategy.

Cognitive Complexity

Research indicates that social perspective-taking ability is related to **cognitive complexity** (Delia & Clark, 1977; Reardon, 1982). Cognitive complexity refers to the number and type of cognitive constructs and schemata people have available for interpreting aspects of their environment. **Constructs** are mental structures by which people interpret the meaning of objects, people, and events. They operate much like yardsticks operate in the measurement of length. A yard is a criterion for identifying length. Constructs are criteria for identifying size, length, height, weight, depth, attractiveness, friendliness, and other qualities. For example, you might wonder at the motive of someone who is excessively friendly when you first meet him. The only way you can determine whether his friendliness is actually excessive is by comparing his behavior to your expectations or schemata for how strangers ought to act. According to George Kelly (1955), originator of the personal construct theory, we have an extensive array of constructs with which we interpret our world. Each of us interprets experiences somewhat differently because our construct systems are different.

Constructs can be depicted as bipolar adjectival scales like those in Figure 5.1. These scales for interpreting a class meeting show how constructs can be used to interpret events. The left side of each construct is the preferred side. If a particular class meeting were ranked near the interesting, informative, and organized side of the constructs, it would be considered a good class by the person using this construct system.

People use different construct systems to interpret different objects, people, and events. If the event to be interpreted were a party rather than a class meeting, the constructs used to interpret it would, in all likelihood, differ from those listed in Figure 5.1. The constructs listed in Figure 5.2 might be used to interpret the quality of a party.

Your construct system for judging parties may be different from that in Figure 5.2. You may consider music a higher priority than number of people. You may have an entirely different set of constructs for determining the quality of a party. You may even have different construct systems for different types of parties.

Construct systems for interpreting objects, people, and events differ among people because different experiences generate different criteria for seeing the world. Interesting, informative, and organized may not be a

```
┌────────────────────────────────────────────────────────────────────────┐
│  Construct System for Interpreting the Quality of a Class Meeting        │
│                                                                          │
│  Interesting    _____  _____  _____  _____  _____   Boring         │
│  Informative    _____  _____  _____  _____  _____   Uninformative  │
│  Organized      _____  _____  _____  _____  _____   Disorganized   │
│                                                                          │
└────────────────────────────────────────────────────────────────────────┘
```

Figure 5.1. Construct system for interpreting the quality of a class meeting.

widely shared system of constructs for interpreting class meetings. Some people may be more concerned with the hour at which the class meets.

Construct systems also differ in terms of the number of constructs used to interpret objects, people, and events and the abstraction and integration of those constructs. **Differentiation** refers to the number of constructs a person uses for interpretation. The construct system in Figure 5.1 has three constructs. Another person's construct system for judging the quality of class meetings may have eight constructs, which would be a more highly differentiated construct system for assessing the quality of classes.

Abstraction refers to the extent to which the constructs used to interpret some object, person, or event subsume other constructs. For example, in the statement "He's jealous," the word "jealous" represents an abstract construct that encompasses a number of specific behavioral descriptions such as "He wouldn't talk to her for a week after seeing her with Ed" and "He broke up with his last girlfriend when she had lunch with another man." These behaviors may indicate that "he" is a jealous person. The following statements illustrate a more abstract construct subsuming less abstract ones: "He's jealous, unreliable, and insulting. I think he's unstable." Unstable encompasses three less abstract concepts: jealous, unreliable, and insulting.

Integration is the extent to which constructs are connected and qualified in a coherent impression. The statement "He is sometimes unpleasant but he is a good person in other ways" represents how the construct "unpleasant," qualified by "sometimes" and linked with "good person," generates a more complex image than does listing the separate constructs "unpleasant" and "good person." We know that the person described is a good person though sometimes unpleasant.

Researchers often select one of these three criteria—differentiation, abstraction, and integration—for assessing cognitive complexity. Delia and his colleagues often use differentiation alone as a criterion for assessing children's cognitive complexity. By counting the number of constructs used by a child in her written descriptions of another child, researchers obtain a measurement of cognitive complexity.

Cognitive complexity is important to competence in interpersonal communication because cognitively complex persons are capable of assessing

```
┌─────────────────────────────────────────────────────────────────┐
│                                                                   │
│   Sample Construct System for Interpreting the Quality of a Party │
│                                                                   │
│   Lively    _____  _____  _____  _____  _____  Dull         │
│   Many                                                Few         │
│   people    _____  _____  _____  _____  _____  people       │
│   Good                                                Bad         │
│   food      _____  _____  _____  _____  _____  food         │
│   Good                                                Bad         │
│   music     _____  _____  _____  _____  _____  music        │
│                                                                   │
└─────────────────────────────────────────────────────────────────┘
```

Figure 5.2.   Construct system for interpreting the quality of a party.

people and situations from a number of perspectives. They have more constructs available for interpretation, and combinations of constructs are more abstract and integrated than those of less complex people. Complexity helps attempts to adjust communication behavior to the peculiarities of the situation at hand and its participants. For example, it appears that "the perceiver with a highly differentiated set of abstract interpersonal constructs is better able to accommodate diverse or newly available information in forming an organized and coherent impression of another" (O'Keefe & Delia, 1982, p. 46). Research also indicates that the level of development of an interpersonal construct system is related to the type of persuasion strategies selected (Clark & Delia, 1977; O'Keefe & Delia, 1979; Delia, Kline, & Burleson, 1979; Applegate, 1980).

To date there is little research indicating that complexity may upon occasion be a detriment to competence. It seems reasonable to conclude, however, that there is such a thing as too much complexity or misplaced complexity. Perhaps extremely complex people think over simple issues longer than necessary. You have no doubt heard the phrase, "He makes a mountain out of a molehill." Highly complex people may be capable of doing just that. Moreover, complexity may be an obstacle when communicating with less complex people. The stereotypical professor who speaks in a manner far beyond the grasp of her audience is an example. The professor's problem may also be one of poor social perspective-taking.

Sensitivity to Relationship Standards

Roloff and Kellerman (1984) argue that communication competence varies across relationships. They explain that over the course of a relationship people develop expectations about what each should and should not say and do. Often people are not even aware that they have expectations until someone does something that offends them.

Why does the same joke work in one situation but not in another? The reason lies in the expectations people have for relationships and situations.

The same jokes that send your friends into frenzies of laughter may produce a smirk from acquaintances.

The type of relationship affects what we expect others to say and do. If you decide that a person is a friend, you expect him to communicate like one. The following conversation demonstrates how defining a relationship sets up certain expectations for behavior:

Barbara: I think Ann is angry with me.
Karen: I don't think so.
Barbara: Oh yes. She hasn't called me in six months.
Karen: She's been very busy with the new baby.
Barbara: I know, but we're friends. Besides, the last time she didn't like something I did, she didn't tell me until it was over. And she's my friend. You'd think she would have said something earlier.
Karen: Maybe you should call her. You may be misjudging her.
Barbara: Yeah. You may be right.

Barbara interpreted Ann's behavior from the perspective of a friendship. She considers six months too long between friends' telephone calls. By deviating from Barbara's expectations, Ann has given Barbara reason to wonder about their friendship. Barbara assumes that she and Ann share a standard for friends contacting friends. Since Ann violated this standard, Barbara believes that Ann is angry at her.

This conversation provides an example of how people use expectations about relationships to judge the communication behavior of others. Competent communicators are sensitive to such expectations and adjust their behaviors to the requirements of their relationships.

Situational Knowledge

Aside from sensitivity to relationship expectations, competent communicators know that there is a time and a place for everything. Recently researchers have begun to study types of social situations. They hope to determine how communicators use information about a situation in their selection of behaviors.

Cody and McLaughlin (1985, p. 265) propose that people use their impressions of situations to understand the behaviors of others and in their own choices of behaviors. People use situational knowledge to determine the rules that they and others should follow. Here are the four uses of situational knowledge described by Cody and McLaughlin:

1. People use knowledge of situations as a framework for evaluating others.
2. People process information, as situations unfold, on the basis of their purposes for being in the situation.

3. People elect to enter into, avoid, or change a situation according to their self-in-situation scenarios, self-knowledge, or perceived competences.
4. People use situational knowledge as a guideline for knowing how to behave.

The first of these four uses of knowledge of a situation suggests that people consider the situation when developing standards for evaluating others' communication. Without some understanding of the context of an interpersonal encounter, people cannot judge the appropriateness and effectiveness of other people's behavior.

If we know that John arrived late to Mary's house, we do not know whether his lateness was incompetent or not. If we learn that Mary planned a surprise party for someone else and arriving on time was important to the surprise, John's lateness becomes more serious. It was inappropriate by the standards of the people at the party.

The second method of using situational information indicates that people interpret the situation in terms of their purposes. For example, if the purpose of your conversation with a friend is to make plans for a weekend trip, you are likely to interpret your friend's actions in terms of that purpose. If your friend changes the subject every time you begin to make definite plans, you might wonder if she really wants to go on the trip. You might wonder whether your friend is hoping for an invitation from someone else to do something more interesting than you have in mind.

The third way people use situational knowledge is to determine whether they can participate without contradicting their self-images or operating beyond their capacities. People often have a general idea about how well they can perform in various types of situations. For example, some people are very uncomfortable meeting strangers. Many people fear public speaking and avoid such situations. Each of us knows, from past experience, how successful we can expect to be in specific types of situations. We may seek to avoid threatening ones or to make changes that ease our discomfort. For example, people who do a lot of public speaking often arrive early to arrange the room in a manner that eases their anxiety.

The fourth way that people use their knowledge of situations involves selecting appropriate and effective behavior. **Appropriateness** and **effectiveness** are meaningless out of context. *Appropriateness* refers to the ability of communicators to meet the requirements of the situation—to do what is right or expected by others (see Wiemann & Backlund, 1980). *Effectiveness* refers to the degree to which behaviors help you attain personal and relational goals in a particular situation. Let's look at an example. How appropriate might it be for a neighbor to invite you, a bachelor, to come over to his home on Christmas morning to watch his children open their presents? This may seem reasonable to you. What if your neighbor extended the invitation by telephone at 6:30 AM on Christmas morning? This actually happened to a friend of mine. When I and others asked how he responded, Charlie said, "I got up from bed and went to watch the little monsters open their presents." He explained, "What else could I do? I couldn't tell him that I couldn't care less about what his kids were doing at 6:30 AM on Christmas morning. So I went over to his house." Charlie considered acceptance of this unusual invitation the appropriate thing to do because it was Christmas morning and his neighbor's intentions were good. Someone else might have been less understanding. Later that day Charlie was relating this story to a few friends. Each had his own version of how he would have responded. One said, "If I were you, Charlie, I would have told him he was nuts." Another said, "You were being a bit unassertive, Charlie. He was clearly wrong to call you at that hour." And a third said, "I think it was a very charitable thing to do on Christmas day."

Obviously consensus on the appropriate and effective ways to respond to situations is not always easily achieved. Nevertheless, situational knowledge helps people decide how to act. It also helps them decide what they can expect from others, which makes situational knowledge an important ingredient of communication competence.

Self-Monitoring

Surely you have known people who frequently say the wrong thing. Such people may be what social scientists call *low self-monitors* (Snyder, 1974; Roloff, 1980). They do not consider the appropriateness of their comments or nonverbal behaviors beforehand. These people seem to lack a filter to catch and reformulate inappropriate behavior before they act. Their behavior is more spontaneous than contrived. Often, without intending to do so, they offend others.

Research indicates that **self-monitors**—people who watch their behavior—pay close attention to the expressions of others and use these observations to guide their own behavioral choices. Turner (1980) found that self-monitors add more humor to their remarks. Sypher and Sypher (1983) found a significant positive correlation between self-monitoring and communication effectiveness. Miller, de Turck, and Kalbfleisch (1983) found high self-monitors better at perpetrating deception than low self-monitors. Douglas (1983) found that self-monitors tend to behave in friendly ways, perhaps due to their interest in having the interaction proceed effectively (Snyder, 1979).

According to Roloff (1980), self-monitoring is important to persuasion. Self-monitors can adjust their strategies to the reactions of other interactants. In public speaking situations, high self-monitors can alter their style of presentation if their audience appears to be inattentive. They might vary their speech—avoiding a monotone—or leave the podium and move among their audience or inject some humor to enliven the presentation.

Japanese businessmen are fully aware of the need to monitor their responses to others (Van Zardt, 1970; Christopher, 1983). Often they use translators even though they understand what their American business counterparts are saying. The reason: this strategy gives them time to consider their responses.

Taking a social perspective and monitoring oneself can work together to enhance communication competence. To the extent that communicators can recognize that others are not responding as they wish, they can alter their presentations if they are adept self-monitors.

Behavioral Skills

Behavioral skills are typically defined in terms of physical behavior during interaction. Because thought is an important part of action, behavioral skills are not totally separate from cognitive skills. We use this somewhat artificial division between cognitive and behavioral skills to organize our discussion.

Interaction Involvement

The behavioral skill of **interaction involvement** concerns the extent to which an individual participates with another in conversation (Cegala, 1981). Cegala and his colleagues (1982, p. 229) explain why interaction involvement influences interpersonal communication competence:

> Highly involved people typically integrate feelings, thoughts, and experiences with the ongoing interaction of which they are assumed to be a part. Their consciousness is directed toward the evolving reality of self, other, and topic of conversation. As such, they are viewed by others as generally competent interpersonal communicators. On the other hand, characteristically low involved people are removed psychologically from the ongoing interaction. When low in interaction involvement, individuals may appear preoccupied with other thoughts or goals, distracted, uncertain, and/or withdrawn from the immediate social context. Their speech may be marked by vagueness, ambivalence, inconsistency, or misunderstanding. Also, they may typically demonstrate poor recollection of details pertaining to past conversations. In general, they appear less competent in their interactions with others.

Cegala and others (1982) found that interaction involvement is composed of three factors: responsiveness, perceptiveness, and attentiveness. **Responsiveness** is "a tendency to react mentally to one's social circumstance and adapt by knowing what to say and when to say it" (p. 233). It is an index of the tendency to say things appropriate to the situation. **Perceptiveness** is "the extent to which one is knowledgeable of (a) the meanings that others assign to one's own behavior, and (b) the meanings that one ought to assign to other's behavior" (p. 230). And **attentiveness** refers to the extent to which a person is aware of stimuli that make up the immediate environment.

Cegala (1981) developed a scale for the assessment of interaction involvement. Research using this scale has provided some support for the relationship between attentiveness and communication competence and between responsiveness and communication competence. However, the strongest relationship was found between perceptiveness and communication competence. (Cegala and others, 1982). This research supports the observation that the person who knows what to say and when to say it has an advantage in competence.

Interaction Management

Aside from being involved in interactions, communicators must know how to manage those interactions to meet their goals. The ability to manage interpersonal interactions develops throughout childhood as rules for effective interaction are learned. In Chapter 4 we discussed children's acquisition of communication skills. Children's communication development is clearly influenced by parents, teachers, peers, and even acquaintances. Few children share exactly the same parents, teachers, peers, and acquaintances, and no two children experience the same events. As a result, every child develops different ideas about what is appropriate and effective behavior in various communication situations—the rules of conversation.

One conversational activity that requires interaction management is taking turns. Early in our lives we learn to identify subtle cues indicating when to talk and when to listen. For example, when people are about to relinquish their turn, their speech tends to slow down a bit. This cues the other person that he may take a turn. An extended pause is another cue. In Chapter 6, we will discuss conversation management in detail.

Behavioral Flexibility

Behavioral flexibility refers to the extent to which communicators know and can perform alternative behaviors to reach the same goal. Bochner and Kelly (1974) described this flexibility as an important aspect of communication competence.

When a conversation begins, there is no way to tell exactly how it will proceed. Communicators who are ill prepared for the unexpected are likely to experience great frustration. They lack the cognitive capacity to create new plans on the spot. We might draw an analogy to a person who buys a map of Missouri so that he might find his way around. He looks at the map and plans a route. He drives along happily until he comes to a detour sign.

What should he do? Some people would be completely lost. Others would be able to take the map and find an alternate route. Some may be capable of finding their way just by keeping the general direction in mind and maintaining that course. The communicator who faces an unexpected response from another communicator is like the map reader who faces a detour.

Reardon (1982) argued that people expect others to follow what they assume to be shared rules of conversation. When a rule is violated—for example, when a speaker is interrupted—the predictability of a conversation is threatened. This is called **conversational deviance;** it takes numerous forms. Standing too near or too far from others, interrupting, and changing topics before others are ready to do so are just a few examples of such deviation. Communicators can recover quite easily from conversational deviances if they have behavioral flexibility—alternative means for achieving their goals.

Communication competence requires the ability to handle deviation without threatening a relationship. If Ellen is telling Joan about her bad day and Joan abruptly changes the subject, Ellen may feel uncomfortable. Ellen might then ask Joan why she changed the topic so abruptly. She might assume that Joan is not interested in her bad day and go along with Joan's change of topic. She could become defensive and leave the conversation. Each of these alternatives has a different potential effect on the conversation and perhaps the relationship.

There are times when a deviation from conversational rules is so unforgivable that saving the relationship may be undesirable. But in most cases, we may assume that people wish to save a relationship or conversation threatened by conversational deviance. Reardon (1982) found that the ability to do so is positively related to the cognitive complexity of communicators and their behavioral flexibility. Cognitively complex communicators adapt to interruptions in their conversational plans. They have the ability to create new plans on the spot, to locate other routes to their communication goals.

Conversational deviance is not unusual. Few conversations proceed as planned. Rules are frequently violated. To the extent that communicators can be flexible in the ways they deal with these violations, they are likely to have fewer conversation disasters. Their level of success is likely to be affected by their abilities to take a social perspective and monitor themselves. It is one thing to know a number of behavioral alternatives and quite another to know with whom to use them and how to monitor your behavior so that you use them effectively.

Listening

Few communicator characteristics are so widely appreciated as listening. A good listener is not easy to find: Bostrom and Waldhart (1980) found that people vary considerably in their listening ability. Some are good at remembering names when they are introduced to others. Some are so self-oriented that they do not attend to the comments of others, but spend that time planning their own response.

Listening enhances communication competence. Without the skill of listening, taking a social perspective and self-monitoring are of little use. In order to adjust one's communication to the needs of the other, one must listen.

Mark McCormack (1984, p. 108), author of *What They Don't Teach You at Harvard Business School*, writes of the value of listening to selling: "Silence has so many different selling applications. If you stop talking and start listening, you might actually learn something, and even if you don't you'll have a chance to collect your thoughts. Silence is what keeps you from saying more than you need to—and makes the other person want to say more than he means to."

All of us are capable of improving our listening abilities. Improvement requires practice. It requires conscious attempts to keep from interrupting or becoming distracted while others are speaking. If good listening were easy, more of us would do it. The effort it requires, however, appears to be positively related to success in communication and persuasion.

Social Style

Style refers to the manner of communication rather than the content. According to Norton (1983), one view of style defines it as a relatively enduring pattern of human interaction associated with an individual. This does not mean that each of us has only one style that never changes. It does mean that most of us have style preferences that recur sufficiently often to be associated with ourselves.

Style also refers to the way something is said. We could say that every message has a style associated with it, which helps the receiver interpret it. When someone asks, "Where'd you get that ugly face?" followed by a big grin, we know to interpret the question as a joke. However, the same statement without a smile is an insult.

Communication scholars use the term *style* in the two ways just discussed: to refer to a person's typical interaction pattern or the manner of presentation at the moment. Both types of style are important to communication competence. A style used in a particular interaction has important implications for the outcomes of that interaction. A person's enduring, typical style has important implications for the outcomes of all of her interactions. Here we will take a brief look at four key types of style: dominance, attentiveness, language features, and self-disclosure.

As a style variable, **dominance** has received much attention from communication researchers, and it may be defined on several levels. One form of dominance is physical. The phrase "Might makes right" describes an attitude often associated with physical dominance. Children are dominated by parents and weaker people are dominated by stronger people.

Courtright, Millar, and Rogers-Millar (1979) argue that dominance and domineeringness are two different variables. They propose that dominance be viewed as a relational pattern rather than as a description of one person's behavior. Dominance from this perspective refers to one-up behavior—as in telling someone what to do—that is accepted by the other interactant. Courtright and others explain that the expression of domineering, one-up messages is unrelated to the actual frequency of being dominant. To be dominant the other person must accept your one-up actions by being submissive.

Someone who is domineering uses one-up types of behavior. Such behavior is not necessarily accepted by another interactant. Behaviors used to control another interactant are domineering behaviors. If the other interactant submits to them, dominance results.

The Courtright, Millar, and Rogers-Millar perspective is an attempt to describe communication in terms of the joint actions of at least two persons. They suggest that a person cannot be dominant unless someone lets him. Some style variables refer only to the actions of one communicator rather than to the result of interaction. For example, it is possible for a person to be attentive whether or not the other interactant cooperates. You can be friendly to someone without that person being friendly in return. Such style variables are **monadic.** Intimacy, on the other hand, is a dyadic variable—it takes two. You can behave in an intimate manner toward someone, but you cannot experience intimacy without the other person's cooperation.

The point made here is an important one. For decades communication scholars have described communication as **transactional**—that is, as involving at least two people, each affecting the behavioral choices of the other. You cannot communicate with other people without their cooperation. You can talk *to* them but not *with* them. It is important to differentiate between types of behavior and types of patterns. For example, a person can behave affectionately toward another but cannot establish a pattern of intimacy with that person without his or her cooperation. An individual can shout all he wants but cannot be dominant unless the other interactant allows it. Perhaps you have heard the phrase, "You can shout till you're blue in the face. I don't care." This indicates that a domineering move has not resulted in a dominant pattern because the other person did not cooperate.

According to Norton (1983), **attentive style** indicates a willingness to show that you are alert to and understand what the other person is saying. It typically refers to the listener's style, but it is possible to be an attentive speaker, one who does not stop observing others' reactions while one is talking.

Attentive communicators convey to the speaker that her contribution is worthy of attention. Attention may be signaled by nods of the head, brief comments of interest, eye contact, posture, and other verbal and nonverbal expressions. The term **nonverbal immediacy** refers to nonverbal behaviors that signal approach, availability for communication, arousal or sensory stimulation, or interpersonal warmth and closeness (Andersen, Andersen, & Jensen, 1979; J. F. Andersen, 1984; P. A. Andersen, 1984). These behaviors may encourage the other speaker to continue speaking by signaling attentiveness to her.

Perhaps you have been the victim of inattentive communicators. Such people look around at others in the room while you are talking with them. They drift in and out of the conversation. Attentive communicators, on the other hand, listen empathically. They react to what is said by signaling that they heard and understood the message. It is, of course, possible to feign attentiveness, but few people do it well.

Another aspect of style that influences communication is the way communicators use language to affect communication outcomes, which is labeled **language features.** Some people just have "a way with words." My sister-in-law has this talent as indicated by this excerpt from her letter describing Buenos Aires:

> Although Buenos Aires isn't as quaint as New Orleans and lacks the architectural exuberance of New York, there are many, many beautifully landscaped parks here all with impressive pieces of public sculpture, some outstanding architecture, tree-lined boulevards, tiny cobbled stone streets. The city has a charm that isn't immediately apparent but rather seeps in slowly.

She is obviously involved with the city. Her language demonstrates involvement and beckons the reader to share her enthusiasm. There are no long, unfamiliar words here, just a melodic description. Some people have the ability to create vivid images both in letters and when they speak. They typically have little difficulty commanding attention because others are captivated by their words.

The way we use language is important to communication, in part because it affects impressions we formulate about each other. Bradac, Bowers, and Courtright (1979, p. 266) explain, "As a result of socialization people develop expectations that particular types of persons will use particular language styles in particular situations." When people use language that falls short of the expectations people have for them, the result can be listener disinterest—the listener tunes out the speaker. When people use language that exceeds others' expectations of them, listener interest may grow.

Communicators can also enhance listener interest by sharing personal information with others, which is termed **self-disclosure.** It is a risky activity because people cannot always be trusted to keep secret what they learn. Margaret Mead once explained that gossip exists in large part because it gives the gossiper status. To know something that others do not know is one way to get attention. It is a social advantage.

The recipients of self-disclosed information can infer several things about the discloser. For example, a recipient of personal information might assume that the discloser trusts him and thinks highly of him or that the discloser has little sense of appropriateness. The latter inference is likely to occur when too much information has been disclosed or when the timing of disclosure is inappropriate.

The effectiveness of any style depends on a host of factors. The situation, the communicators' genders, the nature of the information conveyed, and prior disclosures by the communicators are only a few factors. Baird and Bradley (1979) found, for example, that female and male managers use different styles of supervision with their employees. Female managers give more information, stress interpersonal relations, are receptive to ideas, and encourage employee effort, whereas male managers exceed females in dominance, quickness with which they challenge others, and directing the course of conversation. Female managers are apparently more comfortable with communication styles sensitive to employees.

Studies of style are useful not merely as an academic exercise but also as a means of helping people to see what they do when communicating that hinders achievement of their goals. In this sense, style research is a pragmatic exercise that may, as Norton (1983) suggests, lead to positive changes in the quality of people's lives.

Communication Anxiety

The final behavioral skill is monitoring one's communication anxiety. Some people are afraid to communicate. Their fear affects the way they behave while communicating. McCroskey, Daly, and Sorensen (1976) found that people with high communication anxiety have little sense of control over their environment and lack confidence.

Communication apprehension, one form of communication anxiety, essentially is a fear of real or anticipated communication with others. (See Daly & McCroskey, 1984; McCroskey, 1977, 1982; McCroskey & Beatty, 1984). Some behavioral manifestations of communication apprehension are trembling, inability to look at the other communicator, avoidance of social situations, and hesitancy to participate in conversations.

Reticence is another form of communication anxiety. For a reticent communicator, "anxiety about participation in oral communication outweighs his projection of gain from the situation" (Philips, 1968, p. 40). Philips and Metzger (1973) tell us that reticent communicators see others as more skillful than themselves. Moreover, reticent communicators are indecisive about appropriate behavior. They lack confidence that their behavioral choices are good ones. Burgoon and Koper (1984, p. 618) found that reticent communicators have a style "that can be characterized as simultaneously anxious, tense, depressed, and unanimated; as detached, apathetic, and uninvolved; as nonaffiliative and nonintimate, and possibly as submissive." They also found that strangers perceive reticent communicators as less credible and less attractive than communicators who are not reticent. They explain this problem for those they call "reticents":

> One could speculate that by providing fewer positive reinforcements and affiliative responses to others, reticents engender more negative communication directed to themselves. This would tend to confirm their own feelings of failure and thus contribute to a vicious cycle of the reticent's undesirable communication style triggering negative reactions from others, causing the reticent to become even more withdrawn, uncommunicative, fearful, and alienated [1984, pp. 618–619].

All of us are nervous about communicating at one time or another, but if communication anxiety is recurrent and extensive, its influence on communication competence will be negative.

Situational and Relational Factors in Competence

After reviewing many cognitive and behavioral skills, we could easily conclude that people are either competent or incompetent in situations and relationships. In other words, they either have these skills or they do not. If they do, they are all set. This would be an erroneous view of competence. Let's look once more at our definition of interpersonal communication competence: *Your level of interpersonal communication competence is the degree to which your behaviors are appropriate to the situation and help you attain personal and relational goals.*

According to this definition, competence may vary from situation to situation. While conscientiously monitoring one's communication may be important during a job interview, it can seem out of place with friends. Perhaps you have met someone who is always guarded in her remarks. Such people are often criticized for never being themselves. Appropriate and effective timing and amounts of self-monitoring depend on the situation in which the communication occurs and the relationship between communicators.

A communicator's competence is also affected by the competence of the other communicator. Imagine someone entering a conversation armed with empathy, social perspective-taking, cognitive complexity, a strong desire to be involved in the conversation, attentiveness, and low anxiety only to discover that the other person is rude and uninterested. What good are all these skills with people who have no interest in communicating or with people who merely wish to get a job done?

Different people pose different competence challenges. Since communication is something done *with*, not *to* people, the level of competence achieved by one communicator is influenced by the actions of the other. Competence is easier to achieve when people are cooperative. Perhaps you can think of someone in your own life who strains the limits of your competence. This person may be dragging down your competence average, so to speak, because nothing you say or do seems to work with him.

Competence in interpersonal communication is not just a matter of skills. It is also a relational and situational issue. Communicators carry skills around with them, but they cannot carry competence around with them. Competence is not guaranteed by the presence of skills. It may, however, be facilitated by the cognitive and behavioral skills we have discussed.

Finally, it is important to point out that competence in interpersonal communication is often a matter of trade-offs. There are times when doing what is appropriate in terms of the relationship is ineffective in terms of achieving other goals or vice versa. For example, while allowing a co-worker to digress from the task at hand to tell stories about his problems at home might seem appropriate to the relationship, it might interfere with meeting important deadlines.

Communication competence involves finding ways to deal with challenging trade-offs of appropriateness and effectiveness. In terms of the story-telling coworker, competence may involve showing appreciation for his concerns while also encouraging progress toward the task at hand. A particularly adept communicator might be able to link the coworker's story to the task. For example, she might say, "The moral of that story seems applicable to our task as well." However, unless she is capable of making the connection between the story and the task apparent, such a strategy might well backfire.

Summary

Competence is relationship and situation specific. Some communicators may be competent across all interpersonal communication encounters. If you meet such a person, you might want to take notes because such a person is rare. Most of us do the best we can at getting by and hope that, in some situations and for some relationships, we will be very competent. Even the most heralded communicators throughout history have been specialists in particular types of situations or relationships. Just as it is a rare actor who can play a variety of roles exceptionally well, it is a rare communicator who can communicate exceptionally well in all situations and all relationships.

Despite the difficulties inherent in acquiring communication competence in different types of interactions, knowledge of the social skills that facilitate competence and practice using them can improve communication. Interpersonal communication competence is not something you are born with. It is something that you can improve. To the extent that researchers can identify skills that help communicators achieve personal and relational goals through behavior appropriate to the situation at hand, the path toward improving interpersonal communication competence may be cleared.

CHAPTER 6

Conversation

How do people manage their conversations? This chapter answers that question. As we shall discuss, conversations do not just happen. They are the result of much coordination and cooperation between or among the participants. Each participant brings to a conversation some set of rules about when to talk, how long to talk, amount of eye contact, spatial distance, voice volume, and a host of other considerations. If two people having a conversation are from the same culture, they will likely have many rules in common. Shared rules make an effective conversation easier to achieve. However, as we shall see, conversation is a complex activity even when the people involved share many rules. After all, people bring their moods, biases, personalities, and preferences to conversations. Keeping a conversation on a productive track is not easy.

In this chapter we will look at how people intentionally and unintentionally manage their conversations. Unintentional management involves applying rules without being aware of doing so. For example, people may take turns, choose spatial distances, gesture, and engage in other activities during conversation without really thinking about each behavior's appropriateness. Because we learned during childhood how to engage in conversation, many behaviors are scripted. Of course, each conversation brings with it challenges that may not be handled by scripted behaviors alone. These challenges require contrived behaviors that control the conversation—for example, keeping it from becoming an unwanted conflict or ending prematurely. In this sense, conversation is a demanding activity. Knowing how to engage effectively in conversation is important not only to immediate satisfaction of communication goals but also to long-term relationships. Conversations may be thought of as the building blocks of relationships. It is through conversations that we come to know people. And through conversations we come to have friends, lovers, bosses, acquaintances, colleagues, and other relationships. Moreover, through conversation we maintain, improve, diminish, and destroy our relationships.

The Complex Nature of Conversation

Conversation is a highly complex activity requiring a number of skills. Conversations have highly organized structures—because of participants' cooperative use of rules about how conversations should and should not proceed (see McLaughlin, 1984).

Conversational rules are prescriptions about the verbal and nonverbal behaviors participants ought and ought not to engage in during particular types of interaction (see Pearce & Cronen, 1978; Cushman, 1977; Reardon & Fairhurst, 1979; Shimanoff, 1980). By types of interaction we mean disagreements, discussions, negotiations, greetings, farewells, and so on. If human interaction required us to know exactly how to act in every specific interaction of daily life, our minds would be overextended. Instead, we know ranges of behaviors appropriate to particular types of situations. For example, two people meeting for the first time might shake hands, nod, smile, or provide some other indication of recognition. They might also engage in some combination of these behaviors. Any of these recognition behaviors is an acceptable means of greeting a stranger. They are within the rules for this situation.

Knowledge of the rules allows communicators to manage the course of conversation. Capella (1985, p. 393) explains: "The ability to control conversation depends upon the existence of certain regularities that can be exploited by one or the other conversational partner, and this exploitation depends upon knowledge of the regularity." For example, given the typical conversational rule "It is impolite to interrupt," an abrupt interruption and change of topic by one communicator can signal to the person interrupted that he has been talking too long or that his topic is boring.

Of course, people are not always conscious of the rules they are using to guide their conversations. Many rules are implicit (Shimanoff, 1980). They do not have to be brought to a high level of consciousness for us to use them. Imagine how exhausting conversations would be if we had to consciously consider when to take a turn at talking, when to look at the other person, how loud to speak, and how close to stand to each other. Fortunately, many rules of conversation have been used so often by us that they become second nature, or scripted.

Although communication rules are learned from others, each individual may make alterations in them. Delia, Clark, and Switzer (1979) provided evidence that individuals impose their own influence on "regularities in communicative behavior." Their work suggests that behavioral regularities, or what we are calling **rules,** are not merely learned intact from other people but that people differ in the extent to which they formulate their personal versions of social rules.

We might think of rules as borrowed and owned. **Borrowed rules** are those that people learn from others without much alteration. Such rules typically enjoy high consensus about their use among people of the same subculture or culture. "It's impolite to turn away from a person who is speaking," and "People shouldn't interrupt without good reason" are examples of borrowed rules. Owned rules are personal prescriptions for one's own behavior such as, "When I'm insulted, I don't give the person a chance to explain" or "When people listen to me, I listen to them."

The use of borrowed and owned rules in any conversation depends on each communicator's perceptions of the situation, relationship, and type of conversation. Let's consider a public situation—where people other than the communicators are observing an argument between two friends. Both Robert and Carol see the situation, relationship, and conversation in similar ways. They differ, however, in the amount of borrowed and owned rules with which they are comfortable. Robert feels comfortable relying mainly on personal rules to guide his behavior. He believes in telling people, friends or not, alone or in public, exactly what he is thinking. He doesn't mince words but speaks his mind because that is the type of person he is. Carol relies more on borrowed rules. Perhaps she is more sensitive to public scrutiny than is Robert, who sees much room for self-autonomy—freedom to be oneself—in the situation. Carol speaks politely even when disagreeing with Robert because she has learned from her mother that one should not speak harshly to others in public.

Carol and Robert might change their blend of rule types if the situation were to become private rather than public. Carol, who relied predominantly on borrowed rules in the public situation, now relies mostly on owned rules. She speaks her mind and tells Robert he is an idiot. Robert continues to act as he did in the public situation. Apparently public versus private is not as important a consideration for Robert as it is for Carol. In the private situation, Carol sees nearly as much room for self-autonomy as Robert does.

Carol and Robert's reliance on owned versus borrowed rules could shift again were we to change the type of relationship or type of conversation. Even more complex would be the condition where the two do not agree on the type of relationship they have. For example, if Carol thinks that Robert is a friend, but Robert sees their relationship as one of acquaintances, they are likely to be using different borrowed rules as well as different owned rules. Carol might bring up a personal topic thinking, "Friends should be willing to listen to each other's problems," while Robert is thinking, "Acquaintances should not discuss personal problems." Unless Carol and Robert agree upon the nature of their relationship, they are likely to have considerable difficulty communicating effectively.

These examples demonstrate that, while rules account for regularities in conversation, people often rely on different rules to conduct the same conversation. For this reason, much effort during interaction is expended on negotiating appropriate behavior. The absence of concrete laws about what one can and cannot say and do during conversation renders it a very complex activity. Communicators must coordinate their rules so that they have some knowledge about what to expect from each other.

To the extent that communicators are familiar, much negotiation work has already been done. People married for twenty-five years usually know a good deal about each other's conversational expectations. It is a different case altogether when people converse for the first time. Research on initial interactions indicates that such conversations pose a considerable challenge in terms of knowing how one ought to behave. Since they know little about each other, people meeting for the first time tend to engage in very safe types of interaction. They might discuss the weather, the high price of food, or other impersonal topics relevant to the situation (see Berger & Calabrese, 1975). If their relationship develops, they will learn more about each other. They might observe each other's verbal and nonverbal actions and draw conclusions about the likelihood of their getting along. They might also ask some questions to learn how the other thinks and feels about certain topics. This more active approach is an example of what Berger (1979) calls "knowledge-gaining strategies"—using questions or statements to elicit informative responses from another person.

Whether interaction is with strangers or acquaintances, identical rules are unlikely. There is always the potential for communicators to interpret the situation, relationship, or conversation type differently. A vital part of every conversation is coordinating perceptions about the situation, relationship, and conversation type as well as the rules themselves. Let's now look at several theories about how people achieve this coordination.

Conversational Structure

Before people can coordinate rules about what should or should not be said in a conversation, they must know the structure of conversation—what comes first, second, and so on—the phases of interaction.

Frentz (1976) proposed a model of conversational structure, which has the five phases depicted in the following list:

1. Initiation phase: a phase when people exchange greetings.
2. Rule definition phase: a period of negotiation about the type of interaction or amount of time needed for it.
3. Rule confirmation phase: a phase of agreement between the communicators concerning the type of interaction and amount of time that will be allocated to it.
4. Strategic development phase: a period during which the conversation topic is discussed.
5. Termination phase: a phase that includes farewells or changes of topic.

According to Frentz, some conversations require all five phases. Other conversations may require fewer. The following dialogue includes all five phases:

Jack: Hi, Sharon. What's new with you?
Sharon: Not much. But I do need to talk to you.
Jack: I'm on my way to class, so it'll have to be brief.
Sharon: Give me two minutes. I'll walk with you as we talk.
Jack: Okay. What's on your mind?
Sharon: I had to miss two history classes last week. The exam is coming up and I need to borrow someone's notes. What do you say?
Jack: No problem. I'll give them to you this afternoon. But I need them back tomorrow.
Sharon: Great! Thanks, Jack. I'll see you later.
Jack: Okay. Take care.

In this sample dialogue, the initiation phase includes the greetings. The rule definition phase includes the discussion of whether Jack is willing to talk and for how long. The rule confirmation phase occurs when Jack and Sharon agree to talk briefly and she offers to walk along with him. The strategic development phase, the main part of this conversation, includes the discussion of borrowing notes and arranging to meet later. The farewells constitute the termination phase.

Not all conversations have all five phases. For example, telephone operators do not engage in greetings and rule development and confirmation. There is no need for the caller and operator to discuss how their conversation should proceed. The operator merely asks, "What city, please?" moving the interaction into the strategic development phase without formal discussion of rules. The conversation may be terminated with "Thanks." However, should the caller fail to say thank you, the operator is not likely to call back and ask why.

Some conversations require explicit greetings, rule development, rule confirmation, strategic development, and termination. Others require fewer phases. In any case, the guiding structure exists and we learn it during childhood. It imposes order on conversation and the interaction. Since people generally share the same understanding of basic structure in conversation, it is one less thing for communicators to negotiate in the complex activity of conversation.

Speech Acts

We turn now to the verbal behaviors that make up each phase of conversation. These are called **speech acts** (see Searle, 1969). Speech acts are types of verbal behaviors used to convey a message. They differ according to their purposes. Some types of speech acts are requests, assertions, advice, questions, explanations, interpretations, criticisms, and suggestions. Each type is acceptable or unacceptable for inclusion in particular phases and types of conversation.

For example, if two people want to have a cooperative discussion, accusations and criticisms are probably unacceptable in their conversation. Similarly, while criticism may be acceptable among friends, too much criticism in a casual conversation is usually inappropriate.

Relationship type can affect the type of speech that is appropriate. Fitzpatrick found that marital type influences the types of expressions used by husbands and wives (Fitzpatrick, 1977). Fitzpatrick and Best (1979) found that what they call "traditional" couples express more affection than do "independent" couples and "separate" couples. Independents are more likely to express their feelings openly to their mates. Separates are "emotionally divorced" from their mates; they are the least likely to express their feelings. Although this work has not focused explicitly on speech acts, we may conclude that emotional expressions such as anger are likely to be found more often in conversations of traditional couples than in those of separate couples. Independents are more likely than traditionals are to use frank statements and criticism and less likely than traditionals to exchange private thoughts.

Gender also influences the types of speech acts people use. For example, women tend to interrupt others less often than men do. They use more qualifiers such as "perhaps," "sometimes," and "maybe" and are silent more often than men in female-male interactions (see Zimmerman & West, 1975; Eakins & Eakins, 1978). Research also indicates that supportiveness, nonaggression, affiliation, and dependency are more often expected of females than males, whereas males are expected to use initiative, competency, and dominance (see McLaughlin, Cody, Kane, & Robey, 1981).

Type of relationship, situation, and gender are only a few factors influencing our choices of speech acts. No two persons are ever in total agreement about which speech acts are best suited to the conversation at hand. Sometimes people criticize when they should empathize, assert their positions when they should explain them, or advise when they should listen. When in doubt of their level of agreement or particularly anxious to ensure it, communicators may explicitly discuss what they expect. For example, one person might say, "Criticism is not called for here," or "We'll get along better if you hear me out before you talk." Nonverbal cues can also indicate to others that some type of speech is inappropriate. For example, an angry look can let a conversation partner know that you do not approve of her choice of speech acts.

Coordinated Management of Meaning

When two or several people converse, they enter into an activity of **mutual influence,** in which the behavior of each communicator influences the behavioral options of the other (Capella, 1985). For example, by using remarks such as "That's very interesting" or "How true," a communicator can encourage another to continue to talk. This same communicator might discourage the other from continuing by looking bored.

There are several theories about how people manage their conversations. Each of these tells us something about mutual influence—about the way that each communicator's actions contribute to the course of conversation. One theory of conversation is the **coordinated management of meaning theory** (Pearce, 1976; Cronen, Pearce, & Harris, 1982). According to this theory, communicators can manage their conversations by adjusting their rules or creating new ones when adjustment is impossible. This is called coordinated management of meaning. Coordination is achieved when people agree to conduct a certain type of interaction—a discussion, argument, or debate, for example—in a particular situation. Typically such agreements are implicit rather than explicit. Occasionally, people do explicitly state, "Let's have a discussion, not a fight," or "Would you care to debate that issue?" but most agreements about rules are more subtle.

Pearce (1976) explains that the essential condition of coordination is **consensual rules.** Consensual rules are shared rules, those that communicators have in common. For example, to the extent that two persons planning a party have similar rules about what parties should involve, as well as similar rules for what party planners should do, their interactions are likely to be successful. To the extent that communicators do not share similar rules for how a particular interaction should proceed, the likelihood of satisfying an effective interaction is low, unless they are willing to coordinate their rules.

Coordination of rules can be difficult. Sometimes people who would like to communicate effectively cannot do so because their rules concerning how certain types of interactions should proceed are diametrically opposed. The difficulty associated with rule coordination is one reason why it is often easier to communicate with people who are similar to ourselves. Communicating with people who think as we do makes the job of rule coordination less taxing.

In Chapter 5 we discussed some communicator skills that can facilitate coordination, including social perspective-taking, empathy, self-monitoring, and behavioral flexibility. Being able to see the situation as the other person sees it and monitor your behavior to avoid misunderstanding can be assets to coordination.

Management, the second term in *coordinated management of meaning*, refers to the maintenance of rule coordination throughout the course of interaction. Merely coordinating rules about how a conversation should proceed does not guarantee that the entire conversation will occur without periods of disagreement or discomfort. Communicators manage by attending to verbal and nonverbal cues indicating that something they said or did might have been misconstrued by the other. No doubt you have had conversations in which the other person looked puzzled or annoyed at something you said. If you stopped and asked, "What's the problem? Did I say something wrong?", you were engaging in conversation management.

Convergence

An alternative view of how communicators comprehend and manage their meanings is offered by Rogers and Kincaid's (1981) **convergence model**. While the coordinated management of meaning perspective focuses on how communicators bring their diverse conversational rules into some tolerable range of agreement, the convergence model focuses on how communicators use information, whether in the form of rules or not, to reach a common perspective on some subject.

Rogers and Kincaid define *communication* as "a process in which participants create and share information with one another in order to reach a mutual understanding" (1981, p. 63). They explain that mutual understanding is never perfect since people have different codes and concepts available for understanding. However, by means of cycles of information exchange, communicators may converge toward a greater mutual understanding of each other's meanings, obtain greater accuracy, and come within the limits of tolerance required for the purpose at hand. Figure 6.1 depicts cycles of information exchange leading to mutual understanding. Rogers and Kincaid (1981, p. 65) define *convergence* as "the tendency for two or more individuals to move toward one point, or for one individual to move toward another and to unite in a common interest or focus."

Rogers & Kincaid also propose that, while the purpose of communication is mutual understanding, the results are not always in that direction. They propose four possible combinations of mutual understanding and agreement: (1) mutual understanding with agreement, (2) mutual understanding with disagreement, (3) mutual misunderstanding with agreement, and (4) mutual misunderstanding with disagreement.

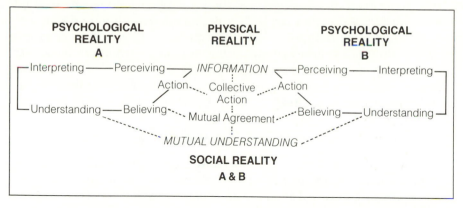

Figure 6.1. Basic components of the convergence model of communication.
Source: Kincaid, D.L. "The Convergence Model of Communication." Honolulu, East-West Communication Institute. Reprinted with permission.

Conversations A and B represent two combinations of understanding and agreement. In which categories would you place each?

Conversation A

Bill: That was a great game.
Ron: I disagree.
Bill: You must have been sleeping.
Ron: You wanted to know my opinion, didn't you?
Bill: Not really. I just said it was a great game.
Ron: It stunk!
Bill: You're crazy.
Ron: Go alone next time.
Bill: Fine.

Conversation B

Bill: Great game, huh?
Ron: I agree.
Bill: Then you'll go to one with me next week.
Ron: No thanks.
Bill: But you said it was great.
Ron: My grandmother is a great lady but I only see her once a year.
Bill: That's an odd comparison.
Ron: Not to me.

What were your decisions? Conversation A involves obvious disagreement and misunderstanding, too. Not only do Bill and Ron disagree about the game, but Ron seems to have misunderstood Bill's intentions. Bill claims to have no interest in Ron's opinion, while Ron believes that Bill wanted to know his opinion. In Conversation B we have a case of agreement but misunderstanding concerning the meaning of the agreement. Bill assumes that Ron's favorable description of the game means that he would like to attend another one. Ron sees it differently. They have mutual misunderstanding with mutual agreement.

The coordination perspective and the convergence model share an important characteristic: they are both relational views of interpersonal communication. Rather than suggesting that communication is the conveyance of a preformulated message from one person to another, these perspectives depict communication as an activity through which people coordinate or converge upon thoughts, feelings, and behaviors as they interact or relate in an effort to understand, to be understood, and to agree.

Managing Conversational Coherence

In addition to coordinating rules or converging upon shared meaning, conversational participants must cooperate in **conversational coherence**—their positioning of verbal and nonverbal behaviors. It is one thing to know what to say and quite another to know when in the conversation to say it.

Stech (1979) states that when acts in conversation are related to prior and subsequent acts, there is coherent discourse. Coherence requires knowing when to take a turn speaking and when to let other persons speak. It also requires that verbal and nonverbal behavior during one's turn be relevant, given what has already transpired in the conversation and given its purpose (see McLaughlin, 1984).

Perhaps the most fundamental aspect of conversational coherence is taking turns. Research indicates that people have an uncanny awareness of when they may speak and when they should be silent in the course of conversation. Some researchers have attempted to identify the subtle verbal and nonverbal signals used by communicators to regulate their turns at speaking (Duncan, 1972). For example, before relinquishing the floor to someone else, a speaker may decrease her rate of speech and look directly at the other person. These cues tell the other person that he may now take a turn at speaking.

Duncan, Bruner, & Fiske (1979) argue that while every turn-taking attempt should be preceded by turn signals, not all turn signals are followed by the other person taking a turn. Whether or not a communicator responds to a turn signal is a decision affected by that communicator's goals and personal style (see Wilson, Wiemann, & Zimmerman, 1984). A speaker may indicate a willingness to relinquish his turn. The listener may decide not to take the turn, a move that could signal disinterest, shyness, or a lack of commitment. Turn-taking signals are necessary but not sufficient conditions for the taking of a turn.

Aside from taking turns, conversational coherence requires that communicators cooperate in the length of their talk and the truth, relevance, and clarity of their comments. In writing about logic and conversation, Grice (1975) states that conversation is the result of cooperation between people with a common purpose or set of purposes or at least a mutually accepted direction:

Our talk exchanges do not normally consist of a succession of disconnected remarks, and would not be rational if they did. They are characteristically, to some degree at least, cooperative efforts; and each participant recognizes in them, to some extent, a common purpose or set of purposes, or at least a mutually accepted direction. This purpose or direction may be fixed from the start (for example, by an initial proposal or a question for discussion), or it may evolve during the exchange; it may be fairly definite, or it may be so indefinite as to leave very considerable latitude to the participants (as in a casual conversation). But at each stage, *some* possible conversational moves would be excluded as conversationally unsuitable [1975, p. 45–46].

Grice suggests that people cooperate to make their conversational contributions appropriate to the purposes of the exchange. He calls this the "cooperative principle" of conversation. He further argues that this cooperation is achieved when communicators attend to four categories of maxims, or what we might term rules, of conversation: quantity, quality, relation, and manner (pp. 45–46).

The quantity maxims are:

1. Make your contribution as informative as is required for the current purposes of the exchange.
2. Do not make your contribution more informative than is required.

Maxim 1 indicates that people share certain expectations about how much information is necessary to conduct the type of interaction in which they are involved. If you meet someone on a train, you may talk for hours about your work activities and never tell one another your names. Names are not required when talking with strangers on trains.

You have probably heard the observation from Shakespeare's *Hamlet*, "The lady doth protest too much." It is an example of the second maxim of quantity. If someone protests excessively, we may wonder if he is hiding his true intentions. When people say more or less than is expected, they break the maxim of quantity and cause us to wonder at their purpose or meaning.

The quality maxims are:

1. Do not say what you believe to be false.
2. Do not say that for which you lack evidence.

The first quality maxim refers to deception. While deception is contrary to quality maxim 1, research indicates that it is a frequent part of conversation (Knapp & Camadena, 1979). It is difficult to tell people the truth if it is likely to cause offense. Instead, people often resort to deception. If you are caught in a lie, the consequences can be serious, since deception, even with good intentions, violates the quality maxim. It may be interpreted as an indication that the relationship is not sound.

Quality maxim 2 requires that people refrain from making claims they cannot support. Situations vary in terms of the accuracy and credibility of information required. Casual discussions do not typically require the mention of highly credible sources of information. Rather than saying, "I read in the *New York Times* that it is supposed to rain today," it is usually acceptable to say, "It's supposed to rain today." One exception might be in agricultural areas where the amount of rainfall is critical to income or sustenance. In such places the credibility of one's weather information source is important.

The relation maxim is:

1. Be relevant.

Each interactant expects the other to speak to the issue at hand. Wandering off on tangents or changing the subject without good reason are violations of the relation maxim.

The manner maxims are:

1. Avoid obscurity of expression.
2. Avoid ambiguity.
3. Be brief.
4. Be orderly.

Manner requires that communicators make the meaning of their contributions clear. To do otherwise suggests that one is hiding something or lacking knowledge. Brevity is important because people's attention spans are short and because others often expect opportunities to speak. Order refers to the structure of remarks—for example, starting at the beginning, rather than the middle, of a story.

Adherence to some maxims can be more important than adherence to others. Among close friends, breaking the brevity maxim may be less offensive than breaking the truth maxim.

A useful metaphor for conversational coherence is provided by Jacobs and Jackson (1983), who compare conversational coherence to a game of chess. Both conversation and chess are accomplished by achieving one or more restricted goals through the use of moves defined by rules. As with chess, conversation is a cooperative activity, even if the people involved are competing with each other, because each interactant adheres to certain rules and assumes that the others will do likewise. Furthermore, just as chess players must anticipate opportunities that their moves will make possible for their opponents, communicators often consider their actions in light of the possibilities they create for others.

Conversations are indeed much like games. Some pass the time; others are a considerable challenge. Each communicator brings to a conversation some understanding of the rules. The ease with which the conversation is conducted depends, to a large extent, on the degree to which the communicators share similar rules for structuring the type of conversation they are in.

Nonverbal Management of Conversations

Aside from managing what they say, communicators also manage what they do. Facial expressions, body movements, eye contact, spatial distance, and conversational regulators such as nods all contribute to the impressions communicators have of each other, their relationship, and the content of the message. As we have noted, nonverbal behaviors are as important to interpersonal communication as verbal behaviors. According to Burgoon (1985), they are more important to communication than indicated by their inclusion in most current theories of interpersonal communication. She points to a number of studies confirming that adults tend to place greater reliance on nonverbal than verbal cues when interpreting communication. Moreover, nonverbal cues are especially likely to be believed when they conflict with verbal messages. In this section we will discuss just a few aspects of the impact of nonverbal behavior on conversation, especially on managing conversation.

Facial Expressions. Much research has focused on the facial expressions of humans. According to Ekman (1978), display rules specify whether facial expressions should be intensified, diminished, or neutralized in appearance or masked with the configurations of another emotion. Research suggests that the rules for female facial displays of emotion, for example, differ from those for men. Women look directly at conversational partners more than men do, smile more than men, and are generally more expressive facially (Henley, 1977; Burgoon, 1985). Cultures also appear to influence rules of facial expression. In some cultures, people mourning the death of a loved one are expected to cry loudly. In other cultures, stoicism is expected. The extent to which one may "wear one's heart on one's sleeve," so to speak, varies across cultures.

Research also indicates that people vary in the capacity to express emotion (see Ekman, 1978; Buck, 1984). Buck and others (1980, 1982) found that women more often exhibited fearful or pleased expressions than men before having opportunities to discuss their feelings about slides depicting frightening scenes and ones depicting beautiful scenes. Research also indicates that children are more spontaneously expressive of positive rather than negative emotions in the presence of an adult (Buck, 1975). Ekman (1978) proposed that families influence the display rules people adopt. He explained that, in extreme cases, people can become "poker-faced," never revealing how they feel. A less extreme reaction might be a "block," the inability to express a certain type of emotion toward a particular group of people. For example, one might be trained to avoid anger when communicating with a female authority figure.

In terms of our purposes here, the key question is, How are facial expressions used to regulate or manage conversation? To answer this question for facial expression without considering other nonverbal behaviors such as body movements and spatial distance could be misleading, so we will look at several modes of expression. During conversation people typically have a full view of each other. They observe many types of nonverbal behavior simultaneously. Yet researchers have tended to study nonverbal behaviors in isolation. For example, we know that gazing can be used to signal status and to encourage others to speak or be silent. We know that it can also be used to signal a willingness to relinquish a speaking turn and to increase attraction (see Burgoon, 1985). We know comparatively little, however, about how eye contact interacts with posture, for example, in the management of conversation.

The context of interaction is also important to interpretations of facial expressions. A smile is not always a positive gesture. It can be used to suggest disbelief of another communicator's words or actions. It can be used to express amusement, when the other person's intentions were serious. It can be used to express a lack of sympathy with someone's dilemma. The same smile used in different contexts has different meanings.

Body Movements. In 1972, Albert Scheflen published *Body Language and Social Order*. In this book, Scheflen described how body movements communicate meaning. He explained that courtship, dominance, submission, and other relational messages are often conveyed by movement. For example, preening one's hair while talking to someone may indicate that one is attracted to that person.

Research on body movements has indicated that, for some movements, meaning is fairly consistent. With few exceptions, however, we cannot look at a person's movements and know exactly what he means (Dittman, 1978). This potential for misreading does not appear to stop people from using inferences drawn from observations of others' body movements in the course of daily conversations.

Verbal language alone is apparently insufficient to the task of communication. We watch others' behaviors to derive inferences about them. Research indicates that people use body movements to determine whether others are attempting to deceive them (Hocking, Bauchner, Kaminski, & Miller, 1979). Movements can also provide information about liking (J. F. Andersen, 1984; P. A. Andersen, 1984).

Eye Contact. Another aspect of nonverbal behavior used in conversation management is eye contact. Argyle and Cook (1976) report that almost no research was done on communication via the eyes until the 1960s. Since then researchers have discovered that the eyes are sources of considerable information during the course of face-to-face interaction.

Exline and Fehr (1978) found that visual attention is more likely to be directed toward the eye region of others while listening to them than while speaking to them. More recent research indicates that this is especially true when talking with peers. Subordinates manifest more visual attention when listening relative to speaking than persons of higher status (Exline, Ellysen, & Long, 1975).

Low levels of eye contact are typically thought to indicate lack of interest or unwillingness to get involved with the other person or the topic under discussion. Too much eye contact, however, can be equally disconcerting. For example, stares can be used to threaten (Argyle & Cook, 1976). Despite these findings, remember that interaction with other nonverbal behaviors and the context of occurrence influence the meaning of eye contact.

Spatial Distance. Another nonverbal behavior that affects interpersonal communication is the spatial distance between people during interaction. Edward Hall (1959, 1963) believes that much information is communicated by spatial distance even though people are generally unaware of how they are using space. Hall coined the term *proxemics* to refer to the study of human beings' unconscious structuring of the space around them.

Culture appears to play an important role in regulations of spatial distance (Hall, 1966). For example, Arabs typically stand closer to others than the English and Americans do. Gender also plays a role in spatial distance, although not a clear-cut one. Physical closeness between same-sex groups has typically been more acceptable for females than for males (Patterson, 1978). Also, females tend to allow others to approach them more closely than do males (Henley, 1977; Burgoon, 1985). Females typically appear to be more reserved than males in approaching someone of the opposite sex (Patterson, 1978). The nature of the relationship between two persons also affects spatial distance. As you might expect, the more intimate the relationship, the closer people stand.

Nonverbal communication is an important aspect of interpersonal communication. In this section we have reviewed only a small part of the research on it. The role nonverbal behavior plays in conveying emotional information is crucial to communication and persuasion. What people say to each other is often not as important as what they do while saying it. Let's now look at what happens when people do the unexpected in conversations.

Repairing Mismanaged Conversations

As we discussed in Chapter 5, breaking conversational rules is called **conversational deviance** (Reardon, 1982). When one person speaks for too long, interrupts, uses an inappropriate speech act, or violates some other rule, conversational deviance occurs. Managing a conversation under such circumstances is a challenge. To recover a conversation from the threat posed by conversational deviance, communicators often engage in **conversational repairs**—behaviors that revise the interpretation of the deviation or minimize its severity (see Schegloff, Jefferson, & Sacks, 1977; and Zahn, 1984). Accounts are one type of conversational repair.

Most of us are good at excusing or justifying our own inappropriate behaviors. According to C. Wright Mills (1940), people only do those things they think they can excuse or justify. With the exception of spontaneous behaviors, people tend to behave in ways they can defend. To protect ourselves and our relationships, we arm ourselves with accounts.

Accounts are excuses or justifications for untoward behavior. They make illogical behavior seem logical. Sometimes people provide accounts before they deliver their message: "I'm tired today, so what I'm about to say may not sound coherent. . . ." is an example of a prospective account. This tells the listener that there is a good reason for not judging too harshly what he is about to hear. Retrospective accounts are those used after the behavior. They can be used to excuse inappropriate expressions of emotion or misguided words. Perhaps you have told a joke that offended more people than it amused. Did you account for it? A useful account for such behavior might be, "Listen, don't mind me. I'm not myself this week. Too much pressure at work."

Accounts are a means of saving a conversation when something inappropriate is said or done. They are a way of managing conversation by making the otherwise unacceptable behavior seem acceptable (see Harre & Secord, 1973; Scott & Lyman, 1968). Some people are highly proficient at providing accounts. They are able to resolve problems coordinating rules through excuses and justifications.

Synthesizing the work of other researchers, Cody and McLaughlin (1984) suggest a taxonomy of account types that includes concessions, excuses, justifications, and refusals. **Concessions** acknowledge guilt and may include an apology. The accounter admits to wrongdoing and may or may not apologize for it. In a concession without an apology, the accounter merely takes responsibility for the offense:

Mom: You interrupted me again, Jim.
Jim: Yeah, I slipped up again.

When apologies are included with admissions of guilt, they may be perfunctory apologies or more sincere attempts to rectify the wrong. Perfunctory apologies are more form than content. You may say "Pardon me" with indifference to a stranger whose path you block. More sincere apologies involve expressions of remorse, offers of help to the offended person, or requests for forgiveness:

Mom: You interrupted me again, Jim.

Jim: I'm really sorry, Mom. It won't happen again.

Cody and McLaughlin's study suggests that simple apologies and admissions of guilt may be two different types of accounts.

Excuses are strategies in which the accounter admits to the offense but denies that he could have done something about it. Accounters who use excuses either deny responsibility for the offense or deny intention to offend.

Tom: That was a nasty thing to say.

Bill: What could I do? She asked me for the truth, so I gave her the truth. I only did what she wanted me to do. *(Denial of responsibility)*

Tom: That was a nasty thing to say.

Bill: I didn't realize she was so sensitive about it. *(Denial of intention)*

Justifications accept responsibility for the offense and attempt to redefine what happened in terms of its positive outcomes. Justifiers may minimize the severity of the offense, deny that anyone was really hurt, claim positive intentions, or insist that the offense was necessary. The following example of justification minimizes the severity of the offense and denies that anyone was hurt:

Michele: You shouldn't call me after eleven at night. I've told you that before.

Sharon: I know, but it really isn't much after eleven and staying up a little later is no big deal for you.

Refusals reject the other's definition of the offense. The accounter imposes his own description on the situation. For example:

Lou: You were very inconsiderate earlier today.

Mike: I'm never inconsiderate and you know it. Perhaps all of you are a little too sensitive.

If these account types seem familiar to you, it is probably because you have used them. We all use accounts now and then. No one is so perfect a communicator that her actions are always inoffensive to others. Through accounts we can redirect the course of a conversation when it is in jeopardy.

Accounts can be provided by the person who deviated from the rules of the conversation or by another interactant: the former is called **self-repair,** the latter **other-repair** (see Schegloff and others, 1977).

Here is an example of other-repair by account:

Lois: Did you hear what he just said?

Alan: Yes. He just says what he thinks.

Lois: What do you mean?

Alan: I mean that most of us think before we speak. He's a great guy, but sometimes he doesn't screen what he says. He just says it. He doesn't mean any harm.

Lois: I suppose you're right. I'll try to remember that. But he does say the strangest things sometimes.

Here Alan has provided an account for a friend's faux pas. He explains that frequent faux pas do not indicate rudeness or nastiness but merely a lack of screening ability. If we like someone, we are often willing to provide accounts for their untoward behavior to avoid having to confront them or end the relationship.

Self-repairs occur when the person who makes the error corrects it. Motley, Camden, and Baars (1979) studied verbal slips. They provide an example of a so-called Freudian slip. Upon being introduced to a competitor at a job interview, a man shook hands and said, "Hello, I'm very pleased to *beat* you." Such accidental slips of the tongue often cause great embarrassment. To avoid extensive offense, the person who slips might provide an account—for example, "I'm a bit nervous." Depending on the nature of the slip, correction may be enough. If the slip is particularly offensive, an apology may be necessary to return the conversation to some semblance of order.

Disclaimers are another means of repairing conversation. Disclaimers deny any negative meaning that might be associated with a comment (Hewitt & Stokes, 1975). For example, if you are about to say something that might be interpreted as gossip, you might say, "Please don't think I'm gossiping, but. . . ." If you are afraid that a statement might be interpreted as an indication of racial prejudice, you might say, "Now, I'm not prejudiced, but. . . ." Such statements disclaim any resemblance to gossip or prejudice that your comments might have. Of course, others may interpret what you say as gossip or bias despite your disclaimer.

Disclaimers are attempts to direct the listener away from possible negative impressions of behavior. We all say things in the course of conversation that may result in poor impressions of us. To avoid looking bad, we may disclaim potential negative impressions before making the statement that is likely to produce them. "What I'm saying may sound silly, but it is very serious" is a disclaimer that tells the listener in advance how a statement is to be interpreted.

Through such conversational repairs, communicators save conversations from going awry or terminating prematurely. Without them there would be little margin for error in conversation. Once something was said or done, there would be no retracting it. Conversations would pose a considerable threat to relationships.

Breaking a Pattern of Mismanagement

In addition to individual slips by communicators, communicators can together fall into dysfunctional patterns of communication, or what Cronen, Pearce, and Snavely (1979) call **unwanted repetitive episodes,** or **UREPs.** These are negative patterns of interaction that two people become accustomed to enacting. Here is a sample UREP:

> *Jim walks in the door of his home. Sandy, the dog, runs over to greet him. Sandy is shedding so Jim's suit pants get covered with dog hair. Lisa is preparing dinner.*

Jim: Get out of here, Sandy! Lisa, that dog needs more discipline. He's uncontrollable.
Lisa: Why don't you train him?
Jim: Me? What about you? You get home before I do.
Lisa: I also fix dinner. I can't do everything.
Jim: Give me a break. "Everything" is not what I'm proposing here.
Lisa: What are you proposing?
Jim: A little more effort, that's all.
Lisa: From whom?
Jim: From you! Listen, I've had a hard day. Let's just drop it before we get into one of our arguments.
Lisa: Fine. *(Silence for the rest of the evening)*

This is not the first time Lisa and Jim have gotten into a conversation of this type right after Jim arrived home. When people frequently fall into a pattern of negative interactions, we call the pattern an UREP.

UREPs can be broken if one communicator is willing to change the pattern. When could Lisa or Jim have changed the course of this conversation? Lisa might have responded to Jim's first comment differently. She might have said, "Perhaps we can work with Sandy this weekend. He does need some training." Jim might have avoided the UREP by saying, "You're right, Lisa. You do fix dinner most nights. I guess I'm just tired."

Parents and children are notorious for having UREPs. Living with someone for a long time and playing a certain role such as parent, child, wife, or husband creates some patterns highly resistant to change. The only way to eliminate UREPs is to say or do the unexpected—break the pattern. Once you realize that patterns are usually the fault of both parties, you can do your part to alter them.

Three Approaches to the Study of Conversation

Now that we have discussed how conversation is structured and how communicators cooperate to create effective conversations, let's look at three approaches used by communication scholars in their study of conversation: the relational approach, the social exchange approach, and the self-presentation approach. The first two are similar in one important respect: they focus on the influence communicators have on each other's actions. The unit of analysis for these two approaches is not the individual communicator but the dyad, triad, or group and participants' patterns of reciprocal action. The third approach, however, focuses on individual communicators and their efforts to influence others. The first two approaches are bidirectional or multidirectional (transactional); the third is unidirectional (source to receiver).

Relational Approach

In this chapter, we have proposed that conversations are structured events involving at least two persons whose cooperation in negotiating and adhering to rules allows the sharing and shaping of information. Millar and Rogers (1976) emphasize, however, that we should not assume that rules account for all that occurs in conversation. Communicators have much autonomy within the rules, and so conversation is a formative process in its own right.

We can understand Millar and Rogers's perspective better if we use a chess analogy again. There are rules for chess known by both players. However, while the rules tell players appropriate types of behaviors available, they do not require specific behaviors at every step in the game. For example, a king can move one space. That still leaves a number of alternatives. Will the king go forward, sideways, or backwards? Similarly, rules tell us, in general, what types of speech acts are appropriate, but our choices within those types are extensive.

Millar and Rogers contend that our choices are guided by the prior moves of other interactants, that each interactant's action is a stimulus for another interactant's action. If, for example, you shout at someone, that person is more likely to shout at you. Your shouting is a stimulus for her reaction.

The following conversation demonstrates how interactants' comments affect each other.

> *Sharon:* All the kids are going to the game tonight.
> *Mom:* Not you.
> *Sharon:* Mom, you can't do that.
> *Mom:* Watch me. You have to study.
> *Sharon:* You never want me to have fun. (*Runs into her room and slams the door*)

Both Sharon and her mother contributed to the unhappy ending of this conversation. Each reacted to the comments of the other. Mom's response, "Not you," may have been interpreted by Sharon as leaving no room for discussion. The emphatic nature of this comment limited Sharon's alternatives. She felt trapped. Her mother's authority coupled with her finality led Sharon to challenge her mother. The mother responded to the challenge by reasserting her authority: "Watch me."

The next example demonstrates how the conversation might have proceeded had Mom and Sharon responded differently:

Sharon: All the kids are going to the game tonight.
Mom: Sharon, let's talk about your homework first.
Sharon: Oh, Mom.
Mom: Well, what would you do if you were me and I were you? I care about your future.
Sharon: I'd let you go if you finished your homework first.
Mom: Seems fair. Better get to work.

In this conversation, the mother's invitation to talk about perspectives created an entirely different situation. The discussion was not closed. Sharon did not challenge her mother because she probably sensed that she still had a chance at persuasion.

If every verbal and nonverbal behavior in conversation can be a stimulus for someone else's behavior, then each of us is at least 50 percent responsible for the way other people treat us. After all, our behavior serves as a stimulus for theirs. If people "walk all over" you, it may be due, at least in part, to your allowing them to do so.

Once we realize that everything we say and do has an impact on what others say and do, we can take responsibility for turning around some misguided conversations. If Sharon had responded to her mother's statement, "Not you," with "Why not, Mom?", she might have managed to keep the discussion open. Had Mom given her a reason, Sharon might have found a way to respond to her mother's concerns and get what she wanted as well.

Millar and Rogers (1976, p. 95) introduced a coding scheme that allows researchers to examine how each interactant's contributions shape the course of the conversation. Using arrows, they coded each comment into one of three categories:

1. An attempt to assert control or definitional rights, designated as one-up ($\uparrow$).
2. A request or an acceptance of the other's definition of the relationship, designated as one-down ($\downarrow$).
3. An undemanding, nonaccepting, leveling movement, designated as one-across ($\rightarrow$).

The code assigned to each message indicates whether or not the interactants are working at cross-purposes. **Complementarity** is the term used to describe those segments of an interaction in which the interactants accept the same definition of the relationship. The following brief exchange is a sample of complementary behavior:

Tom: Let's go to the movies. (↑)
Mike: Whatever you say. (↓)

Mike's acceptance of Tom's suggestion creates a situation of complementarity. Tom's statement is a one-up statement. He is making a move for control by declaring, rather than asking, that he and Mike should go to the movies. Mike's statement is a one-down move, accepting Tom's control move.

Complementarity can also take the form of a one-down move followed by a one-up move. For example:

Tom: I'm not sure I can handle this. (↓)
Mike: It's easy. I'll show you how. (↑)

Complementarity requires opposite rather than parallel directions of control of the two interactants' moves.

Symmetry describes interactants' parallel behaviors, both one-up or both one-down. Frustrating conversations in which all parties refuse to make a decision are examples of symmetrical interaction. This conversation is a sample:

Ellen: What do you want to do tonight? (↓)
Frank: I don't know, what about you? (↓)
Ellen: I'm leaving it up to you. (↓)
Frank: I'm willing to do whatever you want to do. (↓)

Both Ellen and Frank use one-down moves. They engage in what Millar and Rogers term **submissive symmetry.** Below is an example of **competitive symmetry** in which the actions of both interactants are one-up.

Karen: I want to see a movie tonight. (↑)
Bob: Not tonight. (↑)
Karen: We haven't seen one in months. Tonight is a good night for a movie. (↑)
Bob: Forget it. I'm not interested. Some other night. (↑)

Karen and Bob both attempt to control the situation. Neither is willing to give in to the other. The result is competitive symmetry. It is also possible to have neutralized symmetry, where neither party takes or gives away control. Greetings are often characterized by neutralized symmetry. Both persons say "Hi" but neither attempts to assert or reject relational control.

Transition refers to situations where the comments of the interactants are different but not opposite in terms of control directions. Transitions occur when an interactant minimizes the issue of control.

Mike: I'm in charge here. (↑)
Bill: It really doesn't matter much who's in charge. (→)

Here Mike makes a one-up move but Bill diminishes the importance of control with a one-across move. If Bill had said, "Okay, fine," that would have been a one-down move. He would have relinquished control to Mike. If he had said, "No, you're not, Mike," he would have made a one-up move and created a symmetrical situation.

Millar and Rogers's work represents an attempt by communication scientists to map conversations in terms of how each person responds to the other. By coding messages in terms of transaction type (complementary, symmetrical, transitional), we can see how each type influences the communicators' impressions of their relationship, the accomplishment of communication goals, satisfaction with the relationship, and other factors. Millar and Rogers (1976) found that married couples with many one-up moves and few one-down moves in their conversations tended to see their marriage as inequitable. Fisher and Drecksel (1983) used one-up, one-down, and one-across categories to study developing relationships. They were able to identify a cyclical pattern of recurring ebb and flow of competitive symmetry in peer relationships. Fisher (1983) found that competitive dyad patterns of interaction differ markedly from cooperative dyads, with the latter being nearly devoid of competitive symmetry.

The relational perspective of interpersonal communication posits that each action by a communicator is influenced by prior and expected future actions of other communicators. Therefore, the smallest unit of analysis for interpersonal communication scientists is a dyadic unit—two people. Each utterance is seen as the result of prior remarks and the precursor to future ones.

Social Exchange Approach

Common to all the perspectives on conversation described in this chapter is the assumption that people enter into conversations with one or more goals. Even as they are cooperating to achieve mutual understanding, they are attempting to attain certain personal goals. Sometimes they merely wish to pass the time while waiting in line for a movie or riding in an elevator. At other times, explaining a complex idea or learning what is bothering a friend may be the primary goal.

Having goals does not necessarily mean that communicators plan their conversations. Much communication is spontaneous. We do, however, enter into conversations with at least a vague sense of what we wish to obtain. Along with rules for appropriate behavior, we have certain self-interests that guide our participation in conversation.

Social exchange theorists believe that conversation involves the trading of **resources** by communicators in an effort to achieve their goals. By resources we mean attention, concern, support, and other communicator needs that may be met or denied by a cointeractant. Roloff (1981, p. 30) defines interpersonal communication as "a symbolic process by which two people, bound together in a relationship, provide each other with resources or negotiate the exchange of resources."

People suddenly become important when they have information that others want because communicators use information to attain their goals. If one's goal is to get attention, having information that others want can be very useful. People who have valuable information are often granted high status. Gossip is often the result of a communicator's need for attention or status.

Occasionally people are explicit in describing what they want from others in exchange for attention, information, or other resources. The following is an example of explicit exchange of resources:

Thomas: You never pay attention to my opinions.
Marilyn: If you're willing to listen to what I have to say, I'll do the same
    for you.

Often negotiations are not so explicit. For example, one interactant may realize that attention to the other will likely result in reciprocated attention. Giving compliments can be an implicit form of trading resources. Compliments may be said to increase the other person's friendliness and trust or to encourage a compliment in return.

Communicators use nonverbal displays of interest to obtain goals. To encourage self-disclosure, a communicator might nod a great deal while someone is speaking. Nodding, smiling, eye contact, and laughing at the appropriate moments often increase comfort and disclosure of valued information.

These are only a few examples of how communicators exchange resources. The social exchange perspective posits that people expend the energy it takes to communicate in order to get something out of a conversation. To the extent that others can provide what we need, we explicitly or implicitly barter with them. We trade attention for information or laughter for affection. According to social exchange theory, our conversations are a means by which we give in order to get.

Another interesting aspect of social exchange theory is its perspective on obligation. In the course of giving and getting, persons create or incur obligation. Most people sense when someone has given them more than they deserve, or when they themselves have given more than a fair amount of love, interest, or attention. Having this sense of fairness allows us to gauge our giving and receiving and to obligate others. Obligation has its good and bad points. It can be used to obtain resources. It can, however, result in an uncomfortable situation for the indebted party.

People are typically uncomfortable with debt. This is why they often argue about who will pay a restaurant bill. You have no doubt heard people reject compliments on their clothing by saying, "Oh, this old thing.

I've had it for years." Some people have difficulty saying "Thank you" because it is an admission of debt. Because people tend to dislike debt, it can be used to help pressure someone into providing a valued resource. However, it is possible to overdo generosity. If someone at work compliments you on your clothes nearly every day, you may doubt his sincerity or question his motives. Giving too much can also cause an irreparable imbalance of resources that threatens the indebted member of the relationship.

Social exchange theory can be used to explain some aspects of conversation management. For example, how long people talk when they take turns can be divided between or among interactants. If one person talks for a long period of time, she may owe the other. If this long-winded person is of higher status than the other, she may not incur debt. Displays of interest, general attention, and cooperation in establishing and following conversational rules are other aspects of conversation that can be affected by considerations of equity. For example, if someone is willing to listen to your side of a story, you become obligated to listen to his side. If someone sacrifices one of her personal rules, you may be obliged later to sacrifice one of your personal rules. Such is the nature of social exchange in conversation.

Self-Presentation Approach

Unlike relational and social exchange approaches to the study of conversation, Erving Goffman's (1959) **self-presentation approach** focuses on the drama enacted by communicators in the course of conversation. According to Goffman, communicators are like actors, structuring their behaviors to make particular impressions on their audiences. Goffman sees interpersonal communication as the means by which people project various aspects of themselves to others. They essentially take turns presenting dramas to one another.

From Goffman's perspective, interaction with others involves gaining information about others and giving information about oneself. Each person influences the course of conversation by eliciting impressions—performing behaviors that lead others to think of him in a certain way. Goffman explains, "He may wish them to think highly of him, or to think that he thinks highly of them, or to perceive how in fact he feels toward them or to obtain no clear-cut impression; he may wish to insure sufficient harmony so that the interaction can be sustained, or to defraud, get rid of, confuse, mislead, antagonize, or insult them" (1959, p. 3).

Goffman proposes that there are two different "sign activities" used by communicators to create impressions: the expressions that they "give" and the expressions they "give off." The first involves purposeful behaviors used to convey an impression. The latter refers to a wide range of behaviors that others can treat as "symptomatic," or characteristic, of the actor rather than purposely contrived by him.

According to Goffman, communicators influence the definition of the situation by the way they express themselves. The impressions they create influence other communicators' choices. For example, by appearing sad, a communicator may encourage others to behave in a sympathetic manner. In this sense, each communicator has some control over the course of the conversation.

Throughout the course of interaction, communicators use what Goffman calls "defensive" and "protective" practices to safeguard the impressions they and others have fostered. **Defensive practices** are strategies used to save one's own definitions of the situation. **Protective practices** are methods used to save the definitions of the situation projected by others. Such practices are akin to conversational repairs discussed earlier in this chapter.

Goffman argues that people are constantly playing roles during their interactions with others. He refers to their performances of roles as **fronts.** Each of us has several fronts available. Mother, teacher, daughter, son, sibling, and student are all fronts, each having patterns of behavior peculiar to them. To perform these fronts effectively, we often suppress emotions and moods. It is difficult to fire someone from a job if you are sympathetic to that person's plight. It is difficult to be "just a friend" when one is attracted to the friend. So we often suppress our emotions in order to perform the front effectively. As Goffman notes, "Through social discipline, then, a mask of manner can be held in place from within" (1959, p. 57).

According to Goffman, **roles** are the basic units of socialization: "It is through roles that tasks in society are allocated and arrangements made to enforce their performances" (p. 87). When performing a role, the individual must act in a manner that will convey impressions compatible with the "role-appropriate personal qualities" imputed to her. Goffman explains that a judge is supposed to be deliberate and sober, a pilot in a cockpit should be cool, and a bookkeeper accurate and neat.

According to Goffman, people can become enamored with particular roles. When people are forced out of such roles by circumstances, we might expect them to experience considerable upset. The mother whose adult life has been devoted to her children may find their maturity and departure from home a considerable threat because it forces her to relinquish many of the activities associated with the role to which she has been attached.

While some people become attached to roles they play, others are able to "play at" roles. The person who finds himself in a role of authority before feeling confident of his ability to fill that role may play at it for a while by doing things that seem appropriate to the role. A woman taking on a job previously held by men may play at the role for a while—she may, for example, dress in masculine attire. Eventually she may incorporate her own style into the role and play it rather than play at it.

Goffman's perspective is reminiscent of Shakespeare's comment that "All the world's a stage." Each of us plays certain parts and, in so doing, contributes to the definition of our own social environment. Whether we accept Goffman's perspective or not, it is certainly an intriguing image of social interaction.

Summary

In this chapter we have shown that conversations are the creations of at least two people. Each communicator's spontaneous, scripted, and contrived behaviors influence the spontaneous, scripted, and contrived behaviors of the other. Their scripted and contrived behaviors are guided by borrowed and personal rules, which they coordinate in an attempt to reach some level of mutual understanding and agreement.

We have seen that conversations are often threatened by misunderstandings or mismanagement of rules. When such threats occur, conversational repairs may be used to get the conversation back on track. We have also discussed how people slip into unwanted repetitive patterns of interaction that can threaten conversations and relationships.

Finally, we reviewed three approaches to the study of conversation management: relational, social exchange, and self-presentation. Relational and self-presentation approaches share the premise that people create their own definitions of their interactions. The focus of the relational perspective is on how the actions of each communicator influence the actions of the other. Social exchange focuses on distribution of rewards. And the self-presentation approach focuses on how the fronts, or roles, each communicator performs contribute to the course of conversation.

Each of the perspectives described in this chapter assists us in understanding the complex nature of conversation. None of them completely explains conversation, but each has influenced the course of its study in fundamental ways.

CHAPTER 7

Persuasion

Persuasion is an activity that has received much attention from communication theorists and researchers. In fact, prior to 1970, most communication study was focused on persuasion. During the 1970s, however, interest in persuasion waned in part because of dissatisfaction with the then-popular models of persuasion and the post-1960s disdain for anything associated with manipulation. Recently, however, there has been renewed interest in persuasion, and perspectives are being developed that attempt to explain interpersonal as well as public forms of persuasion (see Miller & Roloff, 1980; Cushman & McPhee, 1980; Reardon, 1981; Petty & Cacioppo, 1981; Smith, 1982; Bostrom, 1983).

In this chapter we will examine some classic theories of persuasion and their relevance to interpersonal persuasion. We will also introduce some recent perspectives and discuss their implications for improving one's ability to persuade.

A Definition of Interpersonal Persuasion

In Chapter 2 we defined interpersonal communication as a developmental activity in which at least two persons interact in a coherent manner through the use of spontaneous, scripted, and contrived verbal and non-verbal behavior. We described interpersonal persuasion as an aspect of interpersonal communication having one distinctive feature: the intention by at least one communicator to change the thoughts, feelings, or behavior of at least one other person.

While interpersonal communication can be completely spontaneous, interpersonal persuasion involves scripted or contrived behaviors that have been selected to change another person. Such behaviors are called **strategies.**

Some strategies are scripted—used so often by communicators that they occur without conscious planning or forethought. Other strategies are thought through immediately prior to their use. These are contrived. Whenever you consider how you will approach someone in an attempt to alter their thoughts, feelings, or behavior, you are using contrived strategies. Later in this chapter we will review strategy types used by interpersonal communicators during persuasion. Now let's look at the goals of persuasion.

Types of Persuasion Outcomes

Often we think of persuasion in terms of a dramatic move from one position to an entirely different position. In actuality, this type of outcome constitutes only one of several types of persuasion. Miller (1980) describes three types of persuasion outcomes: response shaping, response reinforcing, and response changing.

Response shaping occurs when an individual does not know how to respond to a situation because of limited experiences or the novelty of the situation. For example, a parent may wish to shape a child's response to escalators. To avoid a reaction of fear, the parent may treat an escalator ride as a game. In this way the child comes to associate escalators with fun rather than fear.

Not all instances of response shaping constitute persuasion. Miller (1980, p. 17) states:

> For instance, it would sound strange to speak of children "being persuaded" to tie their shoes correctly; typically, we assert that they have "learned" to tie their shoes. On the other hand, should children refuse to attempt shoe-tieing behaviors, rebel against feeding themselves, and neglect to pick up clothing or toys, they are likely to be bombarded with messages by parents and teachers aimed at shaping these behaviors. If such messages produce the desired effect, the communicators are likely to claim that they have persuaded the children to become more self-reliant or independent; if not, they will probably lament the failure of their persuasive mission and devise other strategies for coping with the problem.

By response shaping, then, we mean fostering a preference for certain types of behavior. This is accomplished by rewarding the occurrences of the preferred behavior. Parents who clean up after their children are inadvertently rewarding them for making a mess. Thus it is important to remember, especially for long-term relationships, that the way you respond to someone can shape his expectations.

Response reinforcing involves ensuring that currently held attitudes or current behaviors resist change. Attending church or synagogue can serve to reinforce previously learned religious attitudes and behaviors. Renewing marriage vows can remind people of their devotion to each other and encourage renewal of behavior characteristic of early years of marriage. A "Thank you" after someone has done you a favor can encourage him to continue treating you well.

Response reinforcing demonstrates that persuasion is rarely a "one-shot" effort. People must be encouraged to continue behaviors or they may cease to use them. Miller explains that many politicians, as they attempt to gain new supporters, forget to reinforce the behaviors of their current followers. As a result, they find themselves losing the old supporters. Similarly, friends and lovers can forget to reinforce each other. Miller (1980, p. 20) writes:

> Turning to the interpersonal sphere, close relationships may be damaged, or even terminated, because the parties take each other for granted—in the terminology employed here, fail to send persuasive messages aimed at reinforcing mutually held positive attitudes and mutually performed positive behaviors. In short, failure to recognize that being persuaded is an ongoing process requiring periodic message attention can harm one's political aspirations, pocketbook, or romantic relationship.

People often forget that persuasion is usually a long-term process. They think that once persuaded, forever persuaded. Actually, people do that for which they are rewarded and avoid doing that for which they are punished. When rewards cease to be forthcoming, people seek them elsewhere.

Response changing describes the way most of us think of persuasion. Like response reinforcing, response changing is often a long-term process. People prefer to maintain attitudes and behaviors that seem to have worked for them in the past. They are willing to change only if given sufficient justification for doing so. This typically takes time. Thus much persuasion is incremental—it occurs over time.

Acquiescence Versus Private Acceptance

Acquiescence is the act of going along with someone's request, command, rule, or reasoning because to do otherwise would cause problems. A smoker may acquiesce to a no-smoking rule on a bus. A child may acquiesce to his father's request to clean his room. However, their assent may not be long lasting. The smoker who follows the no-smoking rule on a bus is likely to light up a cigarette after the ride. The child who cleans his room may clutter it within a few days.

If the goal is to help a smoker become a nonsmoker or a sloppy child become a neat child, **private acceptance** is required—that is, the person must not only change his behavior but also actually believe in the value of change. Smokers who truly believe that quitting the habit is the best thing they can do for themselves are more likely to quit than those who cease smoking just to please others. Children who recognize that a clean room has important advantages are more likely to keep their rooms clean than are children who simply wish to avoid punishment.

Sometimes persuaders are satisfied with acquiescence. One example might be campaign workers attempting to convince voters to go to the polls. Their goal is immediate. They want the voter to comply with their request. They may prefer that the voter privately accept the importance of voting every year, but their immediate purpose is usually more important to them. They want that voter at the polls for the upcoming election.

Sometimes persuaders want long-term results. Weight loss often requires a long-term commitment. Acquiescing to a friend's suggestion that you refrain from dessert at one dinner is not enough to drop twenty pounds. Rather, private acceptance of the need to lose weight is required— a commitment to the cause that extends beyond the immediate moment.

Long-term persuasion requires internalization of the change— recognition that the new behavior fits one's value system (Kelman, 1961). People must want to change in order for change to be lasting. When private acceptance is the goal, persuasion requires association of the behavioral change with the person's own value system or view of the world.

What Is an Attitude?

We have defined persuasion as an activity in which at least one person consciously intends to change the thoughts, feelings, or behavior of at least one other person. Thoughts and feelings directed at a particular person, object, or event are part of one's attitude toward it. **Attitude** is a predisposition to respond in a certain manner. For decades communication theorists and researchers have attempted to determine the relationship between attitude and behavior. Attitude was assumed to influence behavior. A change in attitude was thought to lead to a change in behavior.

Many theorists have since concluded that attitude is a state of mind that intervenes between a stimulus and a response. A stimulus is anything, such as person, object, or event, that elicits behavior. A red light is the stimulus that makes you press your foot down on the car's brake pedal. Music can be the stimulus that makes you dance or change the radio dial. Attitude was assumed to occur somewhere between the music and the dancing or between the music and the dial changing.

There is no way to prove that this view of attitude is correct. Attitudes are what social scientists call "hypothetical variables." They cannot be seen or touched. We assume their existence in people's minds, and our assumption is based on observable behavior. If, for example, we see a boss respond in anger to an employee who submits a report late, we may assume that the boss has a negative attitude toward lateness or toward the employee. If we observe this behavior in other situations, we may be able to determine which factor best describes the boss's attitude because attitude is also assumed to be an enduring disposition. If the boss expresses anger whenever *any* employee submits a report late, we may, with confidence, assume that this negative attitude is directed at lateness.

We may determine attitude only by observing behavior. We cannot see a person's state of mind. We can only make an educated guess concerning its makeup. To make matters worse, our educated guesses may be based on secondhand information. Often we rely on the opinions of others or secondhand reports about another's behavior rather than directly asking that person what she thinks and feels. Hewes, Graham, Doelger, and Pavitt (1985) conducted an interesting investigation into the way people rely on secondhand information or what they call **second-guessing.** They describe second-guessing as the process by which one person reinterprets a message from another person about some event or person that the former has not experienced directly.

People often rely on indirect information about others when determining what type of people they are—the attitudes they possess and the likelihood of their behaving in particular ways. Hewes and his colleagues (1985) found that people consider their second-guesses about others useful though somewhat inaccurate. Seventy-one percent of their subjects thought that they could debias the information, separate the truth from fiction, and derive an accurate image of the person in question.

In terms of interpersonal interaction, apparently many of our assumptions concerning the attitudes of others come from indirect sources. Moreover, a good number of us believe that we can discern accurate from misleading information about others' attitudes. This may or may not be true.

The Attitude-Behavior Dilemma: Fact or Fallacy?

Much persuasion research is based on the premise that attitude affects behavior. Persuasion researchers have typically assumed that a person with a positive attitude toward chocolate-chip ice cream is likely to choose that ice cream when he buys ice cream. However, research has demonstrated that having a positive attitude toward something does not guarantee positive behavior toward it; similarly, a negative attitude toward something does not guarantee negative behavior toward it.

In a classic study of attitude-behavior linkage, LaPiere (1934) demonstrated that attitudes do not always reliably predict behavior. In a 10,000-

mile motor trip across the United States with a Chinese couple, LaPiere reported that, despite strong anti-Chinese sentiment characteristic of the 1930s, they were received at 66 hotels, auto camps, and tourist homes and were turned away at only one place. They also were served in 184 restaurants and cafes. Six months after the trip, LaPiere sent a questionnaire to each establishment they had visited. Respondents from 92 percent of the hotels, auto camps, and tourist homes and 91 percent of the restaurants and cafes indicated that they would not accept Chinese people as guests.

People do not always act in ways consistent with what they report to be their thoughts and feelings. LaPiere concluded that situational factors must be considered when predicting behavior from attitude reports. If others are watching, people often avoid behaving as they would like to behave. They wish to avoid negative reactions from others.

Miller (1980) argues that the attitude-behavior dilemma should lead not to a disregard of the attitude concept but to a revised view of it. People often have attitudes about things that are not highly important to them. For example, a fondness for chocolate-chip ice cream is not the same as a burning desire for chocolate-chip ice cream. A positive attitude toward arms reduction may not lead someone to picket in front of the White House. In short, our tendency to act upon our attitudes is a function of their intensity. Knowing someone's attitude is not enough to predict his behavior. Knowing the strength of someone's involvement with the attitude in question gives us a better chance of accurately predicting behavior.

Another reason for attitude-behavior inconsistency lies in the probability that people have several behaviors associated with a particular attitude. For example, the employer with a negative attitude toward hiring young women might have several alternatives: (1) hire a woman to satisfy affirmative action but avoid giving her any important projects; (2) hire her to satisfy affirmative action but give her especially difficult jobs so she will want to quit; or (3) refuse to hire her. Here one attitude has three behavioral options associated with it. This example suggests that a single attitude may predict a range of behaviors rather than a single behavior.

O'Keefe and Delia (1980) and O'Keefe (1980) suggest that people differ in their ability to cope with attitude-behavior inconsistency. They propose that cognitively complex people are better able to reconcile what appears to others as inconsistency between their attitudes and behaviors. You may remember from Chapter 5 that cognitively complex people integrate information more efficiently than do less complex people. It follows that they should also be more efficient at integrating inconsistent information into their thinking. They are probably better rationalizers.

All of these reasons for attitude-behavior inconsistency suggest that assessments of attitude are unlikely to yield reliable information about the likely occurrence of particular behaviors. Our research efforts might be more fruitfully directed at identifying factors that influence the links between attitudes and behaviors. In the LaPiere study, a factor that affected the attitude-behavior link was the presence of others. When people are being watched by others, they are less inclined to allow their antisocial attitudes to be reflected in their behaviors.

Major Theories of Persuasion

A theory tells us how events in the world appear to be related. No theory can explain everything about persuasion. All theories have limitations, or scope conditions, beyond which they cannot provide reliable explanations. Each of the theories to be discussed in this section has contributed to our understanding of persuasion, both interpersonal and mass communication. Each belongs to one of three families of theories: learning, consistency, and social judgment. As we describe each theory, we will also describe its contribution to our understanding of interpersonal persuasion.

Learning Theories

Learning theories explain the acquisition of new attitudes and behaviors as well as the way such attitudes and behaviors are changed.

Persuasion researchers of the early and mid-twentieth century believed that people are persuaded to respond positively or negatively to an object, person, or event by pairing it with some other object, person, or event for which they have already learned a positive or negative response. Advertisers pair their products with fun, status, sex appeal, and other positive attributes. They hope that the positive response consumers have to these attributes will be transferred to the products.

Classical conditioning is the term used to refer to a form of learning through association. You have probably read of Ivan Pavlov's experiments with dogs, an example of classical conditioning. Pavlov conducted an experiment in which he rang a bell shortly before blowing meat powder into a dog's mouth. The dog had initially salivated in response to the meat powder alone. Later the dog came to associate the bell with the meat powder and began to salivate at the sound of the bell.

Those persuasion researchers ascribing to the classical conditioning model believe that attitudes are the result of paired associations. We learn to like certain things because, in our minds, they are associated with other things that we like. Chicken soup may be your desire when feeling ill because it reminds you of home and parental attention when you were a child. Similarly, negative attitudes may be the result of the pairing of one object, person, or event with another for which you already have a negative attitude. If you dislike Bill and you see Mike, a relative stranger, associating with Bill, the classical conditioning perspective would predict that you are likely to begin developing a negative attitude toward Mike as well.

Sometimes the purpose of persuasion might be to change someone's attitude rather than to create one. This is called **counterconditioning.** It involves pairing a person, object, or event that evokes a positive response with one that evokes a negative response or vice versa. For example, the child who does not want to go to church might be persuaded by the promise of breakfast at a favorite restaurant right after the service. After several pairings of church with enjoyable family breakfasts, the child may come to consider attending church part of a positive experience. Similarly, a positive attitude stimulus may be paired with a negative stimulus. If the negative stimulus reaction is stronger than the positive one, the positive attitude may become more negative.

For some people in our society, the word *feminist* has come to have negative connotations. The mass media have helped to foster the image of feminist women as militant, radical troublemakers (see Gerbner, 1978). Therefore, this much-abused word can now be used disparagingly. The word *feminist* has acquired some negative connotations through association.

Classical conditioning has come to be viewed as too limited an explanation for all types of learning. As we mentioned earlier, every theory has its scope conditions—limitations on what it can explain. However, if classical conditioning were a complete failure as a form of persuasion, advertisers would cease to associate their products with celebrities and politicians would stop worrying about the clothes they wear to rallies or on television. Many of our first impressions of others are the result of associations. When you cannot describe why you feel uncomfortable around someone you just met, perhaps you have unconsciously drawn an association between her and some person you dislike.

Operant conditioning is a form of persuasion that shares some similarities with classical conditioning. It too depends upon reward or punishment for its success. Operant conditioning, however, does not require that the persuader use a particular stimulus to evoke a reaction from the persuadee such as the meat powder used by Pavlov. With operant conditioning, a behavior occurs for some reason and is rewarded. The second time the same behavior occurs, it is rewarded again. Eventually the behavior becomes associated with reward and increases in frequency. For example, the small boy who picks up a toy from the floor and puts it in the toy box without having been asked to do so might be rewarded by his parents. The next time the child picks up a toy and puts it away, he might be rewarded again. Eventually the child will associate reward with picking up toys.

Albert Bandura (1977) has criticized conditioning models of human

CALDWELL By Caldwell

behavior for their failure to take into account differences in situations, persons, and time. He developed a **social learning** theory of behavior that suggests that behavior, personal factors, and environmental factors all operate as interlocking determinants of each other. Bandura argued that there are times when personal factors are most important in determining behavior and times when environmental factors are most important. He criticized behaviorism for failing to attend to the importance of cognitive factors to behavior. Cognition, Bandura explained, effects behavior and should not be excluded from models that seek to explain human behavior.

One of Bandura's major contributions was his discussion of **modeling.** He explained, "Learning would be exceedingly laborious if people had to rely solely on the effects of their own actions to inform them what to do. Fortunately most human behavior is learned observationally through modeling: from observing others one forms an idea of how new behaviors are performed, and on later occasions this coded information serves as a guide for action" (1977, p. 22). In short, not all, and especially not the most interesting behaviors, are learned through classical or operant conditioning.

Through modeling, people can learn rules or principles of behavior that they may apply in many situations; this is called **abstract modeling.** For example, knowing how to balance oneself on a skateboard may be useful when attempting surfing or water skiing. Another example is language learning. Once you learn grammatical rules, you can apply them across situations. Moreover, once you learn a style of communication, you can apply it in various contexts.

Inoculation theory is another member of the learning theories family. People who are physically unprepared to resist certain infectious diseases, such as smallpox and polio, require inoculation with vaccine to stimulate their bodies' defense mechanisms to resist the disease. This is often done by injection of a strain of bacteria related to the disease or dead bacteria of the disease itself.

Similarly, to the extent that people are uninformed on an issue or unaware of the various positions on that issue, they are typically easier to persuade simply because they are unprepared to refute the persuader's arguments. One way to make them less susceptible to influence is to "inoculate" them with counterarguments.

According to McGuire (1964), people can be inoculated against persuasion. Politicians often attempt to do this. They warn their audience that their opponents will probably attempt to persuade them to some viewpoint. They tell the audience what their opponents are likely to say and then provide reasons why the opponents are wrong. In this way politicians hope to inoculate their followers with counterarguments for future use in refuting their opponents' arguments.

Inoculation theory posits that it is better to arm persuadees with counterarguments than to leave them unprepared to refute an opponent's perspective. If you know that someone you want to persuade is going to be exposed to counterarguments, inoculation may be the answer. The following conversation is an example of how people use inoculation in interpersonal persuasion.

> *Mark:* Would you like to come over for dinner Friday?
> *Sharon:* Aren't you going out with Cindy Parker?
> *Mark:* No. Cindy and I don't date anymore. Do you know her?
> *Sharon:* We live on the same floor at my dorm.
> *Mark:* Oh. Well, Cindy may tell you that I'm not your type. I hope you'll be your own judge of that. After people break up they have some bad feelings for a while. Cindy seems to be in that stage right now. I went through it myself, but it's over for me now.
> *Sharon:* I understand. Why don't you give me a call tonight? I'll let you know about dinner then.

Mark tried to prepare Sharon for remarks she might hear from Cindy that could discourage Sharon from seeing him. You need not be a politician to benefit from an understanding of inoculation theory. Whenever there is a good chance that the persuadee will encounter arguments against your position, inoculation may be useful. However, it may be unwise to inoculate persuadees if there is little chance of them encountering opposing arguments. If, for example, Sharon had not known Cindy, Mark's inoculation attempt would have been unnecessary. If Mark had decided that he should prepare Sharon to refute Cindy's arguments on the slim chance that they might meet, he might actually give Sharon reason to call Cindy to ask her about Mark.

Inoculation can be quite useful in situations where the persuadee is likely to encounter opposing arguments. Dieters who have friends encouraging them to overeat may benefit from being prepared with counterarguments. The child who is likely to encounter peer pressure to smoke might better resist that influence if her parents have already helped her determine how to respond.

Consistency Theories

One of the most popular categories of persuasion theories is **cognitive consistency.** Its premise is that people are uncomfortable with conflicting thoughts. Therefore, one way of persuading people is to point out the inconsistency between what they say and what they do or between what they have done in the past and what they are currently doing.

The major premise of **balance theory,** one of the earliest consistency theories, is that people find inconsistencies between their likes and dislikes irritating. For example, if Judy likes Steven, and Steven likes Rich, but Judy dislikes Rich, Judy likes someone who likes someone whom she dislikes. There is an inconsistency. According to Fritz Heider (1958), who developed balance theory, people prefer balanced cognitions. They seek to avoid or change situations where their preferences conflict.

According to Heider, Judy has two options. Figure 7.1 depicts her dilemma. To solve her discomfort, Judy could decide to like Rich more. If that is difficult, she may decide to dislike Steven. Figure 7.2 depicts these two solutions. Option 1 allows Judy to resolve her discomfort by liking both Rich and Steven. Option 2 allows Judy to solve her dilemma by disliking Steven.

According to Heider, imbalanced cognitive states are susceptible to persuasion. For example, should a staunch Republican discover that his friend is a Democrat, he may become susceptible to arguments directed at

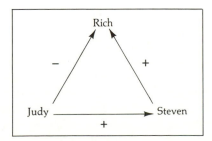

Figure 7.1.   Conflicting preferences that contribute to an imbalanced cognitive state.

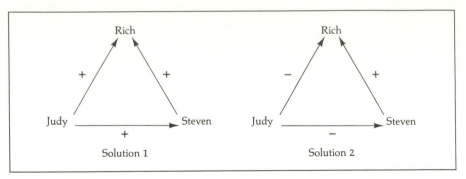

Figure 7.2.   Two options to restore cognitive consistency.

changing his party affiliation or he may become more receptive to criticisms of his friend. Another example of how inconsistent cognitions make us susceptible to persuasion is the encyclopedia salesman who tells his customer how well-behaved her children are. It may be difficult for her to think ill of such a man.

You may be saying to yourself, "Come on, it isn't that easy." That is just what the critics of Heider's theory have said. They argue that people can indeed tolerate inconsistency. They can reason that the salesman is just using compliments to sell encyclopedias. Judy could decide to continue disliking Rich while continuing to like Steven by reasoning that Rich and Steven have been buddies for years. She might tell herself that Steven is blinded to Rich's faults by their friendship. This relieves Judy's discomfort without her having to change her feelings toward Steven or Rich.

Human beings are capable of reasoning their way out of cognitive imbalance. Does this mean that Heider's theory is useless? No. It means that it cannot explain all types of persuasion. The premise of his theory, however, has some important implications for persuasion. It suggests that creating imbalance—by telling persons that something they dislike is liked by someone they like, for example—can sometimes open the way to persuasion. Their discomfort with the newfound knowledge may cause them to reconsider their attitude toward the disliked object.

Cognitive dissonance theory, developed by Leon Festinger (1957), is derived from the consistency perspective advanced by Heider. According to Festinger, two items are inconsistent, or dissonant, when knowledge of one suggests the opposite of the other. **Dissonance** is an unpleasant motivational tension people feel when they have acted in a manner inconsistent with some cognition. For example, if you know that smoking is hazardous to your health, you should experience dissonance when you light up a cigarette. If you buy a new television even though your family needs the money for food, you will probably experience dissonance.

According to Festinger, dissonance can be a precursor to change: "Just as hunger is motivating, cognitive dissonance is motivating. Cognitive dissonance will give rise to activity oriented toward reducing or eliminating the dissonance. Successful reduction of dissonance is rewarding in the same sense that eating when one is hungry is rewarding" (1957, p. 70).

The magnitude of dissonance felt depends upon the ratio of consonant, or harmonious, elements to dissonant bits of information. Consonant thoughts support current behavior. Dissonant thoughts challenge it. A boy who smokes may have four reasons, or consonant elements, for smoking: it reduces tension, tastes good, makes me look older, and makes me comfortable with my friends who smoke. He may also be aware of five reasons why he should not smoke: it makes my clothes smell awful, is dangerous to my health, wastes my money, annoys my girlfriend, and stains my teeth and fingers. Thus he has one more dissonant factor than consonant factor. If these elements were equally important considerations, his ratio of dissonant to consonant items would be five to four. He should, therefore, be more susceptible to antismoking arguments than the smoker who has four consonant and four dissonant elements of information.

The persuader's task is to convince the persuadee that there are more good reasons to change than to continue behaving in the same manner. To do this often involves preventing the persuadee from rationalizing her way out of dissonance. According to Festinger, people can reduce dissonance by adding more consonant items to the ratio. The smoker might add to his list of reasons for smoking, thereby changing the ratio of dissonant to consonant elements. Another method of reducing dissonance is to deny responsibility. Here the smoker might reason that he is the victim of an unbreakable habit begun in childhood when he was ignorant of the consequences of his actions. A third method of reducing dissonance is to alter the importance of the dissonant cognitions. The smoker could decide that staining his teeth is no big deal: coffee causes as much discoloration.

Once again you might ask, "What good is this theory if people can rationalize dissonance?" It's an important theory because persuaders can make it difficult for people to rationalize. They can block the persuadee's attempts to ignore dissonance. Then the only way left to reduce dissonance is to change in the manner advocated by the persuader.

One of the main differences between balance theory and cognitive dissonance theory is that the latter describes human beings as choice makers. Heider's theory imprisoned the individual in triangles of likes and dislikes. This may describe some aspects of our lives, but certainly more often than not, we have more than two choices. What both theories share is the premise that people find inconsistency intolerable.

Another popular theory of persuasion is **counterattitudinal advocacy.** It proposes that people are capable of persuading themselves. Counterattitudinal advocacy is accomplished by convincing people to argue against their own perspectives.

The classic example of this is a father who convinces his son to study the negative effects of marijuana. He then asks the son to write a report on this topic. According to counterattitudinal advocacy, if the son decides to do this and is not rewarded for it or threatened with punishment if he does not do it, he may persuade himself to avoid marijuana in the course of studying its negative effects.

The key factor is that the son must not feel that his father forced him to study the ill effects of marijuana. He must see it as his choice. Otherwise he could rationalize that he was forced to write the report, and none of it represented his own thoughts or feelings. Similarly, if the son were paid to do it, he could rationalize that he only did it for the money. (See Miller & Burgoon, 1973, for a review of counterattitudinal advocacy.)

Counterattitudinal advocacy can be a very effective method of persuasion. When people persuade themselves, the result is likely to be private acceptance. They will probably fit their new views into their current value system.

The problem with counterattitudinal advocacy is that it is difficult to get people to cooperate in self-persuasion. How many sons would write a report about marijuana at their father's request? People are typically reluctant to put themselves in the position of having to refute their own attitudes. Sometimes counterattitudinal advocacy is accomplished in interpersonal communication by encouraging persuadees to empathize—put themselves in the position of someone else. Role playing of this sort is one means by which people can inadvertently persuade themselves to see something as other people see it.

Social and Self Judgment Theories

The third family of persuasion emphasizes the ways in which persuadees judge persuasive appeals. These theories emphasize the role of social norms or standards that guide persuadees as they decide how to respond to a persuasive message. According to Sherif, Sherif, and Nebergall (1965), persuasion involves two steps. First, after hearing or seeing a persuasive message, the persuadee judges the message in terms of how well it matches her own perspective on the issue. Second, the persuadee changes her attitude. However, the amount of change in attitude depends on the degree of discrepancy between the persuadee's initial position and the persuader's position. The persuadee's initial position serves as an anchor or standard for judging whether the persuader's perspective lies within the persuadee's "latitude of acceptance," "latitude of rejection," or "latitude of noncommitment."

Latitude of acceptance refers to the persuadee's preferred position on an issue. Unless the persuadee is very closed minded about the issue, he is likely to accept a range of arguments that agree more or less with his own.

The **latitude of rejection** refers to those ideas the persuadee finds unacceptable. For example, if you are against abortion, you may be unwilling to accept any reasons for terminating a pregnancy.

The **latitude of noncommitment** encompasses all those arguments toward which the persuadee feels neutral. If the issue of persuasion lies within this latitude, the persuader must convince the persuadee to care about the issue before it will be possible to persuade her to adopt the advocated perspective or behavior.

The amount of potential change of attitude depends on the discrepancy between the persuader's position and the persuadee's position. If the persuader's perspective lies within the persuadee's latitude of acceptance but is also discrepant from the persuadee's **primary position,** the attitude change should be greater than if the persuader's position lies within the persuadee's latitude of acceptance and is close to the primary position. As discrepancy increases, the potential for attitude change increases as long as the advocated position lies within the persuadee's latitude of acceptance.

If a persuader's position lies within the persuadee's latitude of rejection, no attitude change is expected. If it lies within the latitude of noncommitment, attitude change is possible. The persuadee's ego is not involved with an issue that lies within this latitude. Without a primary or anchor position, the persuadee is afloat, so to speak, and susceptible to persuasion.

Social judgment theory has been criticized for its view of people as passive recipients of information (Smith, 1982). Ideas are assumed to be automatically categorized, rather than considered. There is no room for reasoning, merely room for responding. The positive side of social judgment theory is the premise that people bring a "frame of reference" to persuasion encounters. They do not merely respond to arguments as if they had had no previous association with them. This theory suggests that people have standards that they use in determining their response to persuasive messages.

Belief Systems Theory of Stability and Change. Ball-Rokeach, Rokeach, and Grube (1984) proposed a model which treats the self as the central focus of judgment. They argued that in virtually every situation people ask themselves implicitly or explicitly whether what they said or did was consistent with their self-images or some enhancement of them. More specifically, whether the behavior fits their images of themselves as competent and moral people. If they discover that their behaviors do not maintain or enhance their self-images, the result is self-dissatisfaction—a harmful, affective state which people will attempt to alleviate or terminate, thus providing an impetus to change their behaviors. If they discover that their behaviors maintain or enhance their self-images, self-satisfaction results and change in behavior is less likely.

Ball-Rokeach, Rokeach, and Grube distinguished between diffuse and focused feelings of self-satisfaction and self-dissatisfaction. Vague or general feelings of self-satisfaction and self-dissatisfaction are not associated with any particular event. Feeling generally satisfied or dissatisfied with oneself without really knowing the cause of those feelings is not a strong impetus for change. More focused states of self-satisfaction or self-dissatisfaction involve conscious awareness of some source or reason for such feelings. That awareness produces greater impetus to change conditions eliciting dissatisfaction and to maintain those eliciting satisfaction.

People may be encouraged to focus on the ways in which some of their behaviors are not self-enhancing. To the extent that a persuader successfully encourages persuadee dissatisfaction with a particular behavior, the persuadee is likely to become receptive to suggestions of alternative behaviors. To the extent that a persuader successfully encourages persuadee satisfaction with a particular behavior, the persuadee is likely to maintain that behavior and resist change.

Ball-Rokeach, Rokeach, and Grube specified seven conditions necessary to initiate persuadee change or maintenance activities:

1. If the information appeals to the curiosity that people have to understand themselves better.
2. If the information is potentially useful, that is, holds out a promise of increasing one's knowledge about something that is truly important to oneself. We assume that the most important information that persons can obtain about themselves is that which directly involves their competence or morality. We further assume that information about one's values, because they are central and because they serve as standards for evaluating self and others, will be more important than information about one's attitudes or behaviors.
3. If the information is unambiguous and does not require too much specialized training or effort to understand.
4. If the information appears credible and intuitively correct.
5. If the information arouses a feeling of self-satisfaction because it reinforces or confirms one's self-conceptions or self-presentations of competence or morality or, alternatively, if it arouses a feeling of self-dissatisfaction because it raises doubts about one's present level of competence or morality and thus becomes an impetus for change.
6. If it is within the repertoire of the person to act upon the information, either to alleviate or eliminate the focused feeling of self-dissatisfaction or to extend and enhance the focused feeling of self-satisfaction.
7. If the information is presented under conditions that minimize ego defense (pp. 35–36).

The ACE Model of Persuasion. A third perspective on persuasion that involves persuadee judgment or reasoning is the ACE model. This model uses both self and social standards or rules as criteria for rejecting persuaders' recommendations.

Capella and Folger (1980) argue that aspects of a given situation cue information in our minds that helps us select among behavioral options. For example, we enter a home and see that there is a party in progress. Our past experiences of parties are cued and we begin to engage in behavior that is appropriate to parties.

As Capella and Folger state, "When a person is faced with a behavioral choice, that person will choose on the basis of information that can be retrieved at the time of decision" (1980, p. 166). They reason that situational cues place certain information at the decision maker's disposal. When you decide whether or not to correct a friend's version of a story as he tells it to others, the knowledge that others are listening and memories of negative social consequences from criticizing others in public might lead you to postpone such criticism.

This information-processing approach to understanding how people choose among behavioral options rests on the belief that people are capable of reasoning. They are able to judge, by some criteria, behavioral alternatives once those options have been cued in memory by aspects of the situation.

One model of the way people reason among behavioral options is the **ACE model,** which suggests that the criteria people use when they consciously select among behavioral options cued by the situation are appropriateness (A), consistency (C), and effectiveness (E). This model does not suggest that people always reason about their behavior, but rather that when they do, appropriateness, consistency, and effectiveness are the three primary criteria they use (Reardon, 1981, 1984).

According to Reardon (1981), people consciously and unconsciously know rules about how appropriate, consistent, or effective a behavioral option is likely to be given the situation and relationship between communicators. **Appropriateness** refers to how the behavior in question might be judged by other people. **Consistency** refers to how the behavior in question "fits" with one's own value system and self-image. Is the behavior something a person like me would do? **Effectiveness** pertains to the likelihood that the behavior will lead to the desired consequence, or outcomes.

An example may be helpful here. If Allen wants to persuade his supervisor to give him a day off (desired consequence) even though he has already reached his limit of vacation days (one major antecedent condition, or factor), he can choose from a number of behaviors. He might simply ask his supervisor for the day off without giving an excuse, he might lie about his reason, or he might just take the day off without asking and face the consequences later.

Each of these alternatives is associated with some possibility of effectiveness—some likelihood of bringing about the desired consequence. For example, lying might be given a low priority because it has never worked for Allen before. Asking without an excuse might be a better choice but asking with an excuse might be preferable. Taking the day off without asking might be the most preferable in terms of getting a day off, but might be ineffective in terms of keeping a job. So the best choice in terms of *effectiveness* might be to lie to the supervisor.

If effectiveness were Allen's only concern, his decision would be considerably simplified. However, effectiveness is probably not Allen's only concern. As with most people, he also has social and personal criteria by which he evaluates behavioral options. He judges his behavioral options not only in terms of the most effective choice but also in terms of appropriateness—what would others consider the right or proper thing to do?—and consistency—what is right for me?

So while Allen may perceive that the most effective way for him to get the day off is to lie, he might consider it immoral and thus inconsistent with his self-image—an element of consistency. He might also wonder what others would think if his lie were discovered—a matter of appropriateness. Given these considerations, Allen might decide to offer his best excuse for wanting the extra vacation day instead of lying.

The ACE model describes the criteria people use when they reason among alternative actions. Figure 7.3 depicts the ACE model of reasoned behavior.

Obligatory, prohibited, preferable, permissible, and *irrelevant* represent how necessary it is for the communicator to perform each behavioral option in order to act appropriately, consistently, and effectively. It may sometimes be necessary to sacrifice one criterion in order to satisfy one or two of the others. For example, while it may be preferable for Allen to lie in terms of effectiveness, it may be obligatory for him to tell the truth in terms of consistency or appropriateness.

Let's take a closer look at each of the three criteria of appropriateness, consistency, and effectiveness and their roots in persuasion research.

Appropriateness. Since human beings are social beings, the opinions of others are important to them. As Donne wrote, "No man is an island." Each of us has what George Herbert Mead called "significant others" whose actions influence our own and whose opinions help us shape our expectations. Even in the physical absence of such significant people, we have some idea of how they would expect us to act, and we use these expectations to help us decide among available behaviors.

Early theories of persuasion focused upon the individual. Consistency perspectives, for example, disregarded the opinions of significant others and treated the person as pushed and pulled by concerns with balance, dissonance, and congruity of cognitions. When these theories failed to

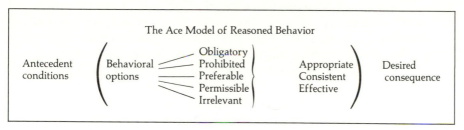

Figure 7.3. The ACE model of reasoned behavior.

adequately explain human action, researchers began to ask why. One answer: consistency theories that treat the individual as a self-contained unit ignore the fact that people are fundamentally social beings. We rely on others to help us decide which behaviors are suitable in particular situations. When others are not present, we can imagine their opinions.

Research by Muzafer Sherif, Solomon Asch, and others on conformity to group norms demonstrated that people are influenced not only by their own individual perspectives but also by the perspectives of others. Sherif (1936) found that when no correct response exists, groups set up norms and people follow them. Asch (1952) found that many people will abandon an obviously correct response in favor of the response chosen by the majority.

Festinger's (1954) theory of social comparison also encouraged persuasion researchers to consider the influence of others on persuadees' actions. According to Festinger, people have a drive to evaluate their attitudes and behaviors. He argued that to behave effectively in society one must be able to judge the reasonableness and appropriateness of one's actions.

The *A* of the ACE model pertains to the influence others exert on our behavioral choices. Given that we are social beings, one criterion for evaluating our actions is the opinions of other people. Rules of appropriateness tell us what others expect. People in the same culture share many appropriateness rules. Without shared rules, society would be impossible. We would not stand in line for movie tickets, stop at stop signs, hold doors open for each other, pay taxes, assist the needy, join the military, attend religious gatherings, or perform many other expected actions.

However, note that people do not always agree on what is appropriate. For example, the American who brings a clock as a gift to a Chinese friend has violated appropriateness rules. The American who crosses his legs and reveals the soles of his shoes in the presence of an Arab may cause offense. If he then asks his Arab counterpart, "How's the wife?", he is not likely to be welcome in that home again.

It isn't necessary for us to cross cultural boundaries in order to find disagreement on appropriateness rules. Each of us belongs to a number of groups from which we have derived our understanding of appropriate actions. We come from different families, regions, and socioeconomic classes. When we consider all the differences we may have from diverse group affiliations, it is a wonder that we share as many rules as we do.

Consistency. The second criterion people use in evaluating their behavior is consistency—how a particular thought, feeling, or behavior fits a person's value system or self-image. We are proposing, as early consistency theorists proposed, that people find inconsistency of thoughts, feelings, and behaviors uncomfortable. We are, however, defining consistency only in terms of personal rules—those in one's own idiosyncratic rule system, which is fundamental to one's self-image.

The value of consistency is something we learn early in life. Children tend to be rewarded for predictable behavior and punished for unpredictable behavior. In this way, children are encouraged to maintain what Goffman (1959) would call particular "fronts." Perhaps parents need to be able to predict their children's actions, even if such actions are not the most appropriate or effective available. Schlenker (1980, p. 232) argues that consistency is maintained when we are adults because it "gives actors a desirable degree of predictability and trustworthiness, and it generates liking and respect." People who are consistent, even if we disagree with them, are often accorded respect for being true to convictions.

Impression management theories posit that people want to appear consistent (Tedeschi, Schlenker, & Bonoma, 1971; Riess & Schlenker, 1977; Snyder & Swann, 1976; Schlenker, 1980). According to Schlenker (1980, p. 204), "Irrespective of whether people have psychological needs to be consistent . . . there is little doubt that the appearance of consistency usually leads to social reward, while the appearance of inconsistency leads to social punishment." This impression management view differs from early cognitive consistency theories in its emphasis on the social punishment derived from the appearance of inconsistency rather than the psychological discomfort derived from inconsistency.

Brehm's theory of psychological reactance suggests that people are motivated to maintain freedom to be themselves—to act in ways consistent with their self-image and value system. According to Brehm (1966), threatening to restrict someone's freedom to act as she chooses arouses in that person a motivational drive called "psychological reactance," which motivates people to reestablish their freedom to act as they please.

Since people value their freedom to act as they please, they can be provoked to use consistency as a criterion by creating the impression that their freedom to act as they please is restricted without legitimate reason. Persuaders use this strategy in all forms of communication. The candidate who reports that an opponent is manipulating the minds of the people can elicit psychological reactance among constituents. The older person forbidden to apply for a job because it is open only to younger people might be motivated by psychological reactance to apply.

At times consistency may be sacrificed for appropriateness or effectiveness or both. Personal rules are sometimes subordinated to please others or achieve goals. When there are few formal rules, a condition of high self-autonomy, people are more likely to use consistency as a criterion for evaluating their behavior. For example, one is more free to rely on personal rules at a party than at a wedding, where formality is more important.

Effectiveness. The third criterion by which people judge their actions is effectiveness. Of the desire to be effective, Abraham Maslow (1970, p. xv) wrote, "Apparently we function best when we are striving for something that we lack, when we wish for something that we do not have, and when we organize our powers in the service of striving toward the gratification of that wish."

Theory and research on achievement motivation have focused primarily on long-term goals. In the study of interpersonal communication, our interest is often focused on short-term goals such as creating a positive image by one's verbal or nonverbal behavior, taking a turn speaking, and encouraging persons to change their behavior. Whether goals are short or long term, however, people strive to locate effective means of obtaining them. Thus effectiveness is one of the criteria they use to evaluate their behaviors.

As with appropriateness and consistency, effectiveness may be superordinate, equal, or subordinate to the other criteria. In some situations and relationships, effectiveness is less important than appropriateness or consistency. For example, people often modify their career goals in order to be good (appropriate) parents or spouses. For a persuader to use an effectiveness appeal successfully, she must understand the persuadee's priorities.

Even if people share an understanding of priorities and agreement concerning their goals, they may differ in the paths they take to obtain them. Maslow stated that ends in themselves are far more universal than the roads taken to achieve those ends since the roads are determined locally in the specific culture. The persuader must be sensitive not only to the importance attached by the persuadee to effectiveness but also to preferred behavior for obtaining it.

Persuasion Strategies

Knowledge of a persuadee's priorities as they pertain to appropriateness, consistency, and effectiveness is of little value unless we also know how to appeal to those priorities. This is where strategies become important.

Strategies provide general guidelines for achieving persuasion goals (Berger, 1985); they are categories of verbal and nonverbal behaviors. For example, threat, promise, altruistic appeals, and reminders of debts the persuadee owes to the persuader are examples of strategies. It is up to the persuader to decide which strategies are likely to be of assistance in achieving her persuasion goals. To do this the persuader may consider the situation, her relationship with the persuadee, past successes with various strategies—particularly with this persuadee—the amount of time available for persuasion, and many other factors. Let's look now at seven specific variables that may play a part in a persuader's choice of a strategy.

Variables in Selecting a Strategy

According to Berger (1985, p. 487), any selection of a strategy may be influenced by a persuader's consideration of one or more of the variables in the following list:*

1. Time available for goal achievement
2. Degree of success
3. Legitimacy
4. Relational consequences
5. Intimacy
6. Relative power
7. Personality

Berger points out, however, that persuaders do not readily consider all or any of these variables when selecting a strategy. Persuaders who attend to the variables in our list must be self-aware. They must think about their actions, an activity that requires energy most of us are reluctant to exert. Berger explained, "Most probably, persons are more likely to say things they 'really don't mean' rather than to restrain themselves from doing so" (p. 489). As with the ACE model, Berger's strategy selection variables are relevant only to reasoned behavior—situations in which the persuader is provoked to consider alternative strategies.

   Time, the first variable in the list, is a crucial factor in strategy selection. When persuaders have the luxury of time, they may consider the persuadee's ranking of priorities for appropriateness, consistency, and effectiveness. Moreover, they may try more than one strategy if the first does not work. When pressed for time or feeling impatient, persuaders may select strategies without considering the consequences, given the situation, relationship, personality of the persuadee, and other important elements of the interaction. Time may be a prime factor in the tendency to, as the saying goes, "put your foot in your mouth."

   Degree of success refers to the utility of the strategy in the past. How successful has the persuader been using a particular strategy? Since we are

*From Berger, "Social Power and Communication," p. 486, in *Handbook of Communication* by M.L. Knapp and G. R. Miller (Eds). © 1985 by Sage Publications, Inc. Reprinted by permission.

capable of remembering the past and using it in current choices, degree of success can play an important role in strategy selection. For example, a child whose pouting and foot stamping gets him an hour alone in his room rather than the desired cookie may think twice before using that strategy again. Of course, there is always the possibility of becoming enamored with a strategy despite its high rate of failure. No doubt you know people who use the same routine to persuade others even though it rarely works. Such people lack the behavioral flexibility needed for effective persuasion.

Legitimacy of a strategy means the persuader's right to use a certain approach. Laws, rules, or status can prohibit some strategies. For example, using violence to gain compliance is typically not legitimate. Commanding a superior to provide a desired raise is typically not legitimate; a polite request might be acceptable. Research suggests that certain strategies legitimate for men are illegitimate for women. For example, Burgoon, Dillard, and Doran's (1983) research suggests that women are expected to use less aggressive strategies than men use. Women are penalized when they are the unexpected source of aggressive strategies.

Relational consequences, the fourth variable on our list, refers to the persuader's perception of the impact of the strategy on his relationship with the persuadee. Some people accept verbal abuse; others do not. Some people will leave a relationship if threatened; others are willing to remain. Before selecting strategies, persuaders may consider the likely response of the targets of their strategies if they are interested in maintaining the relationship.

Intimacy is another factor that may affect strategy selection. Perhaps you have heard the comment "You always hurt the ones you love." This observation suggests that people are less considerate of the people close to them than they are of others. It may be that we feel certain of their love even if we hurt them. We may employ our best manners with acquaintances whose affection or respect is not guaranteed. With total strangers whom we are unlikely to meet again, we may feel free to use threat and other negative strategies because we are not concerned with a future relationship. Research supports the existence of this tendency (Miller, Boster, Roloff, & Seibold, 1977; deTurck, 1985). Apparently when we do not expect to have a long-term relationship with someone, we are more willing to use negative strategies such as threat to persuade them.

Relative power, variable six in the list, refers to the status of the persuader compared to the persuadee. Research suggests that persuaders low in power are likely to use less direct and positive strategies, whereas high-power persuaders are likely to have a wider range of choices among positive and negative and direct and indirect strategies (see Berger, 1985). The more uncertain we are of our ability to control a situation, the less likely we are to use whatever strategy comes to mind.

When others hold the power, persuaders are likely to be more careful in their strategy selections.

Finally, **personality** of the persuader may affect strategy selection. An assertive persuader is likely to feel more comfortable using direct strategies than is a demure persuader. Cognitive complexity also appears to affect strategy choice. Highly complex persons tend to select other-oriented strategies—"If you do this, you'll feel good about yourself"—rather than self-oriented strategies—for example, "Do this for me" (see Reardon & Boyd, 1986).

Figure 7.4 shows how persuaders might use considerations of appropriateness, consistency, and effectiveness and the strategy selection variables to select among strategy options. (The *w* refers to the weight each criterion receives given the situation.)

Aspects of the situation and goal considerations (the change desired by the persuader) cue strategy options. If the persuader has the time, inclination, and ability to consider the strategy options, she may consider the appropriateness, consistency, and potential effectiveness of each option from the persuadee's perspective. When considering appropriateness, the persuader is likely to be concerned with the legitimacy of each strategy option and its utility given the relationship between the persuader and persuadee, as well as how power is distributed. In terms of consistency, the persuader may consider which strategies are consistent with her personality, or self-image. Finally, in terms of effectiveness, the persuader may be concerned with amount of time available, past success of each strategy, the consequences of a strategy, and relational power in terms of who has the advantage.

An Interactional Consideration

An interactional model of interpersonal persuasion means that strategy choices are also influenced by what each person has said and done during the course of the interaction. Each communicator's contributions shape the course of interpersonal persuasion. A persuader capable of taking the perspective of others may consider whether his proposal will appear to the other person as the appropriate, consistent, and effective thing to do.

Let's consider an example. If two friends are involved in interpersonal persuasion, some situational cues that may affect the strategies in their minds are the presence of others, status differences, previous attempts at persuasion, and the long- or short-term nature of their relationship. These cues, along with each communicator's goals and what has already transpired during the interaction, influence the strategies they think to use. Should they be inclined to consider their options, they would do so in terms of each strategy's appropriateness, consistency, or effectiveness or a combination of these factors. A particular strategy, such as threat, might

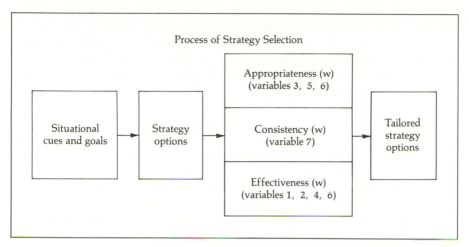

Figure 7.4. Process of strategy selection.

have a high likelihood of effectiveness but might be both inappropriate and inconsistent.

Strategy Taxonomies

Researchers have developed a number of **strategy taxonomies**—lists of strategies available to persuaders. Most of these taxonomies consist of **compliance-gaining strategies**—strategies used to persuade people to comply with requests. Other taxonomies pertain to making friends, avoiding embarrassment, comforting others, and dealing with conflict.

Compliance-gaining strategies are perhaps the most studied persuasion strategies. Marwell and Schmitt (1967) developed a taxonomy of sixteen compliance-gaining strategies, which are explained in Appendix A. Researchers have focused on how and when these strategies are used.

Miller and others (1977) found that the length of the relationship affects strategy choice. They found that people tend to use promises, positive altercasting, and altruism in long-term relationships. (For clarification of these terms, see Appendix A.) Aversive stimulation is unlikely to be used in such situations; apparently we are more positive in our approach to people with whom we must have future dealings. Hecht (1984) looked at the relationship between compliance-gaining strategies and success at changing the persuadee. He found that with friends threat is not as effective a strategy as self-feeling, altruism, and positive altercasting.

Other researchers have focused their efforts on locating strategies in addition to those listed by Marwell and Schmitt (see Wiseman & Schenck-Hamlin, 1981; Schenck-Hamlin, Wiseman, & Georgacarakos, 1982; Boster, Stiff, & Reynolds, 1983; Reardon & Boyd, 1986).

Reardon and Boyd (1986) argue that taxonomies of compliance-gaining strategies should include emotional strategies. They included "empathy," "emotional expression," "compliment," and "insult" in their taxonomy. They also proposed a category labeled "it couldn't hurt," which includes statements about how compliance won't bring any harm—for example, "You don't have anything better to do anyway."

Most research indicates that people select strategies from among a list of possibilities. They use information about the situation and persuadee to determine which strategy is likely to succeed. According to the ACE model, persuaders use three criteria for determining which appeals to use. They consider whether the persuadee cares about being appropriate, consistent, or effective. If the persuadee seems concerned about doing the right thing, appropriateness strategies such as esteem, debt, liking, and pregiving (giving the persuadee a gift or favor before asking him to comply) may be used. If the persuadee's primary concern appears to be consistency, the persuader may use moral appeal, self-feeling, altercasting, or altruism. Finally, if the primary concern is effectiveness, then promise, threat, or expertise might be chosen. Persuaders also consider the appropriateness, consistency, and effectiveness of the strategies they select. It may be out of character for a person to threaten someone or make promises he may be unable to keep.

Of course, persuadees often have more than one motivation. It is not always clear to the persuader which motivation, if any, is the strongest. Usually persuaders make their best guess and select the strategy that seems most likely to succeed.

Many people do not have sixteen strategies available to them. They may have only four or five. Even though Marwell and Schmitt (1967) were able to list sixteen, people are often limited by past learning. Some people use the same persuasion strategy on every occasion. They are in a strategy rut, so to speak. If you wish to improve your persuasive abilities, you might try extending your repertoire of available strategies. The next time you are involved in persuasion, try one of the strategies with which you are unfamiliar. You may find it quite useful.

Persuaders may use **affinity-seeking strategies** to get persuadees to like them. Bell and Daly (1984) argue that people spend considerable energy getting others to feel an affinity or liking toward them and that developing and maintaining affinity is an important function of communication.

Despite the ubiquitous nature of affinity-seeking behavior, little research has been focused on it. It is a relatively new concept for communication study. Bell and Daly have introduced a typology of affinity-seeking strategies, presented in Appendix B. Perhaps you recognize many of these strategies. According to Bell and Daly, people spend much of their daily lives seeking affinity through the use of any number of these twenty-five strategies. Their research suggests that choice of strategies is influenced by such factors as communication apprehension, gender, style, certain personality traits, self-monitoring ability, status, and the nature of the situation.

For example, people with communication apprehension are likely to concede control as a means of gaining affinity. Bell and Daly found that when interacting with someone of the same status, people are more willing to use such strategies as altruism, openness, optimism, and sensitivity than when interacting with a higher-status person.

As with other types of strategies, affinity-seeking strategies are selected with the situation and relationship in mind. Once we know what strategies are available, we can use our perceptions of the situation and relationship to guide our choice among them.

The *A* of the ACE model suggests that people are concerned about the opinions of significant others. Each of us strives to act in ways that will result in approval from people important to us. Sometimes we must settle for satisfying some people and not others. There are also occasions when it seems more important to please oneself, to be consistent, than it is to please others.

But in most cases, we do strive to meet the expectations of people important to us. One way that we can enhance our chances of doing so is to encourage them to think positively of us. This is where affinity-seeking strategies can be useful.

Another category of persuasion methods involves **embarrassment-reducing strategies**—strategies people use when attempting to avoid or reduce embarrassment. From prior work on embarrassment, Petronio (1984) derived eight types of embarrassment-reducing strategies: (1) defensively changing the subject, (2) introducing information excusing the performance, (3) introducing redeeming or self-enhancing information, (4) denying or minimizing failure, (5) implicitly seeking identification, (6) scapegoating; (7) withdrawing, and (8) requesting atonement.

Petronio (1984) divided the eight embarrassment-reducing strategy types into those having a defensive orientation and those with a protective orientation. She based her two-part differentiation scheme on Goffman's (1976) proposition that people tend to have a defensive orientation when they save face for themselves and a protective orientation when they save face for others. Appendix C depicts Petronio's division of defensive and protective embarrassment-reducing strategies.

In a study comparing male and female choices of embarrassment-reducing strategies, Petronio (1984) found that men cite more defensive-oriented strategies as helpful, whereas women cite more protective strategies as helpful. She also found that women tend to use excuse strategies—such as introducing information justifying the performance, implicitly seeking identification, and scapegoating—whereas men tend to use more justification strategies—such as defensively changing the subject, introducing redeeming or self-enhancing information, and denying or minimizing failure.

Comforting strategies are also important to effective interaction with others. Life presents unhappy incidents for all of us. We often expect comfort from friends, family, and some acquaintances to ease our pain.

Because people expect comfort, they must learn to give comfort effectively if they wish to maintain important relationships. Research has indicated a relationship between empathic ability and type of comforting strategies used (Burleson, 1984). The ability to recognize and understand another person's emotions apparently is an important factor in selecting comforting strategies.

Appendix D provides the coding scheme used by Burleson (1984) to assess comforting strategy selections. Notice that the lowest level of comforting is absence of a response. The level of comforting increases with recognition and understanding of the distressed person's perspective.

Take a moment to examine Appendix D. Do you tend to deny the feelings of others or try to understand and deal with distressed people's feelings? For most of us the answer depends on the nature of the situation and relationship. Reardon and Buck (1984) and Sullivan and Reardon (1985) reported that the way we comfort others during their recovery from serious illness affects how they cope with their condition. It appears that comforting is a serious matter. The way we comfort someone tells whether we care, and research indicates that in times of serious crisis expressions of caring by family and friends can influence the extent of the affected person's recovery.

Deception strategies are another group of persuasion tactics. The purpose of deception is to avoid negative reactions that are likely to result from telling the truth. In their article, "Telling It Like It Isn't," Knapp and Camadena (1979) report that white lies, cover-ups, bluffing, euphemisms, masks, pretenses, tall-tales, put-ons, hoaxes, and other forms of falsehoods, fabrications, and simulations are common forms of communication.

Deception is a fact of life. Most people use it to spare the feelings of others or to save themselves pain or embarrassment. Sometimes the deceiver and the deceived collaborate in the falsehood. For example, the guest who says she has had a wonderful time at a party that was a total flop is engaging in deception. The hostess may play along with this deception rather than point out that the guest is a liar.

Once deception has worked, it is likely that the successful deceiver will use it again. It is difficult to determine just what level of deception is too much. Should a doctor tell a dying patient the truth? Should a parent tell a child that she was adopted as soon as the child can speak? The answers to such questions are difficult to determine. We do know that people are not likely to ever stop deceiving each other, because deception works so well for so many.

Conflict resolution strategies are another important group of strategies. Conflict is inevitable in any long-term relationship and possible in short ones. By observing our parents, siblings, friends, television characters, and acquaintances, each of us learns ways to resolve conflict. Some methods of conflict resolution are prosocial—they facilitate growth of relationships; other methods impede it.

Roloff (1976) developed a taxonomy of conflict resolution strategies, which appears in Appendix E. According to Roloff, the least antisocial mode of conflict resolution is **regression,** which "does not rely on intimidation but represents an attempt to resolve the conflict through internalization or consolation from others" (1976, p. 180). The shortcoming of regression is that it results in little contact between the people involved in the conflict. They never fully work things out. Pouting, worrying, and feeling guilty may be low on the antisocial scale, but they do little to guard against future conflict about the same issue.

Antisocial strategies include revenge and verbal aggression, which involves attacks on the self-concept of the target person. Physical aggression, a means of forcing someone to yield, may cause a change of behavior, but not a change of attitude. The result is acquiescence—going along with the aggressor—but not private acceptance.

Prosocial conflict resolution strategies are listed in Appendix E. As Roloff (1976, p. 181) explained, "Prosocial communication strategies reflect people's attempts to obtain relational rewards by techniques that facilitate understanding of their attitudes and needs." Such strategies are expected to enhance the development of relationships.

If people are guided through reasoning to understand the error of their ways, they may decide on their own to change. When persons privately accept the idea of change, they are likely to maintain that changed behavior. When they merely comply because of force or deceit, they are likely to revert to their old ways as soon as the oppressor is gone.

The Role of Emotion in Persuasion

To this point we have treated persuasion as a cognitive activity in which people are pushed and pulled by inconsistency or reason their way through by selections of strategies and tactics. We have done so because persuasion has been studied largely from a cognitive perspective. Until very recently, little attention has been given to the role of emotion in persuasion. However, we know that people often act without conscious consideration of alternatives and that they are capable of feigning emotion or using it to aid their persuasion efforts.

As with the concept of attitude, we often speak of emotions with assuredness of their existence, yet, to date, social scientists have had considerable difficulty defining and studying them. Some have argued that emotions are partly cognitive (Mandler, 1975; Schacter & Singer, 1979; Averill, 1980) in that they consist of physiological arousal and cognitive interpretations of that arousal. For example, when some persons are wronged by others, they may feel their bodies become upset, as evidenced by sweaty palms, a fast heartbeat, trembling, or other behaviors; they might then label this feeling "anger" based on the situation. Others experiencing the same physiological reactions when wronged might label their emotion "hurt." It is in this sense that cognition is a part of emotional experience. The way people think about and label their emotions influences how they respond.

Other social scientists consider emotion capable of effecting behavior without cognitive interpretations. Buck (1984) asserted that emotions are often spontaneous reactions to environmental stimuli and are not voluntarily controlled. Fear, happiness, disgust, sadness, anger, surprise, and interest are what Buck has called **primes**—emotions that elicit spontaneous expressions similar across cultures.

Buck (1984) argued that emotions can be spontaneous or symbolic. Symbolic emotion fits into what we have described in this text as scripted and contrived behaviors. The expression of scripted and contrived emotions is consciously considered at some level before its occurrence. For example, boys and girls are typically encouraged to react differently to some similar emotional stimuli. Boys are usually discouraged from crying, whereas girls are typically allowed to cry without facing as much disapproval. In this way boys and girls learn different reactions to similar physiological arousal. Crying is dropped from boys' repertoires of available responses except in extraordinary circumstances.

Emotions can also be used consciously to achieve interpersonal goals. Emotions do not always just happen. People can use emotions to serve their own ends. They can use them to emphasize a point, gain attention, deceive, manipulate, and so on. Emotional behavior can be strategic behavior. Solomon (1980) suggested that emotion is typically a rational response to situational need. He argued that emotional response only seems irrational to us because our society discourages such expression:

> In a society that places taboos on emotional behavior—condemns it in men and belittles it in women—it is only to be expected that emotions will be counter to ambitions. A society that applauds "cool" behavior will naturally require strategies that are similarly "cool." In such a society, emotional behavior appears "irrational" because it is bad strategy, not because it is not purposive [1980, p. 266].

From Solomon's perspective, emotional behavior does not always represent loss of control. Emotional behavior can be a very rational response to an event. It can also be rationally used to create a lasting or intense impression.

We can also use emotion to deceive ourselves. de Sousa (1980, p. 283) wrote, "Emotion attends self-deception. Vanity, grief, resentment, apprehension, all induce us to connive in the clouding of our vision." We often allow mistaken or purposely inappropriate emotional reactions to guide our behavior because they allow us to retain preferred perspectives or maintain preferred behaviors. An example of emotional self-deception would be holding onto emotional reactions to racial differences merely to avoid having to deal with the knowledge that the target of our reactions is not inferior.

The fact that people do feign emotional reactions and use them in the service of self-deception is testimony to their strategic value. Words alone are often insufficient to the communication task at hand. Emotional expressions frequently fill the void.

What Are Feelings?

Several recent theoretical perspectives on emotion have treated feelings as distinct from emotions. **Feelings** are seen as less intense than emotions and not associated with particular persons, objects, or events. Feelings are also considered more enduring than emotions (see Clark & Isen, 1982; Solomon, 1980; Rorty, 1980).

Feelings are important to persuasion because they influence the types of reactions people have to information. If you are feeling irritable, any attempt to persuade you to do something you would rather not do is likely to be met with antagonism. Under such conditions, the persuader must attempt to change the persuadee's feelings before hoping to change thoughts or behavior with rational appeals.

A concept close to feelings is Rorty's (1980) notion of **magnetizing dispositions,** which involves a tendency to gravitate toward and create conditions that reinforce negative or positive feelings. For example, a magnetizing disposition to negative feelings might involve a low threshold to other peoples' behaviors that are frustrating and aggravating or indicative of betrayal, as well as a tendency to look for frustrating, aggravating, or disloyal behavior. According to Rorty (1980, p. 107), this disposition "not only involves wearing a chip on one's shoulder but involves looking for someone to knock it off." Hormonal, genetic, and social factors and fatigue can contribute to the creation of magnetizing dispositions even in typically reasonable people.

Feelings, whether magnetizing or not, affect the way people interpret events. Research indicates that people experiencing positive feelings behave in ways that reflect a positive outlook. Negative feelings, however, may lead to a negative outlook or attempts to reduce or remove the negative feelings (Clark & Isen, 1982). Isen, Shalker, Clark, and Karp (1978) suggest that the reason why people's behavior is affected by their feelings is that good feelings cue positive material from memory and bad feelings cue negative material. For example, Isen and others (1978) found that people who received unexpected gifts before describing how their cars ran tended to give more positive descriptions than people who did not receive gifts. Receiving an unexpected gift presumably activated in them positive feelings that affected their outlook on other issues.

If feelings do affect the type of information activated in memory, then it is likely that they affect how persuasive messages are interpreted. Attempting to persuade someone who is in a bad mood may require more skill than persuading someone who is in a good mood, because a negative mood is likely to activate uncooperative thoughts and behavior.

It appears that emotions and feelings can influence the course of persuasion by rendering some types of information more accessible than others. Feelings and emotions can enhance or inhibit the chances of persuading someone by stacking the deck for or against the likelihood of the response sought by the persuader.

Changing Emotions and Feelings

Given that emotions and feelings influence the way people interpret persuasive messages, it is often important to change them before attempting any other change. The question is, How can emotions and feelings be changed?

Rorty (1980) contended that emotional behaviors are as difficult to change as old habits. There are a "happy few" who are able to change their own emotional reactions by experiencing a secondary emotional reaction to their emotional behavior. For example, one might feel ashamed about a display of anger.

Sometimes people can be encouraged to reason about emotional behavior. After all, even emotional behavior is supposed to be within reason—appropriate to the situation and relationship. If a parent shouts at a child for pulling boxes from a shelf in a grocery store, observers might decide that shouting under such circumstances is a natural reaction. Should that parent then hit the child, this behavior might be considered rash and inappropriate. People often can reason about emotional behavior. They can critique it as they do rational behavior, according to its appropriateness, consistency, and effectiveness (Reardon & Boyd, 1985; 1986). It follows that much emotional behavior can be changed by convincing the person performing it that it is inappropriate, inconsistent, or ineffective or a combination of these elements.

Another means of changing emotional behavior is to shift the person's attention away from the target of emotion. As we discussed earlier, emotions, unlike feelings, have specific targets. When a person is angry, she is angry *at* someone or something. When someone is sad, it is often *about* something. When a person is allowed to dwell on a target, emotional reactions can become intense and disruptive to behavioral change. Encouraging a change of topic or change of location can diminish the emotional reaction to a level where reasoning about the inappropriateness, inconsistency, or ineffectiveness of the emotion might facilitate change.

Finally, some emotions can be changed by altering the beliefs with which they are associated. To be embarrassed, a person must believe that he has done something foolish. If this person can be convinced that everyone does such things, that the behavior was not foolish, then the emotion may change to relief. Emotions are often associated with beliefs. To the extent that the beliefs supporting them are negated, emotions can be changed.

Feelings, unlike emotions, do not appear to be connected to specific beliefs. It is possible to learn that someone disliked is actually a kind, pleasant person and still have negative feelings toward him without really knowing why. Perhaps this disliked person looks or acts like someone else toward whom you have negative feelings with good reason.

Since feelings are not connected to specific targets as beliefs are, they are difficult to change. One method is to encourage the person to replace negative thoughts with positive ones. Doing entertaining things can cause people to forget their negative feelings. Another method of dispelling negative feelings is to discuss them. An empathic communicator might express concern for others' feelings and encourage them to get it off their chest, so to speak. Sometimes discussing feelings allows one to see that they are not warranted.

Although we are only just beginning to understand what emotions and feelings are, communication scholars as far back as Aristotle have written of their influence on persuasion. It is clear that competent interpersonal persuasion requires the communicator to be sensitive to her own and others' emotions and feelings. Moreover, it is important to know how to use emotions in ways that facilitate persuasion.

Emotional expressions can be spontaneous, scripted, or contrived. Spontaneous emotional expression is the type feared most by a society that prizes reason over emotion. Yet spontaneous emotional expression often aids persuasion by lending additional impact to rational appeals or by revealing cues indicating that what is being said is not what the communicator really thinks.

Scripted emotional expressions allow us to respond appropriately, consistently, and effectively to familiar situations without having to consciously consider alternate behaviors. They save mental energy. Some emotional scripts work against persuasion. For example, the man who reacts with rage to the mention of his mother-in-law's name is not likely to be receptive to her plans to visit no matter how valid the reasons. The child who has learned to cry at every disappointment has an emotional script that is likely to bring social disapproval and also prevent him from learning that he can cope with disappointment.

Finally, contrived emotional behavior is thought through and consciously applied. People with flexible emotional behavioral repertoires and sensitivity to the emotions and feelings of others can effectively choose among emotional behaviors to help them obtain their interpersonal goals.

Summary

We have reviewed a number of perspectives on persuasion in this chapter. Each contributes to our understanding of persuasion while none explains the phenomenon entirely. It is not likely that we will ever develop one theory to explain persuasion entirely. Interpersonal persuasion is especially complex because it typically involves two people engaged in attempts to change each other's thoughts, feelings, or behaviors.

Rather than look for one theory, social scientists might focus on discovering how situations, relationships, personalities, gender, and other factors influence the strategies used in interpersonal persuasion and the success of those strategies. They might identify borrowed and owned rules of interpersonal persuasion and look at how adherence to those rules influences the outcome of persuasive interactions. There is still much research to be done on interpersonal persuasion, a topic that has only recently recaptured the attention of communication scholars.

CHAPTER 8

The Nature of Relationships

Relationships play a crucial role in shaping our lives. We depend on others for affection, understanding, information, encouragement, and many other types of communication that affect our self-images and assist us in knowing what is expected of us. To the question "What is it that makes your life meaningful?", Klinger (1977) found that almost all respondents listed relationships with friends, parents, siblings, lovers, or their children. Most mentioned the importance of "feeling loved and wanted." Other research has provided similar results (see Campbell, Converse, & Rogers, 1976). Indeed, negative experiences in relationships appear to have deleterious affects on health (see Bloom, Asher, & White, 1978; Lynch, 1977; Berkman & Syme, 1979; Peplau & Perlman, 1982). For example, stressful on-the-job relationships and family relationships can increase one's chances of having hypertension. People with loving spouses and those comfortable with their network of friends are less prone to hypertension (Patel, 1984).

Why do human beings need relationships? What is it that makes us different from many other animals that seem content with fleeting, seemingly unintimate relationships? Some researchers believe that our need for attachment and our tendency toward dependency separate us from many other animals (see Gerwirtz, 1972). **Attachment** has typically referred to the emotionally intense relationship of infants and their mothers. **Dependency,** on the other hand, has typically referred to instrumental interpersonal behaviors such as seeking help, seeking approval, and seeking proximity. Although researchers have experienced considerable difficulty in their attempts to separate attachment from dependency in concept and operation, there is at least substantial agreement among them concerning the interdependence of human beings. According to Gerwirtz (1972), the human infant's long period of helplessness—about one sixth of the total lifespan—requires the development of an elaborate set of help-seeking behaviors.

It seems likely that our early needs as infants, which are met substantially by others on whom we become dependent, set up patterns of dependency (Gerwirtz, 1972). Even when adolescents make efforts to break away from parents or guardians, they are typically experimenting with new attachments. According to Gerwirtz, "One might hazard a guess that much of adolescent distress, disorganization, aimlessness, blind seeking for new experiences, searching for sexual partners, and alternating periods of euphoria and despair is an indication of the rootlessness of an existence without attachment" (p. 17).

Lindskold (1982) argued that, aside from what may be inborn human needs for companionship, people need each other for survival. The complexity of contemporary life makes us more interdependent than humans have ever been before. Our elaborate systems of obtaining food, water, and sanitation have made us interdependent. A result of this complexity is a need to share and cooperate. Lindskold contends that the need for sharing and cooperating in the distribution of benefits gives rise to norms and customs such as the norm of reciprocity: "A great deal of social life is regulated by the generally accepted requirement that people should help those who help them" (1982, p. 24). The social responsibility norm ensures that the young, elderly, and ill are not ignored.

Apparently human beings are inextricably enmeshed in relationships. We may vary in the extent to which we need others and the extent to which quality and quantity of relationships are of importance (see Dickson-Markman & Shern, 1985). However, all of us need relationships. In this chapter we will examine the nature of our relationships with others and how communication influences their development, maintenance, and demise. We will look at research on relationships and the influence of networks of friends, relatives, and colleagues on the quality of life.

Factors Affecting Formation of Relationships

One important characteristic of relationships is that many of them are neither created nor broken at will. We are born into many relationships. Others are job related or the result of marriage. We are not always free to form relationships as we please. Such relationships differ from those freely chosen because of constraints on participants' behaviors. One cannot just leave a relationship with a boss, colleague, parent, sibling, or in-law without sacrifice at some level.

This description of relationships is not meant to depress you. Many of our unchosen relationships provide us with affection, care, information, and social support. Throughout our lives people with whom we must have relationships may help us to reach personal and professional goals. Moreover, they provide sociability outlets that we need.

Numerous factors affect the number, types, and quality of relationships that we have with both chosen and unchosen relationship partners. For example, socioeconomic status, age, and gender affect not only who we develop relationships with but also how—and how often—we interact with those people.

Socioeconomic Status

People at different levels of financial comfort also differ in the resources available to them for developing relationships. In the United States, one's socioeconomic status is supposedly less important than in some other cultures where one mingles with and marries within one's own social class. Even in the United States, however, socioeconomic differences affect one's ability to move about and meet people. For example, having a car allows you to maintain relationships outside your locality. The types of occupations held by people of different socioeconomic classes also affect the nature of their relationships. Work is a major source of sociable companions and thus influences the number and types of relationships one experiences.

Age

Research suggests that adults in the child-rearing and retirement stages are most constrained socially (see Allen, 1979). Young children often make sociability difficult. The need to get them bathed and to bed at an early hour, the feeding schedule of infants, the cost of baby-sitters—all conspire to keep parents from frequent socializing in the evenings.

During the retirement stage, possible infirmities and less mobility can make sociability difficult. With more free time on their hands, the elderly often find their limited social outlets a source of dissatisfaction. Cummings and Schneider (1961) found that sibling relationships tend to become more significant at this time, at least in those cases where siblings are accessible. Children and grandchildren often provide needed social relationships. Of course, the extent to which children and grandchildren replace previous associations depends on their geographical location and the strength of the family bond they feel.

Gender

Despite the career advances made by women in the past few decades, the range of sociable pursuits and settings for such pursuits are more readily available to men than women (Allen, 1979). The paucity of female sports, the male bias of many social clubs, and the greater comfort men feel when out alone all serve to limit female socializing. Allen (1979, p. 124) commented on this situation: "Rather than being a 'hiccup' in the inevitable development of equality, many sociologists see this phenomenon as a quite central element of continuing male domination."

In most cultures, further limitations are imposed on female socializing by the domestic division of labor. When a woman is employed outside the home, she also is typically expected to handle the larger share of housework and child-rearing responsibilities. Many of the men who now participate in household tasks more than their fathers did see their participation as "helping the wife out" or "lending her a hand" (Allen, 1979).

The differences in social outlets available to men and women does not mean that women are, on the whole, lonely. If the home is a center for sociability, if relatives live nearby, and if mothers and children attend community programs, women who do not work outside the home may find that they are satisfied with their social relationships. Working women may have the greater challenge especially if they have children, who make it difficult for them to spend some time in the evening with friends. Having money for baby-sitters or having a husband who baby-sits can make socializing easier.

Research also indicates that gender affects the way people communicate (Ickes & Barnes, 1977; Fitzpatrick & Indvik, 1982). Women tend to engage in more talk for talk's sake than men do (Baxter & Wilmot, 1983). They also engage in more intimate talk (Aries, 1976). In general women also display greater concern than do men for smoothness of interactions (Knapp, Ellis, & Williams, 1980).

The potential for relationships and the way relationships develop are influenced by factors beyond the personal dispositions of the individuals involved. Relationships are affected by socioeconomic status, age, gender, mobility, and other factors. Throughout the remainder of this chapter, we will discuss theories of relationship development and demise. We will also look at types of relationships, focusing on characteristics of the interactions between relationship members. While we do so, however, keep in mind that external factors such as those just discussed also affect the course of relationships.

Theories of Relationship Development

The study of relationships is an important aspect of interpersonal communication study. After all, relationships emerge and decline through communication. Throughout the past several decades researchers have attempted to determine how relationships are formed and how they deteriorate. In this section, we will look at a number of theories that address this development. As you will see, each of these theories has contributed to our understanding of relationship development.

Self-Disclosure

Much early communication research and theory on relationships focused on self-disclosure—revealing personal information about yourself to others. Jourard (1971), whose work we discussed in Chapter 3, conceived of healthful communication with others as that characterized by openness. Self-disclosure of one's true self to others who are also willing to disclose their true selves was seen as the ideal relationship.

Joseph Luft (1969) proposed another self-disclosure theory based on a model of human interaction called the Johari Window (see Figure 8.1). According to Luft, people have attributes known to self, to others, to self and others, and unknown to anyone. These types of knowledge constitute the four quadrants of the Johari Window. Ideally quadrant 1, the open quadrant, increases in size over time. If communication is good between two people, disclosure occurs, moving information about the self into the open quadrant. Quadrant 4 is difficult to access but may be reached through such activities as reflection and dreaming.

Can you think of any problems with this model? How do you feel about the idea that healthier relationships are characterized by openness? Is it good to tell people close to you everything about yourself? Should you hold a little back? Openness taken to extremes may be detrimental to relationships. All of us have negative thoughts about relationship partners that, given time, disappear or are reconsidered in light of new or more reliable evidence. If we blurt out our thoughts before we have given ourselves time to question their validity, we may do more harm than good.

Attribution

Another description of how people come to know each other is the attribution theory proposed by Heider (1958) and later revised and elaborated upon by others (see Jones & Davis, 1965; Kelley, 1972). **Attribution theory** focuses on the ways people infer the causes of their own and others'

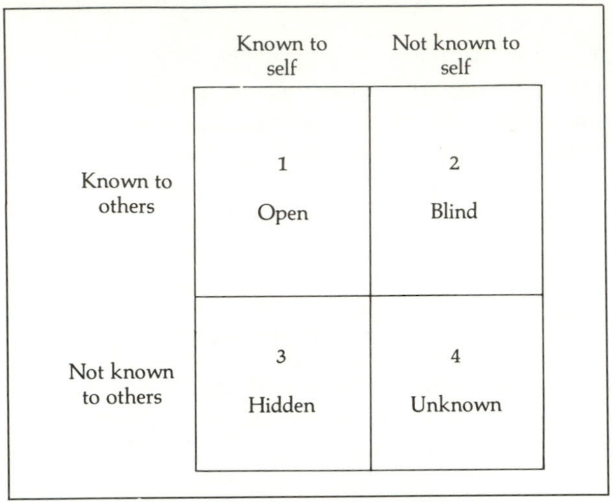

	Known to self	Not known to self
Known to others	1 Open	2 Blind
Not known to others	3 Hidden	4 Unknown

Figure 8.1. Johari Window.

Source: *Of Human Interaction,* by Joseph Luft. Copyright © 1969 by the National Press. Reprinted by permission of Mayfield Publishing Co., formerly Natonal Press Books.

behaviors. According to attribution theory, people attempt to determine the causes of behavior. They want to know why people behave as they do. To accomplish this, they infer causes. For example, if a man runs in front of a car, we might infer that he did not see the car. If he appears to have seen the car, we might infer that he is foolish or in a hurry to get somewhere. Much of our knowledge about others is based on such inferences. These inferences or attributions influence how we behave toward others. For example, if the man did not see the car, we are less likely to yell out the car window, "You idiot. Get out of the road!" than we might be had he seen the car.

The assignment of attributions are often erroneous, but they are how we predict the behavior of others. Without such predictions, interaction would be chaotic. We would have little sense of what the other person might do next. To the extent that we can draw some conclusions about others, we can predict their actions with some degree of confidence. By observing others, we derive information about them from which we may infer their attitudes and likely behavior.

According to Kelley's (1973) attribution perspective, people often use multiple observations of others to draw inferences. In such cases, we examine various possible causes for others' behaviors and draw conclusions based on the best available data. For example, if you know a woman who has two career options—one of which is challenging but not stable and the other stable but dull—you might assign attributes to her based on her choice. If she chooses the challenging but unstable job, you may consider her a risk-taker or a person who does not care about stability. If she chooses the stable, dull job, you might infer that she fears risk or that she is a dull person.

Typically, we have several items of information available from which we may draw conclusions about others. How we select among alternative causal possibilities for others' behaviors shapes our perspectives of them. Applying attribution theory to relationships, we see people as coming to know each other largely through the process of observation and inference. To the extent that a relationship matters to us, we may decide to see even negative behaviors of another in a positive light. For example, we might decide that a friend's seemingly rude behavior is due to his being under pressure at work rather than due to his irascible nature.

Attribution theory describes a process of inferring attributes that occurs when we first meet others and throughout our relationships with them. It shares with self-disclosure theory a focus on discovering the attributes of others as a means of participating in relationships with them.

Social Penetration

Altman and Taylor (1973) proposed a model of relationship development that they term **social penetration,** the process by which people come to know each other. This model involves self-disclosure but also provides a perspective on the timing of self-disclosure in the course of relationship development.

The social penetration process is orderly, with communication progressing from superficial unintimate topics to more intimate ones as relationships develop. People let others come to know them gradually. Moreover, they assess interpersonal rewards and costs—their satisfaction and dissatisfaction—gained from interaction with others. The advancement of the relationship depends heavily on the amount and nature of these rewards and costs. In other words, people use their perceptions of the reward-cost balance of an ongoing exchange to forecast outcomes of future interactions. If such predictions are favorable, they gradually move to successively more intimate levels of encounter.

Altman and Taylor (1973) used an onion as a metaphor to explain how people, through interaction, peel away layers of information about each other. Outer layers of the onion contain superficial information, such as age, location of one's home, and name. As these layers are peeled away, we encounter central layers, which consist of more fundamental characteristics of personality. Altman and Taylor wrote of "breadth" and "depth" dimensions of topical categories, explaining that at any layer of personality, one can refer to breadth of personality in terms of the number of major topical areas, or categories, made accessible to another person in the course of their relationship development. The depth dimension refers to the centrality or superficiality of information provided to another; depth is assumed to increase over the history of a relationship. As people continue to interact, they mutually move toward deeper areas of their personalities.

Altman and Taylor's model describes relationship development as a process. They have suggested that relationships are ongoing, changing phenomena rather than static states. In other words, being married is not just a state of being other than not married. Being married is a process. Early years of marriage may differ markedly in terms of interaction styles from later years of marriage. Also, unlike self-disclosure models, Altman and Taylor's model does not treat self-disclosure as a healthy activity under all circumstances.

Process View

Duck and Sants (1983) have offered a perspective on relationships that does not depend on self-disclosure or the peeling away of layers of information about participants' personal attributes. They have argued that for some fifty years researchers have assumed that the quality and nature of a relationship can be predicted from mere knowledge of the partners' attributes as individuals and from the intermingling of them. They wrote of this perspective, "Ultimately, it represents relationships as created from the chemistry of partner attributes" (1983, p. 30). They argued that we should not focus on the effects of properties such as interactants' similarities but rather on how such properties emerge (see also Roloff & Berger, 1982). For example, the mother who responds immediately to her baby's cries creates a different relationship with her child than the mother who waits before responding. From this perspective, the image of interactants peeling the "onion" of personality attributes constitutes only one aspect of relationship development. Each person's response to the other shapes the course of their relationship. While their individual attributes may affect or mediate their behavioral choices, it is not knowledge of each other's attributes alone that defines the stage of a relationship. Definitions of a relationship emerge as interactants respond to each other's *actions*, not merely to each other's *attributes*.

Note that despite the positive contribution made by models that depict relationships as developmental, there are some warranted criticisms to be levied against them. Duck (1985) argued that researchers should begin to recognize that relationships do not always develop in a smooth and linear fashion and that people do not always actively seek information about their relationship partners rather than obtain it casually or accidentally. In terms of the Altman and Taylor model, people do not always want to peel away layers of information about others, and their relationships do not always progress evenly toward greater intimacy. As Duck (1985, p. 664) explained,

"Not all relationships are intimate; not all relationships develop; and relationships can be both stable and satisfying without taking the tracks or paths presumed in many existing theories of relationships and relationship growth."

Social Exchange Perspective

In Chapter 6 we discussed the social exchange perspective of interaction. Here we will consider this theory as an example of a process view of relationships. Unlike self-disclosure, attribution, and social penetration perspectives, **social exchange** focuses on how the contributions of each member of a relationship influence the contributions of the others.

Thibaut and Kelley (1959; Kelley & Thibaut, 1978) have proposed that people evaluate their relationships with others in terms of the consequences, specifically the rewards versus the costs of remaining in the relationship. They also consider the reward-cost balance in terms of **comparison levels**—that is, what the balance might be were they in a similar relationship with someone else. The comparison level is the level of reward-cost balance above which the person is satisfied with the relationship. For example, friendship carries with it certain obligations. You may feel that the least one can expect from a friend is honesty. Your friends may aggravate you at times, but not enough to cause you to think of seeking friendship elsewhere. Only when the friend is caught attempting to deceive you might you consider leaving the relationship for a better one. Honesty is your bottom line. It is the one factor that can tip the balance so that the rewards of staying in the relationship are outweighed by the costs.

Thibaut and Kelley also introduce the concept of **comparison level of alternatives,** which is the lowest level of outcomes, in terms of rewards and costs, that the person will tolerate, considering her alternatives. Sometimes people lack alternative relationships. In such cases, they are often willing to let small inequities pass. However, should some more attractive person come into their lives, those small inequities may suddenly be enough to tip the reward-cost balance. Perhaps you have heard someone accuse another of having a potential lover "waiting in the wings." This person is being accused of keeping an alternative relationship close by in case he should decide to leave the current one.

Throughout relationships, outcomes vary and comparison levels change. Behavior that is tolerable at one stage in a relationship may be intolerable at another stage. Moreover, when there are few positive alternatives, the relationship one is currently in may be fine. When a positive alternative is available, however, one might become more intolerant of low reward-cost outcomes in the current relationship. People are typically unwilling to relinquish a tolerable relationship if no alternative is available.

Roloff (1981) has written an interesting text on the application of social exchange theory to interpersonal communication. Here he comments on the assumption that the reward versus cost balance influences progress in a relationship:

> This assumption does not mean that people always seek to exploit one another, but that people prefer environments and relationships that provide desirable outcomes. Certainly the self-interests of both individuals can be met providing a mutually satisfying experience rather than an exploitative relationship. An ideal relationship would seem to be one in which two individuals are able to provide one another with sufficient benefits so that the relationship is a dependable source of satisfaction for both [1981, p. 11].

Unlike theories that focus on discovering attributes, social exchange focuses on the patterns of interaction resulting from mutual contributions of the relationship's members. Perhaps all we wish to know about relationships cannot be covered by reward-cost analyses. But the reward-cost perspective seems a viable way to view much relational behavior.

The focus of recent relationship study appears to be moving away from dependence on self-disclosure or discovery of partner attributes through observation of verbal and nonverbal behavior toward an interest in the patterns of interaction that characterize different types of relationships, how they emerge, are maintained, and deteriorate. In the next section, we will look at theory and research on types of relationships.

Types of Relationships

To help impose some order on social life, people tend to categorize their relationships. Such categories help them determine what is expected of them and of others. In this section, we will look at six types of relationships: acquaintances, friends, intimates, spouses, parents and children, and siblings.

Acquaintances

Much research has focused on the way people communicate in early phases of their relationships. Such research suggests that the type of information shared by acquaintances differs from that shared by more familiar persons. According to Duck (1976), information is acquired hierarchically—individuals value information at different levels at different times in their relationship. For example, people meeting for the first time are unwilling to share deep feelings about sensitive topics. Some information is obtained merely by looking at other people in terms of attractiveness (Byrne, 1971) and in terms of associating them with better-known people who look or act similarly. As acquaintances communicate, they make inferences about each other. On the basis of scanty information, they assess whether they have anything in common upon which to build an enduring relationship. According to Duck, acquaintances also consider whether they are interested in moving to the next level of information. That is, do they want to know more about each other? If so, they may become friends.

Research on initial interactions indicates that information shared during the first meeting tends to be rich in factual background information that is exchanged rather rapidly (Berger & Roloff, 1982). There are exceptions to this characterization. Sometimes when people meet, the environment encourages them to exchange personal information. For example, two persons might assume that they possess similar attitudes because they are attending the same religious gathering or political rally. Assumed similarity can alter the typical avoidance of personal information in initial interactions.

Research by Snyder and Swann (1978) indicates that our first impressions of people affect the questions we ask them. We tend to ask questions that are likely to confirm our first impressions. If you assume that someone you have just met is outgoing and friendly, you are more apt to ask them questions that will confirm your hypothesis rather than questions that will contradict it. This does not mean that first impressions are final impressions, but it suggests that first impressions can influence whether a relationship moves from the stage of acquaintance to friend by shaping the types of questions asked of the other person (see also Snyder & Cantor, 1979; Snyder & Campbell, 1980).

Berger and Roloff (1982) have pointed out, however, that research such as that by Snyder and his colleagues may not be representative of what really occurs in initial interactions. In their studies, subjects were given a particular hypothesis to test about another person—for example, he is extroverted or introverted. Berger and Roloff explained that people may develop hypotheses in the course of conversation that they subsequently test, but such development of their hypotheses takes time. Sometimes people simply wish to know something about another person without having any preconceived hypotheses. To acquire this information, people may engage in knowledge-gaining strategies.

There are three general categories of **knowledge-gaining strategies:** passive, active, and interactive (Berger, 1979). Passive strategies involve observing the other person's actions without asking questions or manipulating the situation. Active strategies include manipulating the social environment to learn something about the other. For example, an employer may create a stressful interview to discern how a potential employee will respond. Interactive strategies involve communicating with the other person and gaining information through observations of her behavior.

The image conveyed by most perspectives on initial interactions and acquaintance interactions is that individuals seek to discover information about others they meet. Purposely shared information is typically impersonal for some time. We often acquire information by observations that may be biased by false assumptions or predispositions to see others as we wish to see them (see Sillars, 1982). To the extent that a person is free to walk away from an acquaintance without ever seeing him again, she can choose, on the basis of acquired superficial information, whether to move on to a friendship basis or remain at an acquaintance level. Because, as we shall see in the next section, friendship involves obligations, we cannot be friends with everyone. We must choose friends from among available people via what Duck (1973) describes as a filtering process. We eliminate people who do not seem likely to be the type we want for friends given what we know of them.

Friends

What is a friend? This question has been the focus of plays, novels, poems, and research. The answer has never been simple, because there is no single meaning of *friend*. It is a concept separate from any formal role position. A father or mother can be a friend. Americans use the term more loosely than people of many other cultures. We may refer to someone we have only met once or twice as a friend. There appears to be both a loose and a more limited use of this term. We will focus our attention on the latter—the relationship between "close friends."

A friend is, first of all, unique and not easily replaced. By calling someone friend, we impose on him a special position in our lives. We assume that he can be trusted, and so we admit him to what Goffman (1959) refers to as the "backstage" or "back-region" of our performances. Rawlins (1983) has found, however, that even friends monitor how open they are with private information. Rawlins's research suggests that it is "imprudent" to make our friends excessively vulnerable through conversation.

Friendship also implies a nonexploitive relationship. This does not mean that friends never exploit friends or that they never gain anything from each other. Allen (1979, p. 43) explains: "Friends can quite legitimately make use of one another in instrumental ways without threatening the relationship, provided that it is clear that they are being used because they are friends and not friends because they are useful."

Friendship is also ideally a relationship between equals. This means that neither person has dominance over the other or greater status—one reason why it is difficult to be friends with one's employees. If friendship requires equality while being an employer requires directing employees and evaluating their work, a conflict of roles can emerge. The rules for friends often conflict with those of employer-employee relationships.

Finally, a friend is someone who also considers you a friend. Friendship is reciprocal, not one-sided. The only way we have of determining whether someone is a friend is by observing their behavior. If they abide by the rules of friendship, then we may assume that our feelings toward them are reciprocated. Argyle and Henderson (1984) examined friendship rules and found several that appear to be important to ordinary friendships: (1) sharing news of success with the other, (2) showing emotional support, (3) volunteering to help in time of need, (4) striving to make him or her happy while in each other's company, and (5) standing up for the other person in his absence. Argyle and Henderson argue that such rules exist to keep up rewards characteristic of friendship and to avoid conflict, another characteristic of friendship (see Argyle & Furnham, 1983). At some level of cognition, people know rules like the ones provided by Argyle and Henderson's research. These rules help people to determine whether another person is acting like a friend and also allow them to predict how a friend will respond to requests for help, criticism, or praise.

Given the characteristics of a friend, how do people determine who will be a close friend? Some theorists believe that we select our friends on the basis of interpersonal attraction. Some aspects of attraction are shared attitudes, similarity of behaviors, and physical attractiveness (Byrne, 1971). People who are similar to us provide validation of our beliefs and feelings. They also make us feel liked (Newcomb, 1961) and lower our uncertainty about how to act (Berger & Calabrese, 1975).

Research on physical attractiveness suggests its importance to relationship initiation and development (Berscheid & Walster, 1974). For example, physically attractive people are typically viewed as having positive character traits (Miller, 1970; Strobe, Insko, Thompson, & Layton, 1971) and tend to be more socially skillful (Goldman & Lewis, 1977; Dion & Stein, 1978). On a more encouraging note, recent research suggests that physical attractiveness may not be merely a certain type of face or body but also a function of behavior. For example, Muser, Grau, Sussman, and Rosen (1984) found that individuals appear less socially attractive when their facial expressions are sad. Such research suggests that being attractive is more than having a gorgeous face and body. It is also a product of behaving in attractive ways.

Other research has questioned the importance of similarity to attractiveness. Broome (1983) argued that similarity is not a necessary precursor to positive evaluations of acquaintances. He explained that dissimilar others who we expect to like us are more likely to be positively evaluated than dissimilar others about whom we do not have such assurance. Also, dissimilar others who appear open minded are likely to be evaluated more positively than dissimilar others who appear closed minded. Broome's work suggests that perceived dissimilarity can be reduced by additional information about the acquaintance. It and other research indicates that attraction is a more complex phenomenon than might be assumed on the basis of earlier research (see also Duck, 1985). In terms of social exchange, we cannot assume that dissimilarity is sufficient to threaten the reward-cost balance of relationships.

Social exchange theorists propose that the movement from acquaintance to friend depends upon the balance of rewards and costs (Altman & Taylor, 1973; Roloff, 1981). Based on current interactions, people predict the likely reward-cost balance of future interactions. If the forecast is favorable, the relationship moves to a higher level along the acquaintance-intimate continuum.

The selection of friends is a highly subjective activity. We choose people who reinforce us or who think like us. Over a lifetime, we tend to develop friendships with others who are unlikely to question excessively our views of the world. Of course, friends disagree, but close friendship may require that such disagreements rarely involve a difference of values.

Intimate Relationships

Our next focus in the study of relationship types is on intimate relationships, a category difficult to define because it is more a characteristic of various types of relationships than a type in itself. In other words, spouses, friends, and siblings, may or may not be intimate. Intimacy is a characteristic of interaction more than a type of relationship.

According to Sillars and Scott (1983, p. 154), intimate relationships may be defined as ones "in which there is repeated interaction, high self-disclosure, high interdependence (that is, mutual influence), and high emotional involvement." So defined, intimate relationships encompass many husband-wife and parent-child relationships, some dating couples, close friends, and divorced couples.

Research on intimate partners indicates that they typically overestimate the extent to which they share common attitudes. (see Good, Good, & Nelson, 1973; Knudson, Sommers, & Golding, 1980). At first glance, such findings may seem to suggest that intimates are less critical of each other because they see themselves as very similar. Not so, according to recent attribution research. It appears that intimates tend to minimize their own responsibility for relationship difficulties and blame their partners (see Orvis, Kelley, & Butler, 1976; Thompson & Kelley, 1981). According to Sillars and Scott (1983), this tendency to blame one's intimate partner could eventually lead to negative perceptions between the two. They point to research (Luckey, 1966) indicating that the longer couples are married, the less likely they are to see their spouses as well thought of, respected by others, self-respecting, independent, firm but just, grateful, cooperative, friendly, affectionate, considerate, and helpful.

Research by Parks and Adelman (1983) suggests that the course of intimate relationships involving romance may not be determined solely by the intimate partners themselves. They found that communication with people important to one's romantic partner may enhance stability in a relationship. They explained that becoming involved with a romantic partner's friends and family may make it difficult to terminate a relationship and also limit access to alternative partners.

Intimacy is apparently affected by factors outside the immediate pair as well as factors within it. In terms of romantic partners, love may be only part of the relationship longevity equation. Berscheid (1983) described romantic love as an intense emotion with a swift and sudden onset. Compared with the stability over time of milder positive feelings toward another such as liking, love seems "distressingly fragile." The course of romantic love in early marriage apparently gives way to, at best, a warm afterglow. Berscheid explained that while this may seem pallid and uninteresting compared to the intense flame of love, comfort, contentment, and affection are the best outcomes under the inevitable circumstances of short-lived intense love; they also can be seen as positive outcomes. As Berscheid noted, Western society idolizes elation over contentment. It holds out to its children the view that contentment cannot compare to elation and so we move reluctantly from elation to the relatively safe harbor of afterglow. We may even feel cheated or deprived if every day of our intimate relationship is not fired with passion.

Aside from the belief that love is an intense feeling, people in Western society hold other beliefs about love that affect their behaviors. If people believe that love is a powerful, irrational attraction, two young lovers drawn together despite strong opposition from others have a basis for concluding "We must be in love." If people believe that true love lasts, then they might determine that the best way to test their love is to separate occasionally to see if their feelings persist. Kelley (1983) explained that such beliefs about love shape its course and expression.

Romantic love differs from love felt for parents and siblings. Romantic or **passionate love** is typically considered uncontrollable because it is a matter of pure emotion rather than reason. Thus we might expect passionate love to involve many spontaneous behaviors. The predictability of a partner's actions is therefore low. Boredom is certainly not a characteristic of passionate love.

Kelley (1983, p. 287) observed that passionate love is not a sound basis for a permanent domestic relationship: "The abrasions of ordinary living dull the idealization of the partner, and regular sexual gratification and growing predictability of the partner can reduce high levels of arousal."

He added, however, that passionate love may provide the conditions under which other forms of love may develop. One such form is what Kelley calls **pragmatic love.** Compared to passionate love, pragmatic love develops gradually and is under greater control by the people involved. In such relationships each person sees his or her behaviors of love as reciprocated by the other. Moreover, the partners both feel that the relationship is balanced; that what they get out of it, given what they put into it, is relatively equal.

A third type of love is **altruistic love.** Kelley explained that behaviors elicited by such love are intrisically motivated rather than performed to elicit similar behaviors from the partner. Altruistic love is commonly thought to be epitomized by "mother love," in which the mother sacrifices her own interests for those of her child. It is difficult to separate altruistic love from other more self-motivated forms of love because people know how to make their actions appear altruistic.

Kelley contends that love is typically a blend of various types. A relationship originally characterized by passionate love may become, over time, one characterized by pragmatic love. Passionate love may be revitalized in a relationship that has for some time been characterized by pragmatic love. As Kelley wrote, "It is through its complexity, diversity, and successive changes that we are afforded unending fascination with love" (p. 287).

Other researchers have characterized types of love. Lee (1973) identified three main types of love—eros (romantic love), ludus (game-playing love), storge (friendship love)—and three main secondary styles—mania (possessive, dependent love), pragma (logical love), and agape (all-giving, selfless love). Hatkoff and Lasswell (1979) found that a larger percentage of females than males scored higher on measures of manic, storgic, and pragmatic love, while a larger percentage of males scored higher on measures of ludic and erotic love. Lee's scale may not fully represent types of love. Further research is needed.

An emerging area in the study of intimate communication focuses on immediacy—verbal and nonverbal actions that signal to others that we are close to them physically or psychologically (Andersen, 1985). Such behaviors may be blatant, as in the case of kisses, long gazes, or long amounts of time spent with someone. Other immediacy behaviors are more subtle, like smiles, leaning toward another party, and winks. Immediacy behaviors reduce psychological distance and create feelings of closeness (Andersen, Andersen, & Jensen, 1979).

Marriage

Researchers have given the relationship of marriage considerable attention. Most people contemplate marriage at some time in their lives, and many people are married more than once. Unlike many other types of relationships, marriage typically involves daily contact and sharing one's good and bad moments and moods.

There are several types of marriage. Using a measure for reliably assessing significant aspects of marital life—the Relational Dimensions Instrument—Fitzpatrick (1977) identified three marital types: independents, separates, and traditionals. Independents possess nonconventional marital values and maintain a measure of autonomy from each other in a relationship characterized by novelty, uncertainty, and change. Separates manage to continue their relationship despite very little interdependence. Traditionals are interdependent partners with conventional values concerning marriage.

Fitzpatrick and Best (1979) have also identified mixed types. For example, in "separate-traditional" relationships, the husband classifies himself as a separate, whereas the wife classifies herself as a traditional.

Fitzpatrick and Best (1979) found that traditional couples are significantly higher than the other three types on consensus, cohesion, and satisfaction with the relationship. Independents are significantly lower than the other types on consensus, but this does not appear to impair their ability to get along. Independents are also lower than other couples on satisfaction with their marriages and do not openly demonstrate affection to one another. Separates maintain relatively high consensus on a number of relational issues, affection toward one another in limited ways, and tend to be low on satisfaction and cohesiveness. Separate-traditionals are moderately cohesive, express high satisfaction with their relationship, demonstrate a good deal of affection toward one another, and are low on consensus.

Fitzpatrick and Indvik (1982) found that traditional couples support conventional norms for appropriate male and female behavior. The traditional wife sees herself as expressive and nurturant while her husband rates his communication as predominantly task oriented. Compare this to the separate couples, who support conventional norms about husband and wife behavior but do not report any expressive communication skills. In this type of relationship, the wife is under considerable strain because she is not exhibiting traditional nurturant, expressive behaviors. Fitzpatrick and Indvik (1982, p. 209) explained, "Perhaps the 'emotional divorce' experienced in this couple is related to the lack of expressivity in the wife, a lack not compensated by her husband." The separate-traditionals, like the traditionals, support and enact traditional husband and wife behaviors. However, the wives report even greater expressivity and nurturance than the traditional wives. Finally, independent couples support flexible roles, reflected in the wives' behaviors, which are more instrumental than in other marital types.

Fitzpatrick and her colleagues have made a significant contribution to relationship research. Noting that their approach is not the only one possible or exhaustive of all the important dimensions of ongoing relationships, they explained that the Relational Dimensions Instrument's reliance on self-reports may be problematic (Fitzpatrick & Indvik, 1982). People cannot always be expected to give accurate reports of their own behaviors. Nevertheless, it is only by self-report that we can uncover the "insider's view" of the relationship under study. Through marital typology research, Fitzpatrick and her colleagues have given us this inside view.

Aside from identifying marital types, research has focused on behaviors that affect satisfaction. One such issue is power, construed by researchers in terms of who holds the attention during conversations. Power has also been looked at in terms of the symmetrical and complementary nature of interactions. As we discussed in Chapter 6, symmetrical interaction is characterized by parallel moves by the interactants, both one-up (↑↑) or both one-down (↓↓). Complementary interactions occur when one-up moves are coupled with one-down moves, (↑↓) or (↓↑). Research indicates that complementary couples in which the husband is slightly more dominant report higher levels of satisfaction (Millar & Rogers-Millar, 1976; Courtright, Millar, & Rogers-Millar, 1979). Note, however, that this finding may not pertain to all types of relationships. For example, satisfaction with a dominant husband may vary with financial and educational equality between husbands and wives.

A third method of construing power involves a "who wins" approach—that is, who makes the decisions (Olson & Cromwell, 1975). Fitzpatrick and Badzinski (1985) have suggested that a decision-maker approach to power is misleading; who decides who may make the decisions may also be important.

The concept of power in relationships is still somewhat cloudy. Whether power refers to who talks more, who wins, who decides who wins, or some other behavioral form is not yet clear. Relationships apparently have diverse types of power. Couples may divide power. For example, in a traditional marital relationship, one might expect the wife to have the power to make many domestic decisions. Nontraditional couples, such as Fitzpatrick's independents, probably find themselves negotiating power more often than do traditional couples for whom roles are clear and consensus is high.

Another area of interest to relationship researchers is the effect of children on marital satisfaction. Research indicates that even the knowledge of being pregnant can affect marriage. Expectant mothers typically become more introspective, which puts them at a distance from their husbands (Lamb, 1976). A husband may feel somewhat left out during his wife's pregnancy.

The arrival of a child tends to have a negative impact of marital quality, perhaps because the couple has less time to spend together (Polonko, Scanzoni, & Teachman, 1982). The arrival of a child appears to turn the behavioral pattern of couples toward traditionalism (Hoffman & Manis, 1978; Polonko, Scanzoni, & Teachman, 1982). Although not always the case, marital satisfaction tends to wane. When the children mature and leave the home, marital satisfaction increases somewhat (Rollins & Galligan, 1978). One bright note in this rather gloomy research picture of children's impact on marital satisfaction is provided by Fitzpatrick and Badzinski (1985, p. 22): "The decrease in marital satisfaction during these years may be compensated for by the increase in satisfaction in the parental role."

Some of the tension associated with having children may be alleviated by couples understanding each other's feelings. A number of studies suggest a positive relationship between each partner's understanding of the other and marital satisfaction (Lewis & Spanier, 1979; Sillars & Scott, 1983). This seems reasonable. Being married to someone who does not understand you is typically unpleasant. Research by Sillars, Pike, Jones, and Murphy (1984) suggests, however, that understanding may not be the whole story. They found a negative relationship between understanding spouse feelings and satisfaction, indicating a need to be cautious about exaggerating the importance of communication in marriage to the neglect of other obviously important factors, such as basic compatibility and externally imposed stress. One may have an accurate understanding of a spouse's negative feelings toward some issue, but believe that such feelings are unjustified. Alternately, one may have an accurate understanding of a spouse's negative feelings, but find such feelings annoying in light of current stress levels in the marriage. For example, Maderer and Hill (1983) reported that problems experienced by families often produce unresolved tension and heightened ambiguity in roles, which calls for adaptive behavior and negotiation. If a spouse does not cooperate, as understandable as his feelings might be, relationship satisfaction could be in considerable jeopardy.

Obviously, marriage can be a challenge. The research reported in this chapter is only a small part of attempts being made to understand what communication behaviors enhance marital satisfaction. As Fitzpatrick's work suggests, the answers may differ according to the type of relationship. What works well for traditional couples may not satisfy other types of couples. There are still more questions than answers in this area of study. But our knowledge has been extended in recent years.

Parent-Child Relationships

Much research attests to the important effect communication between parents and children can have on the children's intellectual, emotional, and moral development. During the first several months of a child's life, she forms attachments with her parents or caregivers. Mothers and fathers interact with their children in different ways. Mothers tend to be nurturant, whereas fathers prefer physical "rough and tumble play" (Lamb, 1976; Parke & O'Leary, 1976). Through such interactions, parents or other caregivers set the stage for children's social development.

One factor important to satisfaction with parenthood is a child's compliance. Eliciting compliance while keeping the child happy can be quite a challenge once the child becomes a toddler. During this time, children experience a growing capacity for voluntary self-control. They also learn the meaning of the word *no*.

Marion (1983) explained that cooperative parents and caregivers are adept at arranging their children's environment so that the need to interrupt or control the child is minimized. When control is needed, cooperative parents and caregivers "set the mood" so that the child is willing to accept controls. Compliance appears to be aided when directives are given at a pace that allows the child time to process what he is being told (Marion, 1983). Finally, reinforcement should be timed so that the child makes a connection between it and her compliance. Goetz et al. (1975) found that verbal praise related directly to the requested behavior—for example, "Thank you for picking up your toys"—was more effective than verbal praise unrelated to the request—for example, "Thank you."

Aside from the issue of parent-child compatibility, the parent-child relationship has also been the focus of study in terms of how parents aid children's language development. In Chapter 4 we discussed the important role parents play in this growth. As noted in that review of the literature, parental interest in children's language and conversational development can provide children with a considerable head start in their social development.

Siblings

The sibling relationship, the last relationship to be discussed in this chapter, typically involves both attachment and competition. During childhood siblings tend to compete for love and attention from parents, whereas later in life they tend to feel competitive when one achieves more than the others (Allen, 1979). Research suggests, however, that hostility between siblings may be resolved by consistent parental affection, the development of attachment, and learning how to disagree without aggression (Tsukada, 1979).

Despite the problems associated with sibling competition, recent research suggests that having siblings can enhance one's intellectual and social development. Zajonc and Markus (1975) report that being an older child in a small family has advantages because older children are able to tutor the younger, an activity that appears to have a positive affect on the older child's confidence and development. Mott and Haurin (1982) report that this tutoring advantage is more the case for female older siblings than for males.

Fitzpatrick and Badzinski (1985) report a lack of studies focusing on sibling communication. It appears that birth order, sex, and birth interval (age differences) do not account adequately for sibling differences (Scarr & Grajek, 1982). Such differences may be better explained by communication variables. What types of communication patterns do siblings of different genders and age groups engage in? Do some patterns indicate sibling attachment and others sibling rivalry? Such questions have yet to be answered.

Allen (1979) reports that parents play an important role in encouraging positive feelings between adult siblings. However, because most siblings are merely required to be friendly upon occasion, often in group settings, siblings can often be quite cordial despite any early childhood rivalry. If forced to live together again, however, old patterns of rivalry might reappear. Adult sibling relationships appear to also be affected by the feelings of spouses, who can be a positive or negative influence on sibling relationships.

In this section we have reviewed research on several types of relationships. As social beings we engage in a number of chosen and imposed relationships that affect our daily lives. Let's look now at how such relationships develop.

Stages of Relationship Development and Demise

One of the facts of life is that most of our relationships with others are temporary. One's "best friends" during childhood are unlikely to play a major role in one's adult life. In a highly mobile society such as the United States, it is difficult to maintain friendships. Instead, we start and end relationships frequently.

As we develop and terminate relationships, we pass through a series of stages of intimacy. As you may recall from Chapter 2, Miller and Steinberg (1975) proposed that relationships develop from noninterpersonal relationships, guided by extrinsic rules not unique to the relationship, to interpersonal relationships, those guided by predominantly intrinsic rules peculiar to the relationship.

Exchange theorists believe that relationships progress according to members' perceptions of their reward-cost balance. If a relationship is more rewarding than costly, it is likely to be maintained. If costs exceed rewards, however, the relationship is likely to end (Altman & Taylor, 1973; Roloff, 1981). Reward-cost balances are not easily identified by outside observers. People often stay in relationships despite physical or mental abuse. According to social exchange theory, they do so because they perceive that the costs involved in terminating the relationship exceed the costs of remaining in it.

Whether or not we accept social exchange as a reasonable explanation of the reasons behind relationship development and termination, it appears that relationships proceed through stages. If an initial interaction with an individual is rewarding, we are more likely to move on to a more intimate stage of interaction with that individual than when the initial interaction is negative. Duck (1976) proposed that people filter out those with whom future, more intimate interaction is likely to be a negative experience. Apparently, we move to more intimate stages of relationships with people who are unlikely to put our "faces" in jeopardy, as Goffman (1959) would put it (see Chapter 6).

Relationship Development

Knapp (1978) formulated a model of relational stages suggesting that people take some care in determining whether to move to intimacy with another person. According to Knapp, relationships develop through five stages: initiating, experimenting, intensifying, integrating, and bonding. Knapp proposed these five stages as the way relationships tend to progress rather than the way they must progress. Sometimes people "fall in love," moving rapidly to the bonding stage before having a chance to experience the earlier stages. If the relationship lasts, however, they are likely to return to those earlier stages as a means of getting to know each other. It is also possible for relationships to stabilize at one stage and not proceed to more intimate stages. Equally possible is a recycling through stages.

The first of Knapp's stages, **initiating,** typically involves small talk and greetings. During the **experimenting** stage, relationship partners begin to discover information about each other. Small talk during this stage serves as an audition of sorts for future friendship and assists in uncovering similarities and differences in interests. Stage three, **intensifying,** involves delving deeper into each other's personalities. Each person makes himself more vulnerable by disclosing personal information. Stage four, **integrating,** involves a sense of "coupling"—a sense of "we-ness." The two act as a unit rather than as two disconnected individuals. Decisions tend to be made jointly. The final stage, **bonding,** occurs when the two people go through a formal ritual recognizing the long-term nature of their relationship.

Often two members of a relationship are at different stages. This difference can contribute positively to relationship growth if one person then leads the other to attach greater significance to the relationship.

Relationship Termination

When discrepancies between partners' views concerning the nature of their relationship become obvious, relationship decline is possible. Duck (1982, 1985) proposed that a decline in a personal relationship involves crossing a number of thresholds. The crossing of each threshold leads to shifts in the relationship. These four thresholds and their accompanying states of dissolution (phases) appear in Figure 8.2.

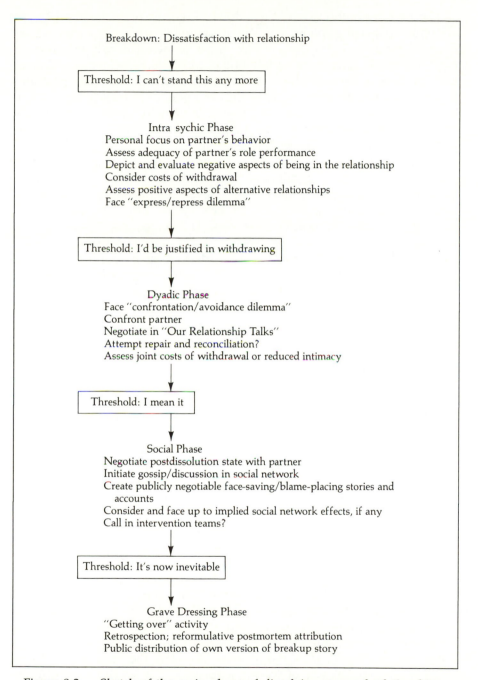

Breakdown: Dissatisfaction with relationship

Threshold: I can't stand this any more

Intra sychic Phase
Personal focus on partner's behavior
Assess adequacy of partner's role performance
Depict and evaluate negative aspects of being in the relationship
Consider costs of withdrawal
Assess positive aspects of alternative relationships
Face "express/repress dilemma"

Threshold: I'd be justified in withdrawing

Dyadic Phase
Face "confrontation/avoidance dilemma"
Confront partner
Negotiate in "Our Relationship Talks"
Attempt repair and reconciliation?
Assess joint costs of withdrawal or reduced intimacy

Threshold: I mean it

Social Phase
Negotiate postdissolution state with partner
Initiate gossip/discussion in social network
Create publicly negotiable face-saving/blame-placing stories and
    accounts
Consider and face up to implied social network effects, if any
Call in intervention teams?

Threshold: It's now inevitable

Grave Dressing Phase
"Getting over" activity
Retrospection; reformulative postmortem attribution
Public distribution of own version of breakup story

Figure 8.2.   Sketch of the main phase of dissolving personal relationships.
Source: *Personal Relationships 4: Dissolving Personal Relationships* (Duck, 1982, p. 16). Reprinted
by permission of Academic Press, Inc., London.

The first dissolution state, breakdown, involves problems with how a relationship is being conducted. The dissatisfied person has a basic acceptance of her partner, but does not like the way the relationship is proceeding. The problem here is typically one of inadequate social skills. One or both persons experience difficulty meshing their behavior together satisfactorily, do not perform the relevant behaviors competently or in accordance with normal social expectations, or actually violate the relevant norms of behavior (for example, by failing in the role of "husband" as defined by either the husband or his wife).

Repair of relationships at this stage involves attempts to increase satisfaction. In this type of repair, the partners are first made aware of their behavior at the "tactical, nuts and bolts level." According to Duck (1982), informed awareness of behavior patterns is an important step toward putting the relationship back on the track. The inadequate behavior is then identified, and with expert guidance, communication skills that facilitate repair are learned. Next, attempts are made to reestablish attraction to the relationship. The relationship, not the partners themselves, is found to be at fault. Finally, partners are encouraged to show affection and express their desire to repair their troubled relationship.

In phase two of Duck's model, the intrapsychic phase, the focus shifts from disaffection with the relationship to disaffection with one's partner. Typically the dissatisfied partner seeks informal help or advice from acquaintances and friends. This person may feel declining affection for the partner, combined with residual attraction to the relationship or inertia about leaving it and psychological detachment from the relationship. There may be reduced effort to sustain the relationship, but no real effort to leave it physically. Duck explained that the most effective strategies for repair prior to psychological withdrawal are those that focus on attributions about the partner and attempt to reestablish a more positive view. For example, the distressed person might be encouraged to keep notes on the pleasing and positive actions of his partner. Once psychological detachment has occurred, however, the distressed person is convinced that his partner's negative attributes outweigh the positive ones. Then the focus of repair should be on revising the distressed person's attitudes about the relationship and its alternatives.

Phase three, the dyadic phase, is when partners face their problems, anxieties, and risks of impending dissolution. Confrontation by the partners has three parts: first, the expression and management of emotion and conflict; second, the identification and negotiation of the issues; third, the subsequent reformulation of beliefs about the problem and the creation of a new, satisfactory form of the relationship. Here the partners need outside help to avoid a cycle of "cross-complaining" in which a complaint by one person is countered by a complaint from the other, and so on. Instead, the partners need to focus on changing routines and relational roles.

Phase four, the social phase, involves gaining social support or allies from among friends and relatives and experiencing the consequences of a breakup of one's social network. Duck described three separate repair goals at this phase, all aimed at handling the wider social consequences of turbulence in a relationship and minimizing its disruptive influence on the network. The first goal is the reconstruction of the relationship by exertion of social influence. For example, friends may attempt to find ways to pressure the couple to reconsider their situation. If this does not work, then social networks can help a person through the breakup by sanctioning it or by taking sides in the case of feuds, vendettas, or victimization of the person they support. In the third goal, networks can help after the breakup—for example, by introducing potential partners.

Phase five, the grave dressing phase, involves the formulation of histories or stories about the dissolved relationship in order to make the dissolution acceptable to the partners and friends. Support groups may place blame by saying things like "He was a bastard" or "I never liked her." Stories typically recall some inherent flaw of the partner or relationship that was present from the start. The person creating the story sees himself as having patiently endured or ignored the partner's flaw for a long time. In this way, the storyteller is able to save face through the creation of an acceptable account.

Duck (1985) proposed that repair of a relationship can benefit from recognition of the stage of dissolution being experienced at the time of intervention. We must know how far along the path of relationship destruction the partners have traveled before we may determine whether and how their relationship might be saved. If we also know the type of relationship, using Fitzpatrick's typology (1977), then reparative strategies suited to the type and stage may be developed. For example, phase three of dissolution often requires revising roles as a repair strategy. Knowing, for example, that the couple is traditional, rather than independent, separate, or separate-traditional, may help determine how the roles might change. The traditional husband might consider taking on some of the child-rearing or domestic chores; the traditional wife might consider getting a full-time job to help with financial burdens.

Summary

Relationships, a fundamental part of human life, respond to different types of social need. As we have discussed in this chapter, maintenance of our relationships involves communication challenges. Among these challenges

are marital partners adjusting to parenthood, adolescents replacing attachment to parents with attachment to friends and intimate partners, children
dealing with sibling rivalry, and elderly people finding new relationships
when partners and friends die.

In this chapter, we have emphasized the changing nature of relationships. With the understanding that people and relationships alter over
time, we can be prepared to adjust to change. Part of relating to others
successfully appears to be a willingness to adjust to inevitable changes.
Such adjustment requires effective communication between partners.

CHAPTER 9

Interpersonal Communication in Various Contexts

In the past eight chapters we focused on the commonalities across contexts of interpersonal communication. In this chapter, we will look at the effects of context—specifically, small groups, organizations, cross-cultural interactions, and health care—on communication. Our purpose is to introduce some recent work and encourage you to read further in areas of interest to you.

Small Group Communication

The study of small group communication was given its greatest impetus by Kurt Lewin. He proposed that each person within a group has a "life space" which she shares, to some extent, with other group members. The group is seen as a "field" in which interdependence of group members' life spaces emerges.

While Lewin took a psychological approach to the study of groups, George C. Homans, a sociologist, proposed a systems perspective of group behavior. Systems theory describes human behavior in terms of interdependencies of persons engaged in regular interaction. According to systems theory, a change in any person's behavior brings about a change in the behavior of other members of the system. The systems perspective on group behavior had a considerable impact on subsequent theory development.

Another group researcher, Moreno (1956), whose work we discussed in Chapter 3, was one of the first scholars to focus on the interpersonal conflicts that occur in small groups. He was interested in discovering and displaying the feelings of liking and disliking that group members had toward each other. Using questionnaires, he was able to assess like and dislike associations among group members, which he displayed with a sociogram such as the one in Figure 3.1 of Chapter 3.

Since Moreno's time, many scholar have studied small group communication. We will review the contributions of several of these scholars in this chapter.

Definition of Small Group

Although small group communication and dyadic communication are both forms of interpersonal interaction, the two are different. The dyad involves coordination of the behaviors of two people. Small groups involve coordination of the behaviors of at least three people. Moreover, members of small groups typically gather with some common purpose in mind. Barker, Cegala, Kibler, and Wahlers (1979, p. 11) proposed the following definition: "A small group is a collection of individuals from three to fifteen in number, who meet in face-to-face interaction over a period of time, generally with an assigned or assumed leader, who possess at least one common characteristic, and who meet with a purpose in mind."

The upper limit of fifteen is somewhat arbitrary. Much research has focused on the size parameters of small groups. The results of such research suggest that it is impossible to specify an ideal number of members. However, the larger the group, the greater the likelihood that few people will monopolize the discussion (Bales & Strodtbeck, 1951). Lopsided monopolization of discussions in small group often results in dissatisfaction among the less active members.

The inclusion of common purpose in our definition suggests that all groups are not alike. Jones, Barnlund, and Haiman (1980) proposed five representative types of discussion groups: casual, cathartic, learning, policy-making, and action. **Casual groups** are those that form anywhere. The purpose of such groups is to establish or maintain relationships. They may be spontaneous discussions or planned social gatherings. **Cathartic groups** allow the exploration and expression of emotions. The focus of discussion is typically on some problem; Alcoholics Anonymous is an example of a cathartic group. **Learning groups** often occur in schools. They help people assimilate new information. **Policy-making groups** consist of people appointed to make decisions concerning some issue. They are usually formed to fix something that has gone wrong or to change current conditions. **Action groups** form to determine when and how the policies set forth by policy-making groups should be implemented.

Although typologies of groups are useful for pointing out the primary purposes of groups, note that groups can have more than one purpose and can also change in type. Typologies are useful guides but should not be viewed as rigid categories.

Group Phases

Researchers have given considerable attention to the identification of developmental phases of group decision making. Bales and Strodtbeck (1951) tested the hypothesis that group problem-solving is characterized by different periods of interaction, each dominated by certain types of communication. They identified three phases: (1) an **orientation phase,** in which there is much asking for and giving of information, orientation, repetition, and confirmation; (2) an **evaluation phase,** in which orienting behaviors decrease while there is an increase in seeking and giving opinions, evaluations, and analyses; and (3) a **control phase** in which orienting statements decline further and seeking and giving suggestions, directions, and courses of action increase.

Based on a review of the literature on group developmental phases, Tuckman (1965) identified four stages of group development: (1) **orientation to the task,** involving identification of the task and determination of how to proceed in gathering information; (2) **emotional response to task demands,** which included members' resistance to the requirements of the task; (3) **open exchange of relevant interpretation,** involving exchanges of opinions and information regarding the accomplishment of the task; and (4) **emergence of solutions,** characterized by constructive attempts to accomplish the task.

Fisher (1970) also attempted to determine whether groups proceed through phases as they move toward consensus. He identified four phases, each blending with the succeeding phase in a continuous and gradual change in interaction patterns. Phase one, **orientation,** involves ambiguity and tentativeness in expressing ideas and opinions. Phase two, **conflict,** includes increased disputes and arguments accompanied by a sharp increase in expression of opinions and ideas. Phase three, **emergence,** is characterized by a decrease in conflict and movement toward resolution of differences. Phase four, **reinforcement,** marks when the group reaches a decision.

It is difficult to select from among these and other phase descriptions. No single set of phases appears to describe all groups. Recent research suggests that groups differ significantly in the types of interaction that emerge over time (Krueger, 1979). Research has also suggested that different types of groups may need different amounts of time to pass through typical sequences of group phases (Beach, 1980) and that different types of groups have different phase patterns (Poole, 1981, 1983a, 1983b). Hirokawa (1981) questioned the value of phase identification research that fails to indicate how the emergence of phases is related to effective group decisions or problem-solving. He found that effective and ineffective problem-solving groups are characterized by different phases of interaction and that no single phase sequence is characteristic of effective or ineffective group problem-solving. And Beach's (1980) research suggests that it may be more fruitful to move beyond defining phases according to the "mere distribution of categories" toward the study of how group members mutually regulate and shape group structure, especially if coding schemes can be developed to capture the subtleties of interaction. Such research suggests that training group members to adhere to any particular preferred phase sequence is no guarantee of effective group problem-solving. Effective interaction is more complex than phase analysis alone can resolve.

Poole (1983a, 1983b) proposed a model of group decision development that is a welcome change from models that treat decision making as a series of phases occurring one after the other in separate and predictable fashion. Instead, Poole offers a model that portrays decision making as "a set of parallel strands or tracks of activity which evolve simultaneously and interlock in different patterns over time" (1983b, p. 326). In other words, this model suggests that coherent, unified phases do not exist at all times during group decision making. Although the model is too complex to adequately describe here, it essentially allows researchers to identify when traditional phases, such as those proposed by Fisher (1970) and discussed earlier in this chapter, occur and when more complex patterns hold. Poole's model is more flexible than the traditional phasic models and, while the jury is still out, appears to provide a more realistic image of group decision making.

Quality Decisions

Aside from understanding the phases that occur during group interaction, it is important to understand how good decisions are made. John Dewey (1910) outlined one of the earliest step-by-step formats of effective decision making. In brief, the five steps included (1) group awareness of the problem, (2) thorough analysis of the nature of the problem, (3) group generation of feasible alternative solutions and consideration of their consequences, (4) careful evaluation of each alternative solution, and (5) adoption of the best alternative solution and determination of ways to implement it.

Since Dewey's contribution, others have studied decision-making steps. Hirokawa (1981) suggested that, while theorists of small group decision making are not in complete agreement concerning the best way to organize a group discussion to maximize its effectiveness, these theorists essentially agree on the specific functions that need to be performed. Hirokawa (1981, pp. 7–8) summarized these functions as follows:

1. *The group must understand and analyze the problem.* They must (a) identify the nature of the problem, (b) determine the extent of the problem, (c) identify the possible causes of the problem, and (d) identify the symptoms of the problem.
2. *The group must establish a set of operating procedures.* They need to decide what needs to be done to solve the problem and how they should go about doing it.
3. *The group must generate alternative solutions to solving the problem.* They must consider as many feasible alternatives as possible before attempting to decide on a final decision or solution.
4. *The group must develop a specific set of criteria for evaluating the worth of a given alternative solution.* They must consider (a) the qualities that a "good" solution must contain, (b) the specific aspects of the problem that the solution must remedy, and (c) the specific negative consequences that need to be avoided in order to prevent further complications and problems.
5. *The group must evaluate each alternative solution before deciding on a final decision or solution.* They must carefully evaluate all alternative solutions, making certain that all important implications and consequences of accepting such a solution have been considered and the one finally selected meets the criteria for a "good" solution.

Hirokawa explained that these five functions may not be the only ones that need to be performed during the problem-solving or decision-making process if a group is to be successful. They do, however, appear to be typical of successful groups.

Hirokawa and Pace (1983) examined how group interaction affects the quality of group decisions. Their research goes beyond listing the types of behaviors that should occur frequently for quality decisions. They attempted to identify consistent differences in the nature and content of interaction within several "effective" and "ineffective" decision-making groups. By analyzing sample interactions from these two types of groups, Hirokawa and Pace identified several features that distinguished effective and ineffective groups. The following list includes some of their findings:

1. Groups that arrived at high-quality decisions tended to examine carefully the opinions of fellow group members rather than accept them without careful consideration.
2. Groups that made high-quality decisions tended to evaluate carefully their alternative choices in light of established evaluation criteria.
3. Groups that reached high-quality decisions selected a particular alternative over others because they believed it logically followed from certain facts, assumptions, or inferences that they considered to be true.

4. Effective groups tended to have one or more members capable of influencing the line of thinking in a positive, helpful manner toward selecting a high-quality decision.

Cohesion

Another issue that has received much attention from researchers is small group cohesion or cohesiveness. **Cohesion** refers to the forces which act on members to remain in the group. Barker and others (1979, p. 168) described *cohesiveness* as "the complex of forces which bind members of a group to each other and to the group as a whole."

From their review of cohesion literature, Evans and Jarvis (1980) concluded that while the typical definition of cohesion has focused on members' attraction to the group, cohesion should be defined in terms of the group as a whole. Although there appears to be a growing acceptance of definitions of cohesion that focus on the group, there have been few attempts to study cohesion from other than the perspective of individual members. (see Drescher, Burlingame, & Fuhriman, 1985).

Drescher and others (1985) also criticized typical cohesion research for its lack of attention to time. Although cohesion is considered a developmental phenomenon, most studies assess it at one point rather than across time. A group that is not initially cohesive may become cohesive as time progresses. Research that fails to take into consideration the element of time widens the gap between conceptual definitions of cohesion and the measurement of it. Drescher and others (1985, pp. 23–24) have suggested that time may interact with the type of member to influence cohesion: For example, if the person and time dimensions are examined simultaneously, it may be that the leader contributes significantly to higher or lower levels of cohesion in the early hours of the group but less so as time passes into the middle and later stages of group life.

Returning for a moment to earlier chapters in this book, we may be able to identify some interpersonal communication activities that might influence group cohesion. For example, several of the competence skills discussed in Chapter 5 could facilitate cohesion. Empathy, social perspective-taking, listening ability, behavioral flexibility, and self-monitoring may be helpful as members attempt to cooperate with each other.

Cohesion is likely a more complex phenomenon than indicated by most research. If it is a group characteristic, can we validly assess it through self-reports of individual members? Is cohesion more than the sum of individual members' perceptions? Future research on cohesion must address such questions if we are to derive useful conclusions.

Leadership

Our final small group topic is leadership. Two assumptions have guided research on small group leadership: (1) leaders emerge in all small groups and (2) all leaders share certain identifiable stable characteristics. Some researchers of groups have questioned whether leadership is always embodied in one group member rather than shared (Gibb, 1969). They have also questioned the assumption that leaders share particular stable characteristics.

Fisher (1985) has proposed a refreshing perspective on leadership. It might be described as a relational perspective because he proposed that leadership is a complex phenomenon involving interaction between leaders and followers. According to Fisher, leaders watch and listen to followers and respond to what they see and hear; good leaders have a variety of responses. In other words, leadership is not characterized by a limited set of behavioral types but by the ability to respond to followers in a variety of ways.

Fisher explained that small groups are complex social phenomena. As such, anyone acting as a leader within a small group must be equipped to respond to complexity: "The key to leadership is thus not in the specific type of action but in performing a variety of specific types of actions" (1985, pp. 184–185). Leadership from this perspective is not the same across groups or even across time within the same group. It requires the ability to respond in complex ways to complex problems.

Organizational Communication

The organization has become an important context in the study of interpersonal communication. Communication, after all, is what makes human organization possible. Through communication, organizational members convey information that facilitates or hinders productivity, interpersonal relations, and individual and group advancement.

Researchers have conceived of **organizations** as systems. **Systems** are "networks of causal relationships, in which many different variables are linked with one another" (Heise, 1975, p. 27). Organizational communication researchers have been faced with the difficult task of determining how best to study systems; however, the most commonly employed statistical models do not do justice to them. They tend to focus on simple or multiple cause-effect relations rather than the system as a whole. Monge (1982) argued that most organizational communication research based on systems theory has failed to support the existence of systems because improper methodological procedures have been used to study them. Contending that the procedures used to study a system should correspond to the logic of the system's properties, he suggested that researchers probably will require different research methods to study different properties of systems.

Organizational Culture

One of the major interests of organizational communication researchers is **organizational culture**—the ways of living, organizing, and communicating developed by groups. Culture includes shared norms, reminiscences, stories, rites, and rituals. For an employee to work effectively in an organization, he or she must learn the culture peculiar to that organization.

Deal and Kennedy (1982) have written an interesting book, *Corporate Cultures*, in which they propose that employees of corporations share certain stories, values, heroes, rules, rites, and rituals that form a culture. They argue that corporate cultures reduce employee uncertainty concerning how he should act. For example, employees of General Electric learn from a story about Charles Steinmetz that people should be treated well:

> A crippled Austrian immigrant, Steinmetz came as a young man to America and worked in Thomas Edison's lab, which he ran after Edison left. He was responsible for dozens of inventions still used by GE and other companies. But Steinmetz is revered for other reasons. Whenever young engineers joined GE, Steinmetz would invite them home for the weekend in order to learn, sincerely and without political intent, what kind of people they were. Once he adopted one of GE's leading engineers as his own son—and the man's whole family. They all moved into Steinmetz's house and lived with him for twenty years [Deal & Kennedy, 1982, p. 45].

Steinmetz was a GE "visionary hero." Such heroes "light the way" for employees, according to Deal and Kennedy. Their influence is broad and philosophical. Companies also have "situational heroes" whose actions inspire employees with the example of their day-to-day success. In fact, companies with a strong culture are adept at recognizing and creating situational heroes. For example, IBM singles out fast-track newcomers and assigns them for one year as assistants to senior managers. During that year, these potential heroes are given the task of answering customer complaint letters. This "ho-hum" function increases their sensitivity to the importance IBM attaches to customer service. Early in their careers, potential heroes are taught the IBM culture, which they will later reinforce by their own example on the job (Deal & Kennedy, 1982).

Rites and rituals also reinforce company culture. Plaques given to employees for their accomplishments are a means of rewarding culture appropriate behavior. Some companies have rituals of social interaction. For example, IBM's Thomas Watson insisted that every employee be addressed as Mr., Mrs., or Miss to indicate that everyone working for IBM is a professional worthy of respect (Deal & Kennedy, 1982).

Some rituals serve to exclude specific types of people. For example, women are often excluded from socializing after work in predominantly male companies. One executive of a New England–based insurance firm who was not overjoyed by the prospect of female competition said, "Women do all right, but they don't jog at lunch with the boss. They miss out on hearing what is going on and how the boss feels about it." According to Deal and Kennedy, this type of exclusion by rituals can be a detriment to a company because it keeps valuable talent on the outside looking in.

Storytellers are another means by which corporate culture is developed and maintained.

> The best storytellers are typically found in positions that give them access to a great deal of information. They are usually in the epicenter of activity and free to be as eccentric as they choose. A storyteller needs imagination, insight, and a sense of details—a story can't be abstract. While the position of storyteller is a powerful one, it's not a leadership role. Many people fear storytellers because everything—and everyone—is grist for their story mills. Yet colleagues revere them and often protect them [Deal & Kennedy, 1982, p. 88].

Research on organizational story telling indicates that it is an important form of employee interaction. Martin (1981) explained that explicit forms of communication are often ineffective in conveying organizational culture, management philosophy, and organizational policies. One solution is the story, an implicit form of communication. Wilkins (1978) conducted research on two organizations within the same industry that differed in employee commitment. He found an association between the number and type of stories told in interviews with employees from these two organizations and the levels of employee commitment; the more committed employees told a larger number of and more favorable stories. Martin and Powers (1979) found that stories can have more of an impact than mere factual information when used as support for abstract policy statements.

Such research suggests that stories can play an important persuasive role in organizations. Managerial philosophies that are difficult to convey via explicit direction may be conveyed effectively via implicit stories. Stored in the mind intact, these stories can be retrieved for behavioral guidance when an employee needs to make a decision. For example, at IBM employees tell a story about a ninety-pound security advisor who dared to challenge Thomas Watson, Sr., the intimidating chairman of the board of the corporation. When Watson approached the doorway to an area where she was on guard, she told him that he could not enter without a green badge. The men accompanying Watson expressed their anger. Watson raised his hand for silence, while one of the party went off to get the appropriate badge (Rodgers, 1969). This story might be interpreted by an employee to mean that following the rules is appreciated at IBM or that pulling rank is not condoned at IBM.

Organizational Networks

Aside from organizational climate or culture, much organizational research focuses on **networks,** which are the emergent structures or patterns through which information travels in the organization (Jablin, 1980a; Albrecht, 1979). Researchers look for links and cliques among organizational members. The assumption guiding network analyses is that organizations are composed of a series of overlapping and interrelated networks. There are various types of networks within each series: friendship, authority, information exchange, task expertise, and status (Guetzkow, 1965). Organizational members have informal roles within these networks. The roles are (1) membership in cliques; (2) bridges—people within a group who link with other groups, thereby providing information between groups; (3) liaisons—people who link groups but who are not themselves members of groups; (4) isolates—people who have little or no contact with other members of the organization (see Farace, Monge, & Russell, 1977; Monge, Edwards, & Kirste, 1978).

Researchers who study networks are able to locate key communicators as well as obstructions to information flow. A number of methodologies have emerged to analyze communication networks (see Roberts & O'Reilly, 1978; Rice, 1979; Jablin, 1980a; Monge, 1982). These methodologies can identify cliques, bridges, liasons, and isolates and provide an image of a particular organization's communication structure.

Rogers and Kincaid (1981) have described how network analysis can be used to study groups of people whether associated with a formal organization or associated because of some common interest, family ties, or common problem. They tell an intriguing story of how networking helped women in Oryu Li, Korea, improve life in their community. They managed, despite many obstacles, to encourage family planning throughout their network, to rid their community of a wine house that drained their husbands' earnings, and to initiate and maintain an impressive number of self-development programs.

According to Rogers and Kincaid, communication networks are "interconnected individuals who are linked by patterned communication flows" (p. 141). They demonstrate how communication network analysis can be used to identify cliques and other communication roles, such as liaisons and bridges, in the network and to measure various indexes of communication structure of the individuals, personal networks, cliques, or systems under study. Doing so allows researchers to see how people get information that influences their behavior. It also allows researchers to propose ways of changing networks to facilitate information flow when desired.

Organizational Relationships

The way people work together in organizations is, in part, a function of the formal and informal rules guiding their actions (Farace, Taylor, & Stewart, 1978). Formal rules are ones that are codified in some fashion. They might be disseminated in monthly reports or daily newsletters for employees. Violations of such rules usually result in some form of punishment. Informal rules are expectations or generally shared beliefs about the ways employees should act. Such rules have not been written down and disseminated to employees; it is understood that employees already know them. Sanctions for violating informal rules also exist. They might take the form of criticism, ostracism, and ridicule and can be as severe as sanctions imposed on violators of formal rules (Farace and others, 1978).

Organizational assimilation is the term used to describe the process by which employees learn the rules of an organization and become part of its culture (Jablin, 1982). During this process, employees learn what is important to the organization—its acceptable values, behaviors, and ways of thinking. While some employees might passively adopt organizational rules, others may influence the organization by bringing some of their own values, styles of behavior, and ways of thinking to their new jobs. Organizational assimilation is therefore not necessarily a one-way street where the employee accepts all organizational rules without question; it may be a process during which the new employee influences the organizational climate by bringing to it novel ways of thinking and acting.

As employees are assimilated into organizations and throughout their employment period, it is important to their satisfaction and productivity that they continue to learn what is expected of them and that they have some means of giving their suggestions to superiors. Some organizations have responded to this need with the development of quality circles— "small groups of employees from the same work area who meet voluntarily on a regular basis to identify, analyze, and solve problems of production and quality" (Stohl, 1986). Members of quality circles brainstorm topics of interest and select a problem to work on. They then contact others outside the circle to find out if anything is being done to solve the problem. The members collect data on the problem and come up with a solution that they think will meet the various needs of diverse members of the organization. They then present their solution to management. Successful quality circles can help to keep organizational communication channels open (Stohl, 1986).

Keeping communication channels open may be useful not only in terms of productivity but also in helping employees learn how others in the organization think. They may, for example, learn about the different approaches that may be taken by males and females to the same job. Because of the increase over the past twenty-five years in women entering the work force and taking positions of authority, research on male-female communication within organizations has received much recent attention. One typical finding of such research is that women who enter pre-dominantly male organizations tend to exclude themselves or be excluded from informal interaction within the organization (see Albrecht, 1983). Fairhurst (1985) described several reasons for female exclusion from impor-tant male interaction within the organizational setting. One reason is the accessibility of mentors, who often facilitate the upward movement of young members of organizations. Boster, Collofello, and Wigand (1984, p. 5) have explained that mentoring "speeds up socialization into the work role, encourages social interaction, provides an opportunity for high-quality interpersonal interaction, and enhances identification with and commitment to the organization." Kanter (1977), author of *Men and Women of the Corporation,* has recommended formal mentoring programs to assist women in male-dominated careers where they may have trouble locating mentors.

A second problem for women in male-dominated jobs is role conflict, which occurs when an individual faces competing expectations. For ex-ample, a woman who displays culturally acceptable female behavior may be rejected as a manager because managerial behavior has been defined in terms of male behavior. Fairhurst (1985) explained that stereotypes are sustained when the majority has few opportunities to test reality and when nontraditional employees act in ways that reinforce the stereotypes because they lack power. Until women in typical male roles and men in typical female roles feel they have enough seniority or power to re-negotiate role definitions, they deal with often uncomfortable role con-flict.

Sexuality is another issue that affects male-female roles and rela-tionships within organizations. Romantic relationships at work are feared because of their potential to disrupt established relations among colleagues (Nieva & Gutek, 1981). Little research exists on this topic, despite the concern it generates within organizations. The literature and research that does exist suggests that love among colleagues can affect organizational structure (Collins, 1983), add excitement to a dull office (Horn & Horn, 1982), or threaten job security (Quinn, 1977).

When attraction between colleagues is not reciprocated, the result may be sexual harassment. In reviewing the literature on this topic, Fairhurst (1985) found that sexual harassment is not uncommon within organiza-tions. While this topic is difficult to research because many employees are unwilling to discuss their experiences, extant research suggests that it can be a significant problem for the targets. Benson and Thompson's (1982) study of sexual harassment on campus indicates the use of several resistance tactics by targets: ignoring advances, directing disclosures away from personal matters, bringing a friend along and leaving office doors open, mentioning a boyfriend, and making direct complaints.

Our last topic of male-female communication within organizations is leadership. Although one might expect females to exhibit less dominant and more nurturant styles of leadership than their male counterparts, recent research suggests that few stylistic differences between male and female leadership communication can be attributed to sex alone (see Fairhurst, 1985). Any differences perceived by employees may be more a function of their expectations than actual behavioral differences. In other words, people expect women and men to act in certain stereotypical ways, so female leaders who act nurturant will have that behavior attributed to their gender, whereas male leaders acting nurturant are likely to have their behavior attributed to their sensitive nature.

Laboratory research indicates that employees are more satisfied with leaders who display gender-consistent behavior (Bartol & Butterfield, 1976; Haccoun, Haccoun, & Sallay, 1978). Field studies have produced inconclusive findings concerning satisfaction with gender-consistent leadership behavior. According to Kanter (1977), dissatisfaction with female managers may be more a function of their lack of influence and less a function of their sex.

As with male-female relationships, superior-subordinate relationships have captured much research attention. Organizational researchers have often concluded that communication between superiors and subordinates must be good if an organization is to function effectively. Much research corroborates this conclusion. For example, research suggests that employees are more satisfied with their jobs when open communication exists between superiors and subordinates (Baird, 1973; Jablin, 1978). Research also suggests that superiors who use a supportive leadership style with their subordinates and who exert influence upward within an organization tend to have more satisfied subordinates (Pelz, 1952; Jablin, 1980b). Other research indicates that an employer's apprehension about communication has a negative affect on employees' satisfaction with supervision (Falcione, McCroskey, & Daly, 1977; Richmond, McCroskey, & Davis, 1982).

The organization, a fascinating context for the study of interpersonal communication, is held together or split apart by communication. The structure of information flow, cultures, climates, relationships, and other topics of organizational study are communication issues. As researchers continue to find ways to study systems such as network analyses, the task of studying organizational communication will become more manageable.

Cross-Cultural Communication

Another context in which the study of interpersonal communication has been important is the cross-cultural context. Surrounded primarily by oceans, Americans are often deficient in their understanding of other cultures. The inevitable result of such lack of understanding is a tendency to believe that others think as we do. The fact is that each culture has its own unique rules for communication. To function effectively in a foreign culture requires a sensitivity to such rules.

Aside from ethnocentrism—the tendency to prefer one's own kind of people—those who communicate with foreigners also face the discomfort of uncertainty. In Chapter 8 we described reduction of uncertainty as an important goal of communication with acquaintances. Because other people can place our "fronts," or preferred roles, in jeopardy, the better we know them, the better we can protect ourselves from embarrassment. Strangers from one's own culture pose considerable uncertainty. Strangers from another culture about which one has little knowledge are even more of a threat to one's sense of communication competence.

Gudykunst and Kim (1984) have identified components of effective communication with cross-cultural strangers. A tolerance for ambiguity, which involves patience and minimal discomfort with novelty, helps communication with cross-cultural strangers. A second component of effective cross-cultural communication is empathy. Gudykunst and Kim explained that empathy surpasses sympathy in facilitating cross-cultural communication because *empathy* involves "imaginative intellectual and emotional participation in another person's experience" (Bennett, 1979, p. 418), whereas *sympathy* involves merely imagining how we would respond were we in another person's position. In cross-cultural interactions, sympathy often leads to misunderstanding because it involves seeing another person's position from one's own cultural perspective.

Of course, empathy cannot occur without some knowledge of the cross-cultural stranger's rules for behavior. The acquisition of such knowledge requires, at the very least, a willingness to learn. Often people believe that learning a language is enough to communicate effectively in another culture. Cultural experts are quick to refute this belief. As we have discussed in previous chapters, language is merely a vehicle of thoughts and feelings. To use a language effectively, one must also study the culture behind it. Let's take a brief look at three cultures to gain a sense of how differently they see the world.

The Japanese

The Japanese have received much recent attention from the United States. Their reputation as exporters of quality goods has skyrocketed over the past decade. Try as we might to understand how Japan has accomplished this feat, the Japanese remain a puzzle to most Americans. According to Robert Christopher (1983), author of *The Japanese Mind*, Americans—with few exceptions—have no idea how the Japanese think and feel. He explains that Americans erroneously assume that they can communicate effectively with the Japanese without understanding Japanese logic and emotion.

For example, the Japanese are nonconfrontational. The group-oriented upbringing of the typical Japanese person equips her to express aggressive feelings in a constructive manner. Moreover, self-assertion is, according to Christopher, "the ultimate 'no-no' in Japan." The Japanese have a saying, "The nail that sticks up gets pounded down." The individual Japanese is always part of a group or organization in which decisions are made by all those who have any competence in the matter under discussion. In Japan, both failure and success are team matters.

As you might imagine, the Japanese group perspective pervades their methods of negotiation. *Nemawashi* is the term used to describe the highly tentative process of feeling out how everyone concerned feels about a particular course of action before proceeding to adopt or reject it. This approach tends to rule out future personal conflict, a form of interaction that the Japanese abhor. To the Japanese, resorting to conflict means that one has lost the game. Even Japanese women who are struggling for women's rights in Japan seldom resort to confrontation.

The Arabs

To understand the Arabs is to understand pride and honor. For most Arabs generosity is the means by which honor is assured. Even when a stranger visits an Arab home, hospitality is likely to be overwhelming. The Arab people, as combative as they tend to be with each other, share a deep sense of pride. Because of this, they are obliged to appear generous and are easily injured if one fails to reciprocate.

The Arab is also sensitive to honor. Typically an Arab man's honor is his wife or sister. Since jealousy is the male Arab's strongest impulse, Arab men are suspicious of women (Almaney & Alwan, 1982). In Westernized countries such as Egypt, Lebanon, Syria, and Iraq, women are freer, but in keeping with traditional Islamic values, Arab women are often separated from men who are not family members.

Although this brief description of Arab concern for pride and honor does not do justice to Arab culture, it points to a source of difference that often makes communication between the Arab and the foreigner difficult. Americans who visit an Arab's home or place of business and refuse to drink coffee during the early phases of discussion are likely to cause offense. The man who asks his Arab business counterpart, "How's the wife?" may find that he is never invited to do business with that man again. Sensitivity to an Arab's pride is an important part of communicating with him.

Latin Americans

Latin American people belong to an associative culture. In contrast to abstract cultures such as the United States where one's family obligations rarely extend to cousins and second cousins, in the associative culture of Latin America, people are very connected to their immediate and even distant relatives. According to Hugo Penata of American University, in the United States one is free to be a loner. In Latin America, "A loner is a looney."

The Latin American people live in a maze of interconnections. The Spanish word for a well-connected man is *enchufado*—a man of influence. He gets things done. He is obligated to his family and friends. If you are related to or a friend of an enchufado, your life is much easier than it would be without him.

The connectedness of the Latin American culture is reflected in their nonverbal communication. Men and women always shake hands and often embrace upon meeting and parting. Such embracing makes many U.S. visitors uncomfortable. Simple handshakes are considered insufficient expressions of warmth with close acquaintances. In order for typical American visitors to become accepted in Latin America, they must develop a sense of comfort with Latin American expressiveness. Also important is comfort with the Latin American tendency to make eye contact and to stand very close during conversation.

The female visitor needs to recognize that machismo is a fact of Latin American male life. U.S. businesswomen in Latin America often find that men are not at all inhibited about making advances unless it is made quite clear to them that such advances are not welcome. The U.S. businesswoman who must give gifts to Latin American business counterparts should be sure that the gift does not imply more than she intends. The wise move is to give a gift to the family rather than to the man alone (Reardon, 1985).

Although our descriptions of Japanese, Arab, and Latin American cultures are brief and general, they suggest the challenge of communication across cultures. It is not enough to learn the language of another culture; the typical thought processes of the people must also be understood. The typical American is ill prepared to communicate effectively with people from foreign cultures. We often expect that others should know our language and tolerate our inadvertent insults. Perhaps we should ask ourselves if we would be tolerant of people expecting that of us. In most cultures, attempts to speak the local language and to abide by local rules is a head start toward positive communication experiences.

Health Communication

Another important context for the study of interpersonal communication concerns health. The sources people use for information about their health, their willingness to comply with physicians' recommendations, patient relationships with health practitioners, and therapeutic relationships are only a few of the communication issues to be studied in the health context. Each of these issues has received increased research attention over the past decade.

Sources of Information

In terms of the sources people use to learn about health issues, research has been conducted using both interpersonal and mass media channels. Such research suggests that people often learn about health issues from the mass media, but determine how to act through interpersonal communication with family, friends, and doctors. Flay and Sobel (1983, p. 5) explained that changing peoples' behavior in regard to health requires more than mass media information programs: "Changes in knowledge, which such programs sometimes do accomplish well, are only at the beginning of a long probabilistic chain, and many other factors must be examined if behavior is to be changed." Flay and Sobel have reported increasing recognition by researchers that the primary influences on adolescent drug use are social, particularly peer and family influence. It is difficult to counter immediate, important social influence with impersonal media campaigns alone. But mass media and interpersonal communication together can disseminate health information:

> To the extent that an issue is already salient, people will be discussing it with each other, and any new information or program is likely to be attended to and also discussed. To the extent that an issue is not already salient, the ultimate effectiveness of a mass media program will be enhanced if it gets people talking to each other about the issue. . . . Interpersonal communication then spreads the message, or reactions to it, to a wider audience. Diffusion of an issue may lead, in turn, to demands for more information on it or for new policies or laws [Flay & Sobel, 1983, p. 21].

Other researchers have also reported benefits of joint mass and interpersonal health campaigns (Maccoby & Farquhar, 1975; Best, 1980; Danaher, Berkanovic, & Gerber, 1982). Moreover, Cook and Flay (1978) have contended that interpersonal communication is important for ensuring the maintenance or persistence of changes in health behavior. People need reinforcement from others. To the extent that family and friends encourage certain changes toward healthy behavior, those changes are likely to be maintained. Reardon and Buck (1984) proposed that the coping styles chosen by cancer patients may be more conducive to health when supported by family and friends. It may not matter so much whether a cancer patient decides to be stoic, deny the disease, fight it, or feel helpless as much as it matters that people important to the patient support the chosen coping style.

Physician-Patient Communication

Research on the relationship between physicians and patients is another key area of interpersonal communication study. It appears that patients are more satisfied with doctors they perceive to be caring and concerned about patients and who alleviate patients' anxiety. Sharf (1986) explains, however, that most patient-physician interactions are dominated by the doctor over a relatively passive patient. The traditional doctor-patient relationship may thus prohibit informative interaction. When this happens, patient satisfaction decreases.

Adler (1977) indicated that the physician is only one source of information about illness. People have informal channels through which they learn about how they should respond to or prevent illnesses. Physicians need to recognize that such informal channels exist and that patients often need to be given accurate information to avoid having them rely on the inaccurate information they may get via informal channels. Williams and Meredith (1984) reported that in recent years there has been a trend toward doctors being more open with their patients and for more patient participation in medical decisions. They described the physician-patient relationship as becoming one of allies rather than adversaries. For example, obstetricians and expectant mothers are negotiating preferences for normal birth and contingency plans for the unexpected (Simkin, 1983). This type of doctor-patient interaction is an important area of health communication research.

Patient Compliance *yield to*

Another area of research is patient compliance. Once a physician has communicated her recommendations, how can the patient be persuaded to follow them? Richardson, Anderson, Selser, Evans, Kishbaugh, and Lavine (1983) studied cancer patients' compliance with chemotherapy. They studied various interventions, or means of encouraging compliance, and concluded that "to be effective, the intervention must overcome what may already be a learned habit of noncompliance" (p. 382). For example, providing patients with information about ways to cope with stressful medical procedures appears to be useful. Fear appeals, on the other hand, often reduce rather than increase compliance of an already frightened patient.

Helpful Communication

Part of health communication study involves styles of communication. Researchers have looked at (1) how frequently people listen to the patient as compared to the amount of time devoted to giving advice (Arnston, Droge, & Fassl, 1978), (2) ways of communicating conducive to creating positive therapeutic environments (Pettigrew & Thomas, 1978; Thompson, 1982a,b), (3) what constitutes helpful communication (Mayton & Andersen, 1985), (4) communicating with the dying (Miller & Knapp, 1985), and (5) the value of candor in discussing illness with the patient (Hudson-Jones, 1986; Northouse, 1986). These are only a few of the help-related issues relevant to health communication. What we assume to be helpful to a patient may be harmful. For example, Peters-Golden (1982) reported that people feel they must "cheer up" cancer patients, a type of behavior that discourages cancer patients from expressing their true feelings. Getting help from people when one is ill is often difficult because often what people think is helpful is not (see Segal, 1985).

Recent research suggests that one way to help people dealing with challenging illnesses is to encourage in them a sense of self-efficacy. **Self-efficacy** refers to personal judgments about how well one can organize and implement patterns of behavior in situations that may contain novel, unpredictable, and stressful elements (Bandura, 1982; Schunk & Carbonari, 1984). People with a low sense of self-efficacy are likely to avoid or postpone dealing with their illnesses. A strong sense of self-efficacy is associated with more vigorous efforts to succeed in coping with difficult situations such as severe illness.

Encouraging patients to feel a sense of self-efficacy is a valuable goal. It can, however, backfire. It is important to avoid encouraging patients to take risks before they are ready. Repeated failure can dampen anyone's sense of self-efficacy. For example, the patient encouraged to go back to full-time work before he is ready may interpret small daily frustrations as indications that he will never be able to work effectively again. Patients can also overestimate their self-efficacy. In such cases, friends and family can be of assistance by encouraging the patient to pace his recovery (see Schunk & Carbonari, 1984).

Another way that people can be helpful to seriously ill patients is by providing social support. House (1981) has divided social support into four types. The first type involves getting the patient to believe that she is loved and cared for and that someone is prepared to listen and understand. The second type of social support involves material assistance given by family, friends, or society. The third type of support is easy access to advice, directions, and suggestions in time of need. The fourth type of social support concerns expressions of approval from friends, family, acquaintances, colleagues, and others. Illness can cause considerable loss of self-esteem in a society that puts a high premium on health and fitness. Social support can enhance a patient's health by providing him with affiliation, approval, and affection (Patel, 1984).

Health communication, an important and interesting area of study, affects us all. As people become increasingly aware that they are in large part responsible for their own health, they may seek more information about how they can increase their chances for long lives. Patients may become conscientious consumers. Mass media and interpersonal channels can increase awareness and change behavior in ways that facilitate health. Much research remains to be done in this area, but it has a promising future.

Summary

In this chapter we have looked briefly at four contexts of interpersonal communication study: small group, organizational, cross-cultural, and health. These four only begin to suggest the contexts in which interpersonal communication is an important factor, but these contexts have received considerable research attention over the past two decades.

This chapter has given us an opportunity to see how interpersonal communication research can provide useful information for our everyday use. Group meetings, communicating at work, meeting people from other cultures, and coping with illness are not only of interest to researchers but a part of most peoples' lives. Research such as that reviewed in this chapter provides us with some clues about how we might improve our communication in these contexts. With this thought, we close our overview of interpersonal communication.

Appendix A

Marwell and Schmitt's Compliance-Gaining Taxonomy

Strategy	Type of statement or action used by persuader
1. Promise:	"If you comply, I will reward you."
2. Threat:	"If you do not comply, I will punish you."
3. Expertise (positive):	"If you comply, you will be rewarded because of the nature of things."
4. Expertise (negative):	"If you do not comply, you will be punished because of the nature of things."
5. Liking:	Actor is friendly and helpful to get target in a good frame of mind so that he will comply with request.
6. Pregiving:	Actor rewards target before requesting compliance.
7. Aversive stimulation:	Actor continuously punishes target, making cessation contingent on compliance.
8. Debt:	"You owe me compliance because of past favors."

9. Moral appeal: "You are immoral if you do not comply."

10. Self-feeling (positive):   "You will feel better about yourself if you comply."

11. Self-feeling (negative):   "You will feel worse about yourself if you do not comply."

12. Altercasting (positive):   "A person with 'good' qualities would comply."

13. Altercasting (negative):   "Only a person with 'bad' qualities would not comply."

14. Altruism: "I need your compliance very badly, so do it for me."

15. Esteem (positive):   "People you value will think better of you if you comply."

16. Esteem (negative):   "People you value will think worse of you if you do not comply."

From *Sociometry*, Vol. 30 (1967). Reprinted by permission of the American Sociological Association.

Appendix B

Bell and Daly's Typology of Affinity-Seeking Strategies

1. Altruism: The affinity seeker strives to be of assistance to the target in whatever she is currently doing.

2. Assume control: The affinity seeker presents himself as a person who has control over whatever is going on.

3. Assume equality: The affinity seeker strikes a posture of social equality with the target.

4. Comfortable self: The affinity seeker acts comfortable and relaxed in settings shared with the target

5. Concede control: The affinity seeker allows the target to assume control over relational activities.

6. Conversational rule-keeping: The affinity seeker adheres closely to cultural rules for polite, cooperative interaction with the target.

7. Dynamism: The affinity seeker presents herself as an active, enthusiastic person.

8. Elicit others' disclosures: The affinity seeker encourages the target to talk by reinforcing the target's conversational contributions.

9. Facilitate enjoyment: The affinity seeker tries to maximize the positiveness of relational encounters with the target.

10. Inclusion of other: The affinity seeker enthusiastically participates in an activity the target is known to enjoy.

11. Influence perceptions of closeness: The affinity seeker engages in behaviors that cause the target to perceive the relationship as closer than it has actually been.

12. Listening: The affinity seeker listens actively and attentively to the target.

13. Nonverbal immediacy: The affinity seeker signals interest in the target through various nonverbal cues.

14. Openness: The affinity seeker discloses personal information to the target.

15. Optimism: The affinity seeker presents herself to the target as a positive person.

16. Personal autonomy: The affinity seeker presents himself to the target as an independent, free-thinking person.

17. Physical attractiveness: The affinity seeker tries to look and dress as attractively as possible in the presence of the target.

18. Present interesting self: The affinity seeker presents herself to the target as someone who would be interesting to know.

19. Reward association: The affinity seeker presents himself in such a way that the target sees that the affinity seeker can reward the target for associating with him.

20. Self-concept confirmation: The affinity seeker demonstrates respect for the target and helps the target to feel good about herself.

21. Self-inclusion: The affinity seeker arranges the environment to come into frequent contact with the target.

22. Sensitivity: The affinity seeker acts in a warm, empathic manner toward the target.

23. Similarity: The affinity seeker seeks to convince the target that the two of them share many similar tastes and attitudes.

24. Supportiveness: The affinity seeker supports the target in the latter's social encounters.

25. Trustworthiness: The affinity seeker presents himself to the target as an honest, reliable person.

Source: Bell, R. A., and Daly, J. A. (1984). The affinity-seeking function of communication. Reprinted with permission of *Communication Monographs.*

Appendix C

Petronio's Strategies to Reduce Embarrassment

Defensive orientation	Protective orientation

Defensively changing the subject (justification)

Person changes the topic	Wants other to change the topic
Person verbally blames the incident on something else	Wants others to verbally blame the incident on something else

Introduce information excusing the performance (excuse)

Person pretends he is physically injured	Wants others to pretend that he was only clowning around
Person states she was not really trying to do that which caused embarrassment	Wants others to apologize to her, thus shifting responsibility
Person gives an excuse, thus minimizing the incident	

Introduce redeeming or self-enhancing information (justification)

Person tells information about himself that would cause others to see him in a positive light	Wants others to give him a chance to try again

Person looks for a chance to try again, thus redeeming herself

Person apologizes to those present, thus taking responsibility

Wants others to point out she is a good person in many ways

Denying or minimizing failure (justification)

Person laughs at the incident to deny failure

Person pretends nothing inappropriate happened

Wants others to indicate nothing inappropriate happened

Wants others to ignore the incident

Implicitly seeking identification from others (excuse)

Person laughs at her own behavior

Wants others to become embarrassed too

Wants others to express sympathy for her

Scapegoating (excuse)

Person verbally blames incident on others present

Person makes someone else the focus of attention

Wants others to make themselves center of attention

Wants others to verbally blame the incident on themselves

Withdrawal (escape)

Person retreats from the situation

Wants others to leave the situation

Requests for atonement

Person criticizes herself

Wants others to demand that she make amends for the situation

Wants others to become angry and yell

Wants others to laugh at what she did to cause her own embarrassment

From Petronio's communication strategies to reduce embarrassment, *Western Journal of Speech Communication*, 1984, pp. 31–32. Used by permission.

Appendix D

Burleson's Hierarchical Coding System for Sensitivity of Comforting Strategies

"What would you say to make a friend feel better about not receiving an invitation to another child's party?"

  0. *No response*

   Subject is unable to think of anything to say.

  I. *Denial of individual perspectivity*

   The speaker condemns or ignores the specific feelings that exist in the situation for the person addressed. This denial may be either explicit or implicit.

  II. *Implicit recognition of individual perspectivity*

   The speaker provides some implicit acceptance of or positive response to the feelings of the other, but does not explicitly mention, elaborate, or legitimize those feelings.

III. *Explicit recognition and elaboration of individual perspectivity*

The speaker explicitly acknowledges, elaborates, and legitimizes the feelings of the other. These strategies may include attempts to provide a general understanding of the situation. Coping strategies may be suggested in conjunction with explication of the other's feelings.

These levels of comforting strategies represent the three primary divisions. Each level contains three sublevels in the coding scheme used by researchers.

Source: Burleson, B. R. (1984). Age, social-cognitive development, and the use of comforting strategies. Reprinted with permission of *Communication Monographs*.

Appendix E

Roloff's Modes of Conflict Resolution and Their Items

Revenge

Hate the person
Destroy something that the person has
Cheat the person
Get drunk
Take a pill
Take something from the person
Turn others against the person
Chase the person away
Lie to the person
Give the person something for returning the object
Ignore the missing object
Joke about it

Regression

Ask someone what to do
Cry

Physical Aggression

Shoot the person
Hit the person

Plead with the person
Pray for return of the object
Worry
Pout
Feel guilty that someone took
something from you
Not know what to do
Run away

Stab the person
Kick the person
Punish the person
Shove the person

Verbal Aggression

Argue with the person
Trick the person
Shout at the person
Insult the person
Take the object back
Threaten the person
Tell someone about it
Make the person feel guilty
Ask others' help

Prosocial

Help the person reform
Feel sorry for the person
Forgive the person
Talk to the person
Be honest with the person
Think about what to do
Try to persuade the person
Let the person alone

From Communication strategies by M.E. Roloff in G.R. Miller (Ed.)
Explanations in Interpersonal Communication. Copyright © 1976 by Sage Publications, Inc.
Reprinted by permission of the publisher.

References

Chapter 1

Bateson, G. (1972). *Steps to an ecology of mind.* New York: Ballantine.

Bochner, A. P. (1985). Perspectives on inquiry: Representation, conversation, and reflection. In M. L. Knapp & G. R. Miller (Eds.), *Handbook of interpersonal communication* (pp. 27–58). Beverly Hills: Sage.

Dervin, B. (1983). Information as a User Construct: The Relevance of Perceived Information Needs to Synthesis and Interpretation. In S. A. Ward & L. J. Reed (Eds.), *Knowledge, Structure, and Use: Implications for Synthesis and Interpretation* (pp. 155–183). Philadelphia, PA: Temple University Press.

Kelly, G. (1955). *The psychology of personal constructs.* New York: Norton.

Krippendorff, K. (1975). Information theory. In G. Hanneman & W. McEwen (Eds.), *Communication and behavior* (pp. 164–178). Reading, MA: Addison-Wesley.

Miller, G. R. (1981). Tis the season to be jolly: A yuletide 1980 assessment of communication research. *Human Communication Research, 7,* 361–370.

Poole, M. S., & McPhee, R. D. (1985). Methodology in interpersonal communication research. In M. L. Knapp & G. R. Miller (Eds.), *Handbook of interpersonal communication* (pp. 100–170). Beverly Hills: Sage.

Popper, K. (1982). *The open universe: An argument for indeterminism.* Totowa, NY: Rowman and Littlefield.

Chapter 2

Abelson, R. (1976). Script in attitude formation and decision making. In J. Carroll & T. Payne (Eds.), *Cognition and social behavior* (pp. 33–45). Hillsdale, NJ: Erlbaum.

Berlo, D. K. (1977). Communication as process: Review and commentary. In B. D. Ruben (Ed.), *Communication yearbook 1* (pp. 11–27). Rutgers, NJ: Transaction Press.

Bochner, A. P. (1978). On taking ourselves seriously: An analysis of some persistent problems and promising directions in interpersonal research. *Human Communication Research, 4*, 179–191.

Buck, R. (1984). The *communication of emotion*. New York: Guilford Press.

Goffman, E. (1967). *Interaction ritual: Essays on face-to-face behaviors*. New York: Doubleday.

Hewitt, J. P., & Stokes, R. (1975). Disclaimers. *American Sociological Review, 40*, 1–11.

Jacobs, S., & Jackson, S. (1983). Speech act structure in conversation: Rational aspects of pragmatic coherence. In R. T. Craig & K. Tracy (Eds.), *Conversational coherence* (pp. 47–66). Beverly Hills: Sage.

Langer, E. (1978). Rethinking the role of thought in social interaction. In H. Harvey, W. Ickes, & R. Kidd (Eds.), *New directions in attribution research* (Vol. 2, pp. 35–58). Hillsdale, NJ: Erlbaum.

McLaughlin, M. L. (1984). *Conversation: How talk is organized*. Beverly Hills: Sage.

Millar, F. E., & Rogers, L. E. (1976). A relational approach to interpersonal communication. In G. R. Miller (Ed.), *Explorations in interpersonal communication* (pp. 87–103). Beverly Hills: Sage.

Miller, G. R. (1978). The current status of theory and research in interpersonal communication. *Human Communication Research, 4*, pp. 164–178.

Miller, G. R., & Steinberg, M. (1975). *Between people: A new analysis of interpersonal communication*. Chicago: Science Research Associates.

Parks, M. (1985). Interpersonal communication and the quest for personal competence. In M. L. Knapp & G. R. Miller (Eds.), *Handbook of interpersonal communication*. Beverly Hills: Sage.

Reardon, K. K. (1981). *Persuasion: Theory and context*. Beverly Hills: Sage.

Roloff, M. E. (1980). Self-awareness and the persuasion process. In M. E. Roloff & G. R. Miller (Eds.), *Persuasion: New directions in theory and research* (pp. 29–66). Beverly Hills: Sage.

Sanders, R. E. (1983). Tools for cohering discourse and their strategic utilization: Markers of structural connections and meaning relations. In R. T. Craig & K. Tracy (Eds.), *Conversational coherence* (pp. 67–80). Beverly Hills: Sage.

Scott, M. B., & Lyman, S. M. (1968). Accounts. *American Sociological Review, 33*, 46–62.

Snyder, M. (1974). Self-monitoring of expressive behavior. *Journal of Personality and Social Psychology, 30*, 526–537.

Watzlawick, P., Beavin, J., & Jackson, D. (1967). *Pragmatics of human communication: A study of interactional patterns, pathologies, and paradoxes*. New York: Norton.

Chapter 3

Argyle, M. (1967). *Psychology of interpersonal behavior*. Middlesex, England: Penguin Books.

Aristotle. *Rhetoric*. John Henry Freese (Trans.) (1967). Loeb Classical Library. Cambridge, MA: Harvard University Press.

Asch, S. E. (1951). Effects of group pressure upon the modification and distortion of judgments. In H. Guetzkow (Ed.), *Group leadership and men* (pp. 177–190). Pittsburgh: Carnegie Press.

Bales R. F. (1950). A set of categories for the analysis of small group interaction. *American Sociological Review, 15*, 257–263.

Bales, R. F. (1950). *Interactive process analysis: A method for the study of small groups*. Reading, MA: Addison-Wesley.

Bales, R. F. (1970). *Personality and interpersonal behavior*. New York: Holt, Rinehart and Winston.

Bandura, A. (1977). *Social learning theory*. Englewood Cliffs, NJ: Prentice-Hall.

Bateson, G. (1972). *Steps to an ecology of mind*. New York: Ballantine.

Bem, D. (1967). Self-perception: An alternative interpretation of cognitive dissonance phenomena. *Psychological Review, 74*, 183–200.

Berlo, D. (1960). *The process of communication*. New York: Holt, Rinehart and Winston.

Birdwhistell, R. L. (1952). *Introduction to kinesics*. Louisville, KY: University of Louisville Press.

Birdwhistell, R. L. (1970). *Kinesics and context*. Philadelphia: University of Pennsylvania Press.

Bogardus, E. S. (1925a). Measuring social distance. *Journal of Applied Psychology, 9*, 299–308.

Bogardus, E. S. (1925b). Social distance and its origins. *Journal of Applied Psychology, 9*, 216–277.

Brownell, J. (1983). Elwood Murray's interdisciplinary view. *Western Journal of Speech Communication, 47*, 244–252.

Campbell, G. (1823). *The philosophy of rhetoric*. Boston: Charles Ewer. (Originally published 1776.)

Chaffee, S. H. (1982). Mass media and interpersonal channels: Competitive, convergent or complimentary? In G. Gumpert & R. Cathcart (Eds.), *Inter/Media: Interpersonal communication in a media world* (2nd Ed.). New York: Oxford University Press.

Cicero. *DeOratore*. H. Rackham (Trans.) (1942). Loeb Classical Library. Cambridge, MA: Harvard University Press.

Cicero. *Orator* (1939). In J. L. Hendrickson and H. M. Hubbell (Trans. and Eds.), *Brutus and Orator*. Loeb Classical Library. Cambridge, MA: Harvard University Press.

Coleman, J. S., Katz, E., & Menzel, H. (1966). *Medical innovation: A diffusion study*. New York: Bobbs-Merrill.

Cooley, C. H. (1909). *Social organization*. New York: Scribner's.

Cooley, C. H. (1918). *The social process*. New York: Scribner's.

Dahling, R. L. (1962). Shannon's information theory: The spread of an idea. In E. Katz et al. (Eds.), *Studies of innovation and of communication to the public*. Stanford, CA: Institute for Communication Research.

De Quincey, T. (1877). *Beauties selected from the writings of Thomas De Quincey*. New York: Hurd & Houghton.

Deutsch, M., & Krauss, R. M. (1965). *Theories in social psychology*. New York: Basic Books.

Doob, L. W. (1947). The behavior of attitudes. *Psychological Review, 54,* 135–156.

Ekman, P., & Friesen, W. (1969). The repertoire of nonverbal behavior categories, origins, usage and coding. *Semiotica, 1,* 48–49.

Ekman, P., Friesen, W., & Ellsworth, P. (1972). *Emotion in the human face.* Elmsford, NY: Pergamon Press.

Ewbank, H. L. (1964). The art of conversing: Informal speech education, 1828–1860. *Today's Speech, 12,* 7–9 & 36.

Festinger, L. (1957). *A theory of cognitive dissonance.* Evanston, IL: Row Peterson.

Festinger, L. (1954). A theory of social comparison processes. *Human Relations, 7,* 117–140.

Fishbein, M. (1963). An investigation of the relationship between beliefs about an object and an attitude toward that object. *Human Relations, 16,* 233–240.

Fishbein, M. (1967). *Readings in attitude theory and measurement.* New York: John Wiley.

Gerbner, G., & Gross, L. (1976a). Living with television: The violent profile. *Journal of Communication, 26,* 173–199.

Gerbner, G., & Gross, L. (1976b). The scary world of television. *Psychology Today, 89,* 41–45.

Gerbner, G., Gross, L., Signorielli, N., & Morgan, M. (1980). Aging with television: Images on television drama and conceptions of social reality. *Journal of Communication, 30,* 37–47.

Goffman, E. (1961). *Encounters: Two studies in the sociology of interaction.* Indianapolis, MI: Bobbs-Merrill.

Goffman, E. (1963). *Behavior in public places.* New York: Free Press.

Goffman, E. (1967). *Interaction ritual: Essay on face-to-face behavior.* Garden City, NJ: Doubleday.

Goffman, E. (1971). *Relations in public.* New York: Basic Books.

Golden, J. L., Berquist, G. E., & Coleman, W. E. (1976). *The rhetoric of Western thought.* Dubuque, IA: Kendall/Hunt.

Hall, E. T. (1959). *The silent language.* Greenwich, CT: Fawcett.

Hall, E. T. (1966). *The hidden dimension.* New York: Random House.

Harper, N. L. (1979). *Human communication theory: The history of a paradigm.* Rochelle Park, NJ: Hayden.

Heider, F. (1958). *The psychology of interpersonal relations.* New York: Wiley.

Hovland, C. I., Janis, I. L., & Kelley, H. H. (1953). *Communication and persuasion: Psychological studies of opinion change.* New Haven, CT: Yale University Press.

Jones, E. E., & Davis, K. E. (1965). From acts to dispositions: The attribution process in person perception. In L. Berkowitz (Ed.), *Advances in experimental social psychology* (Vol. 2, pp. 219–266). New York: Academic Press.

Jourard, S. (1964). *The transparent self.* New York: Van Nostrand Reinhold.

Katz, E., & Lazarsfeld, P. (1966). *Personal influence.* New York: Free Press.

Kelley, H. H. (1973). The process of causal attribution. *American Psychologist, 28,* 107–128.

Kiesler, C. A., Collins, B. E., & Miller, N. (1969). *Attitude change: A critical analysis of theoretical approaches.* New York: Wiley.

Laing, R. D. (1969). *Self and others.* London: Tavistock.

Laing, R. D., Phillipson, H., & Lee, A. R. (1966). *Interpersonal perception.* New York: Springer.

Laing, R. D. (1967). *The politics of experience.* New York: Pantheon Books.

LaPiere, R. T., & Farnsworth, P. R. (1936). *Social psychology.* New York: McGraw-Hill.

Lavine, T. Z. (1984). *From Socrates to Sartre: The philosophic quest.* New York: Bantam Books.

Lewin, K. (1935). *A dynamic theory of personality.* New York: McGraw-Hill.

Lewin, K. (1947a). Frontiers in group dynamics. *Human Relations, 1,* 1–28.

Lewin, K. (1947b). Frontiers in group dynamics II. *Human Relations, 1,* 143–153.

Littlejohn, S. W. (1983). *Theories of human communication.* Belmont, CA: Wadsworth.

Lumsdaine, A. A., & Janis, I. L. (1953). Resistance to "counterpropaganda" produced by one-sided and two-sided "propaganda" presentations. *Public Opinion Quarterly, 17,* 311–318.

McDougall, W. (1908). *An introduction to social psychology.* London: Methuen.

Mead, G. H. (1934). *Mind, self and society.* Chicago: University of Chicago Press.

Miller, G. R. (1983). Taking stock of a discipline. *Journal of Communication, 33,* 31–41.

Murray, E. (1948). Personality, communications, and interpersonal relations. *The Southern Speech Journal, 13,* 79–83.

Oliver, R. T. (1961a). Conversational rules. *Today's Speech, 9,* 19–22.

Oliver, R. T. (1961b). Conversation and personality. *Today's Speech, 9,* 2–3 & 32.

Ogden, C. K., & Richards, I. A. (1923). *The meaning of meaning.* New York: Harcourt Brace Jovanovich.

Plato. *Phaedrus.* W. C. Helmhold & W. G. Rabinowitz (Trans.) (1956). Library of Liberal Arts. New York: Liberal Arts Press.

Quintilian. *Institutes of Oratory.* J. S. Watson (Trans.) (1888). Bohn Library. London: G. Bell.

Reardon, K. K., & Rogers, E. (1986). Interpersonal and mass communication: A false dichotomy. Unpublished manuscript, University of Southern California.

Roberts, D. F., & Maccoby, N. (1984). Effects of mass communication. Unpublished manuscript. Stanford University.

Rogers, E. (1983). *Diffusion of innovations.* (3rd Ed.). New York: Free Press.

Rogers, E., & Chaffee, S. (1983). Communication as an academic discipline. *Journal of Communication, 33,* 18–30.

Rokeach, M. (1968). *Beliefs, attitudes and values: A theory of organization and change.* San Francisco: Jossey-Bass.

Ross, E. A. (1908). *The foundations of social psychology.* New York: Macmillan.

Sahakian, W. S. (1982). *History and systems of social psychology.* (2nd Ed.) New York: Hemisphere.

Schramm, W. (1959). Comments on the state of communication research. *Public Opinion Quarterly, 23,* 6–9.

Shannon, C. E. (1948). A mathematical theory of communication. *Bell Systems Technical Journal, 28,* 379–423.

Shannon, C. E., & Weaver, W. (1949). *The mathematical theory of communication.* Urbana: University of Illinois Press.

Sherif, M. (1936). *The psychology of social norms.* New York: Harper & Row.

Simons, H. (1980). Are scientists rhetors in disguise? An analysis of discursive processes within scientific communities . In E. G. White (Ed.), *Rhetoric in transition: Studies in the nature and usage of rhetoric.* University Park: Pennsylvania State University Press.

Spencer, H. (1953). *The philosophy of style.* New York: Pageant Press. (Originally published 1882.)

Sullivan, H. S. (1953). Interpersonal theory of psychiatry. H. S. Perry & M. L. Gawel (Eds.). New York: Norton.

Thibaut, J. W., & Kelley, H. H. (1959). *The social psychology of groups.* New York: Wiley.

Thurstone, L. L. (1928). Attitudes can be measured. *American Journal of Sociology, 33,* 529–554.

Thurstone, L. L., & Chave, E. J. (1929). *The measurement of attitude: A psychological method and some experiments with a scale for measuring attitude toward the church.* Chicago: University of Chicago Press.

Watson, J. B. (1925). *Behaviorism.* New York: Norton.

Watzlawick, P., Beavin, J., & Jackson, D. D. (1967). *Pragmatics of human communication: A study of interactional patterns, pathologies and paradoxes.* New York: Norton.

Whately, R. (1855). *Elements of rhetoric.* Boston: James Monroe. (Originally published 1828).

Wilder, C. (1979). The Palo Alto Group: Difficulties and directions of the interactional view for human communication. *Human Communication Research, 5,* 171–186.

Chapter 4

Allen, R., & Brown, K. (1976). *Developing communication competence in children.* Skokie, IL: National Textbook Co.

Alvy, K. (1973). The development of listener-adapted communications in grade-school children from different social-class backgrounds. *Genetic Psychology Monographs, 87,* 33–104.

Bernstein, B. (1958). Some sociological determinants of perception. *British Journal of Sociology, 9,* 159–174.

Bernstein, B. (1959). A public language: Some sociological implications of a linguistic form. *British Journal of Sociology, 10,* 311–326.

Bernstein, B. (1960). Language and social class. *British Journal of Sociology, 11,* 271–276.

Bernstein, B. (1971). *Class, codes and control* (Vol. 1). London: Routledge & Kegan Paul.

Burleson, B. (1986). Communication skills and childhood peer relationships: An overview. In M. L. McLaughlin (Ed.), *Communication Yearbook 9* (pp. 143–180). Beverly Hills: Sage.

Chomsky, N. (1969). *Syntactic structures.* The Hague: Mouton.

Chomsky, N. (1975). *Reflections on language.* New York: Pantheon Books.

Clark, E. (1978). Strategies for communicating. *Child Development, 19,* 953–959.

Clark, R. A. (1977). What's the use of imitation? *Journal of Child Language, 4,* 341–358.

Dale, P. (1972). *Language development: Structure and function.* Hinsdale, IL: Dryden Press.

Delia, J. G., & Clark, R. A. (1977). Cognitive complexity, social perception, and the development of listener-adapted communication in six-, eight-, ten-, and twelve-year-old boys. *Communication Monographs, 44,* 326–345.

Delia, J. G., & O'Keefe, B. J. (1976). Social construal processes in the development of communicative competence. Mimeograph, Department of Speech Communication, University of Illinois at Urbana-Champaign.

DePaulo, B., & Jordan, A. (1982). Age changes in deceiving and detecting deceit. In R. Feldman (Ed.), *Development of nonverbal behavior in children.* New York: Springer-Verlag.

Ekman, P., & Friesen (1974). Detecting deception from the body or face. *Journal of Personality and Social Psychology, 29,* 288–298.

Ekman, P., Friesen, W. V., & Ellsworth, P. (1972). *Emotion in the human face.* Elmsford, NY: Pergamon Press.

Elliot, A. J. (1981). *Child language.* Cambridge, England: Cambridge University Press.

Elliot, N. (1984). Communicative development from birth. *Western Journal of Speech Communication, 48,* 184–196.

Flavell, J. (1963). *The developmental psychology of Jean Piaget.* Princeton, NJ: Van Nostrand.

Haslett, B. (1984). Acquiring conversational competence. *Western Journal of Speech Communication, 48,* 107–124.

Irwin, E. (1975). Play and language development. *The Speech Teacher, 24,* 15–23.

Johnson, F. (1977). Role-taking and referential communication abilities in first- and third-grade children. *Human Communication Research, 3,* 135–145.

McLeod, J. M., & Chaffee, S. R. (1971). The construction of social reality. In J. Tedeschi (Ed.), *The Social influence process.* Chicago: Adline-Atherton.

McNeil, D. (1966). Developmental psycholinguistics. In F. Smith & G. Miller (Eds.), *The genesis of language.* Cambridge, MA: M.I.T. Press.

Piaget, J. (1959). *The language and thought of the child.* New York: Humanities Press.

Piaget, J. (1960). *The moral judgment of the child.* Glencoe, IL: Free Press.

Reardon, K. (1982). Conversational deviance: A structural model. *Human Communication Research, 9,* 59–74.

Reardon-Boynton, K., & Henke, L. (1978). Conversational expansion in young children. *Communication Education, 27,* 202–211.

Robinson, W. P. (1981). Some problems for theory, methodology, and methods for the 1980s. In W. Robinson (Ed.), *Communication in development.* New York: Academic Press.

Robinson, W. P., & Rackstraw, S. J. (1978). Social class differences in posing questions for answers. *Sociology, 12,* 265–280.

Rodnick, R., & Wood, B. (1973). The communication strategies of children. *The Speech Teacher, 22,* 114–125.

Rosenthal, R., & DePaulo, B. (1979). Sex differences in accommodation in nonverbal communication. In R. Rosenthal (Ed.), *Skill in nonverbal communication* (pp. 68–103). Cambridge, MA: Oelgeschlager, Gunn, & Hain.

Sachs, J., Goldman, J., & Chaille, C. (1983). Planning in pretend play: Using language to coordinate narrative development. In A. Pellegrini & T. Yawkey (Eds.), *The development of oral and written language in social contexts.* Norwood, NJ: Ablex Publishing Corp.

Schaeffer, H. R. (1979). Acquiring the concept of dialogue. In M. Bernstein & W. Kesson (Eds.), *Psychological development from infancy: Image to intentions* (pp. 219–225). Hillsdale, NJ: Earlbaum.

Shennum, W., & Bugental, D. (1982). The development of control over affective expression in nonverbal behavior. In R. Feldman (Ed.), *Development of nonverbal behavior in children*. New York: Springer-Verlag.

Skinner, B. F. (1957). *Verbal behavior*. New York: Appleton-Century-Crofts.

Stone, V., & Chaffee, S. (1970). Family communication patterns and source-message orientation. *Journalism Quarterly, 47*, 239–246.

Vygotsky, L. (1962). *Thought and language*. Cambridge, MA: M.I.T. Press. (Originally published 1934.)

Wood, B. (1981). *Children and communication*. Englewood Cliffs, NJ: Prentice-Hall.

Zajonc, R. B. (1980). Feeling and thinking: Preferences need no inferences. *American Psychologist, 35*, 151–175.

Chapter 5

Andersen, J. F. (1984). Nonverbal cues of immediacy and relational affect. Paper presented at the Central States Speech Association Convention, Chicago.

Andersen, J. F., Andersen, P. A., & Jensen, A. D. (1979). The measurement of nonverbal immediacy. *Journal of Applied Communication, 7*, 153–180.

Andersen, P. A. (1984) An arousal-valence model of nonverbal immediacy exchange. Paper presented at the Central States Speech Association Convention, Chicago.

Applegate, J. L. (1980). Adaptive communication in educational contexts: A study of teachers' communicative strategies. *Communication Education, 29*, 158–170.

Aronfreed, J. (1968). *Conduct and conscience*. New York: Academic Press.

Baird, J. E., & Bradley, P. H. (1979). Styles of management and communication: A comparative study of men and women. *Communication Monographs, 46*, 101–111.

Berger, C. R., & Roloff, M. E. (1982). Thinking about friends and lovers: Social cognition and relational trajectories. In C. R. Berger & M. E. Roloff (Eds.), *Social Cognition and Communication* (pp. 151–192). Beverly Hills: Sage.

Bochner, A. P., & Kelly, C. W. (1974). Interpersonal competence: Rationale, philosophy and implementation of a conceptual framework. *Speech Teacher, 23*, 270–301.

Bostrom, R., & Waldhart, E. (1980). Components of listening behavior: The role of short-term memory. *Human Communication Research, 6*, 211–227.

Bradac, J. J., Bowers, J. W., & Courtright, J. A. (1979). Three language variables in communication research: Intensity, immediacy, and diversity. *Human Communication Research, 5*, 257–265.

Burgoon, J. K., & Koper, R. J. (1984). Nonverbal and relational communication associated with reticence. *Human Communication Research, 10*, 601–627.

Cegala, D. J. (1981). Interaction involvement: A cognitive dimension of communication competence. *Communication Education, 30*, 109–121.

Cegala, D. J., Savage, G. T., Brunner, C. C., & Conrad, A. B. (1982). An elaboration of the meaning of interaction involvement: Toward the development of a theoretical concept. *Communication Monographs, 49*, 229–248.

Christopher, R. C. (1983). *The Japanese mind*. New York: Fawcett Columbine.

Clark, R. A., & Delia, J. (1976). The development of functional persuasive skills in childhood and early adolescence. *Child Development, 47*, 1008–1014.

Clark, R. A., & Delia, J. (1977). Cognitive complexity, social perspective taking and functional persuasive skills in second- to ninth-grade children. *Human Communication Research, 3*, 128–134.

Cody, M. J., & McLaughlin, M. L. (1985). The situation as a construct in communication research: Review and synthesis. In M. L. Knapp & G. R. Miller (Eds.), *Handbook of interpersonal communication* (pp. 263–313). Beverly Hills: Sage.

Courtright, J. A., Millar, F. E., & Rogers-Millar (1979). Domineeringness and dominance: Replication and expansion. *Communication Monographs, 46,* 179–192.

Daly, J., & McCroskey, J. C. (1984). *Avoiding communication: Shyness, reticence, and communication apprehension.* Beverly Hills: Sage.

Delia, J., & Clark, R. A. (1977). Cognitive-complexity, social perception, and listener-adapted communication in six-, eight-, ten-, and twelve-year-old boys. *Communication Monographs, 44,* 326–345.

Delia, J., Kline, S., & Burleson, B. (1979). The development of persuasive communication strategies in kindergarten through twelfth-graders. *Communication Monographs, 46,* 241–256.

Deutsch, F. (1974). Female preschoolers' perceptions of affective responses and interpersonal behavior in video-taped episodes. *Developmental Psychology, 10,* 733–740.

Deutsch, F., & Madle, R. A. (1975). Empathy: Historic and current conceptualizations, measurement, and a cognitive theoretical perspective. *Human Development, 18,* 267–287.

Douglas, W. (1983). Scripts and self-monitoring: When does being a high self-monitor really make a difference? *Human Communication Research, 10,* 81–96.

Fenigstein, A. (1979). Self-consciousness, self-attention, and social interaction. *Journal of Personality and Social Psychology, 37,* 75–86.

Flavell, J. H., Botkin, P.T., Fry, C. L., Jr., Wright, J. W., & Jarvis, P. E. (1968). *The development of role-taking and communication skills in children.* New York: Wiley.

Kalisch, B. (1973). What is empathy? *American Journal of Nursing, 73,* 1548–1552.

Katz, R. L. (1963). *Empathy: Its nature and uses.* London: Free Press of Glencoe.

Kelly, G. A. (1955). *The psychology of personal constructs.* New York: Norton.

Kohler, W. (1929). *Gestalt psychology.* New York: Liveright.

Kohler, W. (1947). *Gestalt psychology.* New York: New American Library of World Literature.

McCormack, M. H. (1984). *What they don't teach you at Harvard Business School.* New York: Bantam Books.

McCroskey, J. C. (1977). Oral communication apprehension: A summary of recent theory and research. *Human Communication Research, 4,* 78–96.

McCroskey, J. C. (1982). Oral communication apprehension: A reconceptualization. In M. Burgoon (Ed.), *Communication yearbook 6.* Beverly Hills: Sage.

McCroskey, J. C., & Beatty, M. J. (1984). Communication apprehension and state anxiety. *Communication Monographs, 51,* 79–84.

McCroskey, J. C., Daly, J. A., & Sorensen, G. A. (1976). Personality correlates of communication apprehension: A research note. *Human Communication Research, 4,* 376–380.

McLaughlin, M., & Cody, M. (1982). Awkward silences: Behavioral antecedents and consequents of the conversational lapse. *Human Communication Research, 8,* 299–316.

Mead, G. H. (1934). *Mind, self, and society.* Chicago: University of Chicago Press.

Miller, G. R., Boster, F., Roloff, M. E., Seibold, D. (1977). Compliance-gaining message strategies: A typology and some findings concerning effects of situational differences. *Communication Monographs, 44,* 37–51.

Miller, G. R., de Turck, M. A., & Kalbfleisch, P. J. (1983). Self-monitoring, rehearsal and descriptive communication. *Human Communication Research, 10,* 97–118.

Norton, R. (1983). *Communication style.* Beverly Hills: Sage.

O'Keefe, B. J., & Delia, J. G. (1979). Construct comprehensiveness and cognitive complexity as predictors of the number and strategic adaption of arguments and appeals in persuasive messages. *Communication Monographs, 46,* 321–340.

O'Keefe, B. J., & Delia, J. G. (1982). Impression formation and message production. In M. E. Roloff & C. R. Berger (Eds.), *Social cognition and communication* (pp. 33–72). Beverly Hills: Sage.

Parks, M. R. (1985). Interpersonal communication and the quest for personal competence. In M. L. Knapp & G. R. Miller (Eds.), *Handbook of interpersonal communication* (pp. 171–204). Beverly Hills: Sage.

Philips, G. M. (1968). Reticence pathology of the normal speaker. *Speech Monographs, 35,* 39–49.

Philips, G. M., & Metzger, N. J. (1973). The reticence syndrome: Some theoretical considerations about etiology and treatment. *Speech Monographs, 40,* 220–230.

Reardon, K. K. (1982). Conversational deviance: A structural model. *Human Communication Research, 9,* 59–74.

Roloff, M. E. (1980). Self-awareness and the persuasion process. In M. E. Roloff & G. R. Miller (Eds.), *Persuasion: New directions in theory and research.* Beverly Hills: Sage.

Roloff, M. E., & Kellerman, K. (1984). Judgments of interpersonal competence: How you know, what you know and who you know. In R. N. Bostrom (Ed.), *Competence in communication.* Beverly Hills: Sage.

Rothenberg, B. (1970). Children's social sensitivity and their relationship to interpersonal competence, intrapersonal comfort, and intellectual level. *Child Development, 2,* 335–350.

Snyder, M. (1974). Self-monitoring of expressive behavior. *Journal of Personality and Social Psychology, 30,* 526–537.

Snyder, M. (1979). Self-monitoring processes. In L. Berkowitz (Ed.), *Advances in experimental social psychology* (Vol. 12). New York: Academic Press.

Spitzberg, B. H., & Cupach, W. R. (1984). *Interpersonal communication competence.* Beverly Hills: Sage.

Spitzberg, B. H., & Hecht, M. L. (1984). Component model of relational competence. *Human Communication Research, 10,* 575–600.

Stotland, E., Sherman, S. E., & Shaver, K. G. (1971). *Empathy and birth order.* Lincoln: University of Nebraska Press.

Sypher, B. D., & Sypher, H. E. (1983). Perceptions of communication ability: Self-monitoring in an organizational setting. *Personality and Social Psychology Bulletin, 9,* 297–304.

Turner, R. (1980). Self-consciousness and memory of trait terms. *Personality and Social Psychology Bulletin, 6,* 273–277.

Van Zandt, H. F. (1970). How to negotiate in Japan. *Harvard Business Review,* Nov.–Dec.

Wiemann, J. M. (1977). Explication and test of a model of communicative competence. *Human Communication Research, 3,* 195–213.

Wiemann, J. M., & Backlund, P. (1980). Current theory and research in communicative competence. *Review of Educational Research, 50,* 185–189.

Chapter 6

Andersen, J. F. (1984). Nonverbal cues of immediacy and relational affect. Paper presented at the Central States Speech Association Convention, Chicago.

Andersen, P. A. (1984). An arousal-valence model of nonverbal immediacy exchange. Paper presented at the Central States Speech Association Convention, Chicago.

Argyle, M., & Cook, M. (1976). *Gaze and mutual gaze.* Cambridge, England: Cambridge University Press.

Berger, C. R. (1979). Beyond initial interaction: Uncertainty, understanding, and the development of interpersonal relationships. In H. Giles and R. St. Clair (Eds.), *Language and social psychology* (pp. 439–99). Oxford, England: Blackwell.

Berger, C. R., & Calabrese, R. J. (1975). Some explorations in initial interaction and beyond: Toward a developmental theory of interpersonal communication. *Human Communication Research, 1,* 99–112.

Buck, R. (1975). Nonverbal communication of affect in children. *Journal of Personality and Social Psychology, 31,* 644–653.

Buck, R. (1984). *The communication of emotion.* New York: Guilford.

Buck, R., Baron, R., & Barrette, D. (1982). The temporal organization of spontaneous nonverbal expression: A segmentation analysis. *Journal of Personality and Social Psychology, 42,* 506–517.

Buck, R., Baron, R., Goodman, N., & Shapiro, N. (1980). The utilization of spontaneous nonverbal behavior in a study of emotion communication. *Journal of Personality and Social Psychology, 39,* 522–529.

Burgoon, J. K. (1985). Nonverbal signals. In M. L. Knapp & G. R. Miller (Eds.), *Handbook of interpersonal communication* (pp. 344–390). Beverly Hills: Sage.

Capella, J. N. (1985). The management of conversations. In M. L. Knapp & G. R. Miller (Eds.), *Handbook of interpersonal communication* (pp. 393–438). Beverly Hills: Sage.

Cody, M. J., & McLaughlin, M. L. (1984). Models for the sequential construction of accounting episodes: Situational and interactional constraints on message selection and evaluation. Unpublished manuscript, Department of Communication Arts and Sciences. University of Southern California.

Cody, M. J., & McLaughlin, M. L. (1985). Models for the sequential construction of accounting episodes: Situational and interactional constraints on message evaluation. In R. L. Street & J. N. Capella (Eds.), *Sequence and pattern in communicative behavior.* London: Edward Arnold Press.

Cronen, V. E., Pearce, W. B., & Harris, L. M. (1982). The coordinated management of meaning: A theory of communication. In F.E.X. Dance (Ed.), *Human communication theory: Comparative essays.* New York: Harper & Row.

Cronen, V. E., Pearce, W. B., & Snavely, L. (1979). A theory of rule-structure and types of episodes and a study of perceived enmeshments in undesired repetitive patterns (UREPS). In D. Nimmo (Ed.), *Communication yearbook 3.* New Brunswick, NJ: Transaction Press.

Cushman, D. P. (1977). The rules perspective as a theoretical basis for the study of human communication. *Communication Quarterly, 25,* 30–45.

Delia, J. G., Clark, R. A., & Switzer, D. E. (1979). The content of informal conversations as a function of interactants' interpersonal cognitive complexity. *Communication Monographs, 46,* 274–281.

Dittman, A. (1978). The role of body movement in communication. In A. Siegman & S. Feldstein (Eds.), *Nonverbal communication and behavior* (pp. 69–95). Hillsdale, NJ: Erlbaum.

Duncan, S. D. (1972). Some signals and rules for taking speaking turns in conversations. *Journal of Personality and Social Psychology, 23,* 283–292.

Duncan, S. D., Bruner, L. J., & Fiske, D. (1979). Strategy signal in face-to-face interaction. *Journal of Personality and Social Psychology, 37,* 301–313

Eakins, B. W., & Eakins, R. G. (1978). *Sex differences in human communication.* Boston: Houghton Mifflin.

Ekman, P. (1978). Facial expression. In A. Siegman & S. Feldstein (Eds.), *Nonverbal communication and behavior* (pp. 97–116). Hillsdale, NJ: Erlbaum.

Exline, R. V., Ellyson, S. L., & Long, B. (1975). Visual behavior as an aspect of power role relationships. In P. Pilner, L. Kramer, & T. Alloway (Eds.), *Advances in the study of communication and affect* (Vol. 2). New York: Plenum.

Exline, R., & Fehr, B. (1978). Applications of semiosis to the study of visual interaction. In A. Siegman & S. Feldstein (Eds.), *Nonverbal communication and behavior* (pp. 117–158). Hillsdale, NJ: Erlbaum.

Fisher, B. A., and Drecksel, G. L. (1983). A cyclical model of developing relationships: A study of relational control interaction. *Communication Monographs, 50,* 68–78.

Fisher, B. A. (1983). Differential effects of sexual composition in interactional context on interaction patterns and dyads. *Human Communication Research, 9,* 225–38.

Fitzpatrick, M. A. (1977). A typological approach to communication in relationships. In B. Rubin (Ed.) *Communication yearbook 1* (pp. 263–275). New Brunswick, NJ: Transaction Press.

Fitzpatrick, M. A., & Best, P. (1979). Dyadic adjustment in relational types: Consensus, cohesion, affectional expression and satisfaction in enduring relationships. *Communication Monographs, 46,* 167–178.

Frentz, T. (1976). A generative approach to episodic structure. Paper presented at the Western Speech Association Convention, San Francisco.

Grice, H. (1975). Logic and conversation. In P. Cole and J. Morgan (Eds.), *Syntax and semantics,* Vol. 3: *Speech acts* (pp. 45–46). New York: Academic Press.

Goffman, E. (1959). *Presentation of self in everyday life.* New York: Doubleday/Anchor Books.

Hall, E. T. (1959). *The silent language.* Greenwich, CT: Fawcett.

Hall, E. T. (1963). A system for the notation of proxemic behavior. *American Anthropologist, 65,* 1003–1026.

Hall, E. T. (1966). *The hidden dimension.* New York: Random House.

Harre, R., & Secord, P. (1973). *The explanation of social behavior.* Totowa, NJ: Littlefield, Adams.

Henley, N. M. (1977). *Body politics; Power, sex and nonverbal communication.* Englewood Cliffs, NJ: Prentice-Hall.

Hewitt, J., & Stokes, R. (1975). Disclaimers. *American Sociological Review, 40,* 1–11.

Hocking, J. E., Bouchner, J., Kaminski, E. P., & Miller, G. R. (1979). Detecting deceptive communication from verbal, visual, and paralinguistic cues. *Human Communication Research, 6,* 33–46.

Jacobs, S., & Jackson, S. (1983). Speech act structure in conversation. In R. Craig & K. Tracy (Eds.), *Conversational coherence: Form, structure, and strategy.* (pp. 47–66). Beverly Hills: Sage.

Knapp, M. L., & Camadena, M. E. (1979). Telling it like it isn't: A review of theory and research on deceptive communication. *Human Communication Research, 5,* 270–285.

McLaughlin, M. (1984). *Conversation: How talk is organized.* Beverly Hills: Sage.

McLaughlin, M. L., Cody, M. J., Kane, M. L., & Robey, C. S. (1981). Sex differences in story receipt and story sequencing behaviors in dyadic conversations. *Human Communication Research, 7,* 99–116.

Millar, F., & Rogers-Millar, E. (1976). A relational approach. In G. R. Miller (Ed.), *Explorations in interpersonal communication* (pp. 87–103). Beverly Hills: Sage.

Mills, C. W. (1940). Situational actions and vocabularies of motives. *American Sociological Review, 5,* 904–913.

Motley, M. T., Camden, C. T., & Baars, B. J. (1979). Personality and situational influences upon verbal slips: A laboratory test of Freudian and prearticulatory editing hypotheses. *Human Communication Research, 5,* 195–202.

Patterson, M. (1978). The role of space in social interaction. In A. Siegman & S. Feldstein (Eds.), *Nonverbal communication and behavior* (pp. 265–290). New York: Wiley.

Pearce, W. B., & Cronen, V. E. (1978). *Communication, meaning, and action: The creation of social relations.* New York: Praeger.

Reardon, K. K. (1982). Conversational deviance: structural model. *Human Communication Research, 9,* 59–74.

Reardon, K. K., & Fairhurst, G. T. (1979). Elaboration of the concept "rule": A case study with the military. Paper presented at the International Communication Association Convention, Philadelphia.

Rogers, E. M., & Kincaid, D. L. (1981). *Communication networks: Toward a new paradigm for research.* New York: Free Press.

Roloff, M. (1981). *Interpersonal communication.* Beverly Hills: Sage.

Scheflen, A. E. (1972). *Body language and social order: Communication.* Englewood Cliffs, NJ: Prentice-Hall.

Schegloff, E. Jefferson, G., & Sacks, H. (1977). The preference for self-correction in the organization of repair in conversation. *Language, 53,* 361–382.

Scott, M. B., & Lyman, S. (1968). Accounts. *American Sociological Review, 33,* 46–62.

Searle, J. (1969). *Speech acts: An essay in the philosophy of language.* Cambridge: The University Press.

Shimanoff, S. B. (1980). *Communication rules.* Beverly Hills: Sage.

Stech, E. (1979). A grammar of conversation. *Human Communication Research, 5,* 158–170.

Wilson, T. P., Wiemann, J. M., & Zimmerman, D. H. (1984). Models of turn-taking in conversational interaction. *Journal of Language and Social Psychology, 3,* 159–183.

Zahn, C. (1984). A reexamination of conversational repair. *Communication Monographs, 51,* 56–66.

Zimmerman, D. H., & West, C. (1975). Sex roles, interruptions and silences in conversation. In B. Thorne & N. Nenley (Eds.), *Language and sex: Difference and dominance* (pp. 105–129). Rawley, MA: Newbury House.

Chapter 7

Asch, S. E. (1952). *Social psychology.* Englewood Cliffs, NJ: Prentice-Hall.

Averill, J. (1980). A constructivist view of emotion. In R. Plutchik & H. Kellerman (Eds.), *Emotion: Theory, research and experience* (Vol. 1). New York: Academic Press.

Ball-Rokeach, S., Rokeach, M., & Grube, J. (1984). *The great American values test.* New York: Free Press.

Bandura, A. (1977). *Social learning theory.* Englewood Cliffs, NJ: Prentice-Hall.

Bell, R. A., & Daly, J. A. (1984). The affinity-seeking function of communication. *Communication Monographs, 51,* 91–115.

Berger, C. R. (1985). Social power and interpersonal communication. In M. L. Knapp & G. R. Miller (Eds.), *Handbook of interpersonal communication* (pp. 439–499). Beverly Hills: Sage.

Boster, F. J., Stiff, J. B., & Reynolds, R. A. (1983). Do persons respond differently to inductively derived and deductively derived lists of compliance-gaining message strategies? A reply to Wiseman and Schenck-Hamlin, presented to the International Communication Association, Dallas.

Bostrom, R. (1983). *Persuasion.* Englewood Cliffs, NJ: Prentice-Hall.

Brehm, J. A. (1966). *Theory of psychological reactance.* New York: Academic Press.

Buck, R. (1984). *The communication of emotion.* New York: Guilford Press.

Burgoon, M., Dillard, J. P., & Doran, N. E. (1983). Friendly and unfriendly persuasion. *Human Communication Research, 10,* 283–294.

Burleson, B. (1984). Age, social-cognitive development, and the use of comforting. *Communication Monographs, 51,* 140–153.

Capella, J., & Folger, J. (1980). An information-processing explanation of attitude-behavior inconsistency. In D. Cushman & R. McPhee (Eds.), *Message-attitude-behavior relationship.* New York: Academic Press.

Clark, M. S., & Isen, A. M. (1982). Toward understanding the relationship between feeling states and social behavior. In A. H. Hastord & A. M. Isen (Eds.), *Cognitive social psychology.* New York: Elsevier/North Holland.

Cushman, D., & McPhee, R. (Eds.) (1980). *Message-attitude-behavior relationship.* New York: Academic Press.

de Sousa, R. (1980). Self-deceptive emotion. In A. Rorty (Ed.), *Explaining emotions.* Berkeley: University of California Press.

deTurck, M. A. (1985). A transactional analysis of compliance-gaining behavior. *Human Communication Research, 12,* 54–78.

Festinger, L. (1954). A theory of social comparison processes. *Human Relations, 7,* 117–140.

Festinger, L. (1957). *A theory of cognitive dissonance.* New York: Harper & Row.

Gerbner, G. (1978). The dynamics of cultural resistance. In G. Tuchman (Ed.), *Hearth and home: Images of women in the mass media* (pp. 46–50). New York: Oxford University Press.

Goffman, E. (1959). *Presentation of self in everyday life.* New York: Doubleday/Anchor Books.

Goffman, E. (1976). On face-work: an analysis of ritual elements in social interaction. In J. E. Combs & M. W. Mansfield (Eds.), *Drama in life: The use of communication in society.* New York: Hastings House.

Hecht, M. L. (1984). Persuasive efficacy: a study of the relationship among types and degrees of change, message strategies, and satisfying communication. *Western Journal of Speech Communication, 48,* 373–389.

Heider, F. (1958). *The psychology of interpersonal relations.* New York: Wiley.

Hewes, D., Graham, M., Doelger, J., & Pavitt, C. (1985). Second-guessing message interpretation in social networks. *Human Communication Research, 11,* 299–334.

Isen, A. M., Shalker, T. E., Clark, M. S., & Karp, L. (1978). Affect, accessibility of material in memory and behavior: A cognition loop? *Journal of Personality and Social Psychology, 36,* 1–12.

Kelman, H. (1961). Processes of opinion change. *Public Opinion Quarterly, 25,* 57–58.

Knapp, M., & Camadena, M. (1979). Telling it like it isn't. *Human Communication Research, 5,* 270–285.

LaPiere, R. (1934). Attitudes vs. action. *Social Forces, 13,* 230–237.

Mandler, G. (1975). *Mind and emotion.* New York: Wiley.

Marwell, G., & Schmitt, D. (1967). Dimensions of compliance-gaining behavior: An empirical analysis. *Sociometry, 30,* 350–364.

Maslow, A. H. (1970). *Motivation and personality.* 2d ed. New York: Harper & Row.

McGuire, W. (1964). Inducing resistance to persuasion: some contemporary approaches. In L. Berkowitz (Ed.), *Advances in experimental and social psychology* (Vol. 1.). New York: Academic Press.

Miller, G. R. (1980). On being persuaded: some basic distinctions. In G. R. Miller and M. E. Roloff (Eds.), *Persuasion: New directions in theory and research* (pp. 11–28). Beverly Hills: Sage.

Miller, G. R., Boster, F., Roloff, M. E., & Seibold, D. (1977). Compliance-gaining message strategies: A typology and some findings concerning effects of situational differences. *Communication Monographs, 44,* 37–51.

Miller, G. R., & Burgoon, M. E. (1973). *New techniques of persuasion.* New York: Harper & Row.

Miller, G. R., & Roloff, M. E. (1980). *Persuasion: New directions in theory and research.* Beverly Hills: Sage.

O'Keefe, D. (1980). The relationship of attitudes and behavior: A constructivist analysis. In D. Cushman & R. McPhee (Eds.), *Message-attitude-behavior relationship.* New York: Academic Press.

O'Keefe, D., & Delia, J. (1980). Cognitive complexity and the relationship of attitudes and behavioral intentions. Unpublished manuscript, Department of Speech Communication, Pennsylvania State University.

Petronio, S. (1984). Communication strategies to reduce embarrassment. *Western Journal of Speech Communication, 48,* 28–38.

Petty, R., & Cacioppo, J. (1979). Effects of forewarning of persuasive intent and involvement on cognitive responses and persuasion. *Personality and Social Psychology Bulletin, 5,* 173–176.

Petty, R., & Cacioppo, J. (1981). *Attitudes and persuasion: Classic and contemporary approaches.* Dubuque, IA: W. C. Brown.

Reardon, K. (1981). *Persuasion: Theory and context.* Beverly Hills: Sage.

Reardon, K. (1984). Emotion and reason in persuasion. Paper presented to the Central States Speech Association, Chicago.

Reardon, K., & Boyd, B. R. (1985). Emotion and compliance in two types of relationships. Unpublished manuscript, University of Connecticut and Annenberg School of Communication.

Reardon, K., & Boyd, B. R. (1986). Emotion and cognitive complexity in compliance gaining. Paper presented to the International Communication Association, Chicago.

Reardon, K., & Buck, R. (1984). Emotion, reason and communication in coping with breast cancer. Paper presented to the International Communication Association, San Francisco.

Reiss, M., & Schlenker, B. (1977). Attitude change and responsibility avoidance as modes of dilemma resolution in forced-compliance situations. *Journal of Personality and Social Psychology, 35,* 21–30.

Roloff, M. (1976). Communication strategies, relationships, and relational change. In G. Miller (Ed.), *Explorations in interpersonal communication* (pp. 173–190). Beverly Hills: Sage.

Rorty, A. (1980). Explaining emotions. In A. Rorty (Ed.), *Explaining emotions.* Berkeley: University of California Press.

Schacter, S., & Singer, J. E. (1979). Comments on the Maslach and Marshall-Zimbardo experiments. *Journal of Personality and Social Psychology, 37,* 989–995.

Schenck-Hamlin, W., Wiseman, R. L., & Georgacarakos, G. N. (1982). A model of compliance-gaining strategies. *Communication Quarterly.*

Schlenker, B. (1980). *Impression management: The self-concept, social identity, and interpersonal relations.* Monterey, CA: Brooks/Cole.

Sherif, C., Sherif, M., & Nebergall, R. (1965). *Attitude and attitude change: The social judgement-involvement approach.* Philadelphia: Saunders.

Sherif, M. (1936). *The psychology of social norms.* New York: Harper & Row.

Smith, M. J. (1982). *Persuasion and human action.* Belmont, CA: Wadsworth.

Smith, M. J. (1984). Contingency rules theory, context and compliance behaviors. *Human Communication Research, 10,* 489–512.

Snyder, M., & Swann, W. (1976). When actions reflect attitudes: The politics of impression management. *Journal of Personality and Social Psychology, 34,* 1034–1042.

Solomon, R. (1980). Emotion and choice. In A. Rorty (Ed.), *Explaining emotions.* Berkeley: University of California Press.

Sullivan, C., & Reardon, K. (1985). Social support and health locus of control: discriminators of breast cancer coping style preference. In M. McLaughlin (Ed.), *Communication Yearbook 9.* Beverly Hills: Sage.

Tedeschi, J., Schlenker, B., & Bonoma, T. (1971). Cognitive dissonance: Private ratiocination or public spectacle? *American Psychologist, 26,* 685–695.

Wiseman, R. L., & Schenck-Hamlin, W. (1981). A multidimensional scaling validation of an inductively derived set of compliance-gaining strategies. *Communication Monographs, 48,* 251–270.

Chapter 8

Allen, G. A. (1979). *A sociology of friendship and kinship.* London: Allen & Unwin.

Altman, I., & Taylor, D. A. (1973). *Social penetration: The development of interpersonal relationships.* New York: Holt, Rinehart and Winston.

Andersen, P. A. (1985). Nonverbal immediacy in interpersonal communication. In Seigman & Feldstein (Eds.), *Nonverbal Behavior.* Lawrence Erlbaum.

Andersen, J. F., Andersen, P. A., & Jensen, A. D. (1979). The measurement of nonverbal immediacy. *Journal of Applied Communication Research, 7,* 153–180.

Argyle, M., & Furnham, A. (1983). Sources of satisfaction and conflict in long-term relationships. *Journal of Marriage and the Family, 45,* 481–493.

Argyle, M., & Henderson, M. (1984). The rules of friendship. *Journal of Social and Personal Relationships, 1,* 211–237.

Aries, E. (1976). Interaction patterns and themes of male, female and mixed groups. *Small Group Behavior, 7,* 7–18.

Baxter, L. A., & Wilmot, W. W. (1983). Communication characteristics of relationships with differential growth rates. *Communication Monographs, 50,* 264–272.

Berger, C. R. (1979). Beyond initial interaction: Uncertainty, understanding, and the development of interpersonal relationships. In H. Giles & R. St. Clair (Eds.), *Language and social psychology.* Oxford, England: Blackwell.

Berger, C. R., & Calabrese, R. J. (1975). Some explorations in initial interaction and beyond: Toward a developmental theory of interpersonal communication. *Human Communication Research, 1,* 99–112.

Berger, C. R., & Roloff, M. E. (1982). Thinking about friends and lovers: Social cognition and relational trajectories. In C. R. Berger & M. E. Roloff (Eds.), *Social Cognition and Communication* (pp. 151–192). Beverly Hills: Sage.

Berkman, L. S., & Syme, S. L. (1979). Social networks, host resistance, and morality: A nine-year follow-up study of Alameda County residents. *American Journal of Epidemiology, 109,* 186–204.

Berscheid, E. (1983). Emotion. In H. H. Kelley et al. (Eds.), *Close relationships* (pp. 110–168). New York: Freeman.

Berscheid, E., & Walster, G. (1974). Physical attractiveness. In L. Berkowitz (Ed.), *Advances in experimental social psychology* (Vol. 7, pp. 157–215). New York: Academic Press.

Bloom, B. L., Asher, S. J., & White, S. W. (1978). Marital disruption as a stressor: A review and analysis. *Psychological Bulletin, 85,* 867–894.

Broome, B. J. (1983). The attraction paradigm revisited: Response to dissimilar others. *Human Communication Research, 10,* 137–151.

Byrne, D. (1971). *The attraction paradigm.* New York: Academic Press.

Campbell, A., Converse, P. E., & Rogers, W. L. (1976). *The quality of American life.* New York: Russell Sage Foundation.

Courtright, J., Millar, F. E., & Rogers-Millar, L. E. (1979). Domineeringness and dominance: Replication and expansion. *Communication Monographs, 46,* 179–192.

Cummings, E., & Schneider, D. (1961). Sibling solidarity: A property of American kinship. *American Anthropologist, 63,* 498–507.

Dickson-Markman, F., & Shern, D. L. (1985). Social support and health in the elderly. Paper presented to the International Communication Association, Hawaii.

Dion, K. K., & Stein, S. (1978). Physical attractiveness and interpersonal influence. *Journal of Experimental Social Psychology, 14,* 97–108.

Duck, S. W. (1973). *Personal relationships and personal constructs: A study in friendship.* Chichester, England: Wiley.

Duck S. W. (1976). Interpersonal communication in developing acquaintance. In G. R. Miller (Ed.), *Explorations in interpersonal communication* (pp. 127–148). Beverly Hills: Sage.

Duck, S. W. (1982). A topography of relationship disengagement and dissolution. In S. W. Duck (Ed.), *Personal relationships 4: Dissolving personal relationships* (pp. 1–30). London: Academic Press.

Duck, S. W. (1985). Social and personal relationships. In M. L. Knapp & G. R. Miller (Eds.), *Handbook of interpersonal communication* (pp. 655–686). Beverly Hills: Sage.

Duck, S. W., & Sants, H. K. A. (1983). On the origin of the specious: Are personal relationships really interpersonal states? *Journal of Social and Clinical Psychology, 1,* 27–41.

Fitzpatrick, M. A. (1977). A typological approach to communication in relationships. In B. D. Ruben (Ed.), *Communication yearbook 1* (pp. 263–275). New Brunswick, NJ: Transaction Press.

Fitzpatrick, M. A., & Badzinski, D. M. (1985). All in the family: Communication in kin relationships. In M. L. Knapp & G. R. Miller (Eds.), *Handbook of interpersonal communication* (pp. 22, 687–736). Beverly Hills: Sage.

Fitzpatrick, M. A., & Best, P. (1979). Dyadic adjustment in traditional, independent and separate relationships: A validation study. *Communication Monographs, 46,* 167–178.

Fitzpatrick, M. A., & Indvik, J. (1982). The instrumental and expressive domains of marital communication. *Human Communication Research, 8,* 195–213.

Gerwirtz, J. L. (1972). *Attachment and dependency.* Washington, DC: Winston.

Goffman, E. (1959). *The presentation of self in everyday life.* New York: Doubleday.

Goldman, W., & Lewis, P. (1977). Beautiful is good: Evidence that the physically attractive are more socially skillful. *Journal of Experimental Social Psychology, 13,* 125–130.

Good, L. R., Good, K. C., & Nelson, D. A. (1973). Assumed similarity and perceived intrafamilial communication and understanding. *Psychological Reports, 32,* 3–11.

Hatkoff, S., & Lasswell, T. E. (1979). Male-female similarities and differences in conceptualizing love. In M. Cook & G. Wilson (Eds.), *Love and attraction: An international conference.* Oxford, England: Pergamon Press.

Heider, F. (1958). *The psychology of interpersonal relations.* New York: Wiley.

Hoffman, L. W., & Manis, J. D. (1978). Influences of children in marital interaction and parental satisfaction and dissatisfaction. In R. M. Lerner & G. B. Spanier (Eds.), *Child influences on marital and family interaction* (pp. 165–214). New York: Academic Press.

Ickes, W. K., & Barnes, R. D. (1977). The roles of sex and self-monitoring in unstructured dyadic interactions. *Journal of Personality and Social Psychology, 35,* 315–330.

Jones, E. & Davis, K. (1965). From acts to dispositions: The attribution process in person perception. In L. Berkowitz (Ed.), *Advances in experimental psychology* (pp. 220–226). New York: Academic Press.

Jourard, S. (1971). *The transparent self.* New York: Van Nostrand.

Kelley, H. H. (1972). Attribution in social interaction. In E. E. Jones et al. (Eds.), *Attribution: Perceiving the causes of behavior.* Morristown, NJ: General Learning Press.

Kelley, H. H. (1973). The process of causal attribution. *American Psychologist, 28,* 107–128.

Kelley, H. H. (1983). Love and commitment. In H. H. Kelley et al. (Eds.), *Close relationships* (pp. 265–314). New York: Freeman.

Kelley, H. H., & Thibaut, J. W. (1978). *Interpersonal relations: A theory of interdependence.* New York: Wiley.

Klinger, E. (1977). *Meaning and void: Inner experience and the incentives in people's lives.* Minneapolis: University of Minnesota Press.

Knapp, M. L. (1978). *Social intercourse: From greeting to goodbye.* Boston, MA: Allyn & Bacon.

Knapp, M. L., Ellis, D., & Williams, B. (1980). Perceptions of communication behavior associated with relationship terms. *Communication Monographs, 47,* 262–278.

Knudson, R. A., Sommers, A. A., & Golding, S. L. (1980). Interpersonal perception and mode of resolution in marital conflict. *Journal of Personality and Social Psychology, 38,* 251–263.

Lamb, M. E. (1976). *The role of the father in child development.* New York: Wiley.

Lee, J. A. (1973). *The colors of love: An exploration of the ways of loving.* Ontario: New Press.

Lewis, R. A., & Spanier, G. B. (1979). Theorizing about the quality and stability of marriage. In W. Burr, R. Hill, & I. R. Reiss (Eds.), *Contemporary theories about the family* (Vol. 1, pp. 268–294). New York: Free Press.

Linskold, S. (1982). *You and me: The why and how of interpersonal behavior.* Chicago: Nelson-Hall.

Luckey, E. B. (1966). Number of years married as related to personality perception and marital satisfaction. *Journal of Marriage and the Family, 28,* 44–48.

Luft, J. (1969). *Of human interaction.* Palo Alto, CA: Mayfield.

Lynch, J. J. (1977). *The broken heart: The medical consequences of loneliness.* New York: Basic Books.

Maderer, H., & Hill, R. (1983). Critical transitions over the family life span: Theory and research. *Marriage and Family Review, 6,* 39–60.

Marion, M. (1983). Child compliance: A review of the literature with implications for family life education. *Family Relations, 32,* 545–555.

Millar, F. E., & Rogers-Millar, E. (1976). A relational approach to interpersonal communication. In G. R. Miller (Ed)., *Explorations in interpersonal communication* (pp. 87–103). Beverly Hills: Sage.

Miller, A. G. (1970). Role of physical attractiveness in impression formation. *Psychonomic Science, 19,* 241–243.

Miller, G. R., & Steinberg, M. (1975). *Between people: A new analysis of interpersonal communication.* Chicago: Science Research Associates.

Mott, F. L., & Haurin, R. J. (1982). Being an only child. *Journal of Family Issues, 3,* 575–593.

Muser, K. T., Grau, B. W., Sussman, S., & Rosen, A. J. (1984). You're only as pretty as you feel: Facial expression as a determinant of physical attractiveness. *Journal of Personality and Social Psychology, 46,* 469–478.

Newcomb, T. (1961). *The acquaintance process.* New York: Holt, Rinehart and Winston.

Olson, D.H.L., & Cromwell, R. E. (1975). Power in families. In R. E. Cromwell &

D.H.L. Olsen (Eds.), *Power in families* (pp. 3–14). New York: Russell Sage Foundation.

Orvis, B. R., Kelley, H. H., & Butler, D. (1976). Attributional conflict in young couples. In J. H. Harvey, W. J. Ickes, & R. F. Kidd (Eds.), *New directions in attribution research* (Vol. 1, pp. 353–386). Hillsdale, NJ: Erlbaum.

Parke, R. D., & O'Leary, S. (1976). Family interaction in the newborn period: Some findings, some observations and some unresolved issues. In K. Riegel & J. Meacham (Eds.), *The developing individual in a changing world* (Vol. 2, pp. 653–666). The Hague: Mouton.

Parks, M. R., & Adelman, M. B. (1983). Communication networks and the development of romantic relationships: An expansion of uncertainty reduction theory. *Human Communication Research, 10,* 55–80.

Patel, C. (1984). A relaxation-centered behavioral package for reducing hypertension. In J. D. Matarazzo, S. M. Weiss, J. A. Herd, N. E. Miller, & S. M. Weiss (Eds.), *Behavioral health* (pp. 846–861). New York: Wiley.

Peplau, L. A., & Perlman, D. (Eds.) (1982). *Loneliness: A sourcebook of current theory, research and therapy.* New York: Wiley-Interscience.

Polonko, K., Scanzoni, J., & Teachman, J. (1982). Childlessness and marital satisfaction. *Journal of Family Issues, 3,* 545–573.

Rawlins, W. K. (1983). Negotiating close friendships: The dialectic of conjunctive freedoms. *Human Communication Review, 9,* 255–266.

Rollins, B. C., & Galligan, R. (1978). The developing child and marital satisfaction of parents. In R. M. Lerner & G. B. Spanier (Eds.), *Child influences on marital and family interaction: A life-span perspective* (pp. 71–106). New York: Academic Press.

Roloff, M. E. (1981). *Interpersonal communication: A social exchange approach.* Beverly Hills: Sage.

Roloff, M. E., & Berger, C. R. (1982). *Social cognition and communication.* Beverly Hills: Sage.

Scarr, S., & Grajek, S. (1982). Similarities and differences among siblings. In M. E. Lamb & B. Sutton-Smith (Eds.), *Sibling relationships: Their nature and significance across the life-span* (pp. 357–382). Hillsdale, NJ: Erlbaum.

Sillars, A. L. (1982). Attributions and communication: Are people "naive scientists" or just naive? In M. E. Roloff & C. R. Berger (Eds.), *Social cognition and communication* (pp. 73–106). Beverly Hills: Sage.

Sillars, A. L., Pike, G. R., Jones, T. S., & Murphy, M. A. (1984). Communication and understanding in marriage. *Human Communication Research, 10,* 317–350.

Sillars, A. L., & Scott, M. D. (1983). Interpersonal perception between intimates. *Human Communication Research, 10,* 153–176.

Snyder, M., & Campbell, B. (1980). Testing hypotheses about other people: The role of the hypothesis. *Personality and Social Psychology Bulletin, 6,* 421–426.

Snyder, M., & Cantor, N. (1979). Testing hypotheses about other people: The use of historical knowledge. *Journal of Experimental Social Psychology, 15,* 330–342.

Snyder, M., & Swann, W. B. (1978). Hypothesis-testing processes in social interaction. *Journal of Personality and Social Psychology, 36,* 1202–1212.

Strobe, W., Insko, C. A., Thompson, V. D., & Layton, B. D. (1971). Effects of physical attractiveness, attitude similarity, and sex on various aspects of interpersonal attraction. *Journal of Personality and Social Psychology, 18,* 79–91.

Thibaut, J. W., & Kelley, H. H. (1959). *The social psychology of groups*. New York: Wiley.

Thompson, S. C., & Kelley, H. H. (1981). Judgment of responsibility for activities in close relationships. *Journal of Personality and Social Psychology, 41,* 469–477.

Tsukada, G. K. (1979). Sibling interaction: A review of the literature. *Smith College Studies in Social Work, 3,* 229–247.

Zajonc, R. B., & Markus, G. B. (1975). Birth order and intellectual development. *Psychological Review, 82,* 74–88.

Chapter 9

Adler, K. (1977), Doctor-patient communication: A shift to problem-oriented research. *Human Communication Research, 3,* 179–190.

Almaney, A. J., & Alwan, A. J. (1982). *Communicating with the Arabs*. Prospect Heights, IL: Waveland Press.

Albrecht, S. L. (1983). Informal interaction patterns of professional women. In J. R. Gordon (Ed.), *A diagnostic approach to organizational behavior*. Boston: Allyn & Bacon.

Arnston, P., Droge, D., & Fassl, H. (1978). Pediatrician-parent communication: Final report. In B. S. Ruben (Ed.), *Communication yearbook 2* (pp. 502–522). New Brunswick: NJ: Transaction.

Baird, J. (1973). An analytic field study of "open communication" as perceived by superiors, subordinates and peers. Unpublished doctoral dissertation, Department of Communication, Purdue University.

Bales, R. F., & Strodtbeck, F. L. (1951). Phases in group problem-solving. *Journal of Abnormal and Social Psychology, 46,* 485–495.

Bandura, A. (1982). Self-efficacy mechanism in human agency. *American Psychologist, 37,* 122–147.

Barker, L. L., Cegala, D. J., Kibler, R. J., & Wahlers, K. J. (1979). *Groups in process: An introduction to small group communication*. Englewood Cliffs, NJ: Prentice-Hall.

Bartol, K. M., & Butterfield, D. A. (1976). Sex effects in evaluating leaders. *Journal of Applied Psychology, 61,* 446–454.

Beach, W. A. (1980). A reflexive analysis of conversational sequencing in group systems. Paper presented at the International Communication Association Convention, Acapulco.

Bennett, J. (1979). Overcoming the golden rule: Sympathy and empathy. In D. Nimmo (Ed.), *Communication yearbook 3*. New Bruswick, NJ: Transaction.

Benson, D. J., & Thompson, G. E. (1982). Sexual harassment on a university campus: The confluence of authority relations, sexual interest and gender stratification. *Social Problems, 29,* 236–251.

Best, J. A. (1980). Mass media, self-management and smoking modification. In P. O. Davidson & S. M. Davidson (Eds.), *Behavioral medicine: Changing health lifestyles*. New York: Bruner/Mazel.

Boster, F. J., Collofello, P. M., & Wigand, R. T. (1984). Mentoring, social interaction and commitment: An empirical analysis of a mentoring program. Paper presented at the International Communication Association, San Francisco.

Christopher, R. C. (1983). *The Japanese mind*. New York: Fawcett.

Collins, E. G. C. (1983). Managers and lovers. *Harvard Business Review*, Sept.–Oct., 142–153.

Cook, T. D., & Flay, B. R. (1978). In persistence of experimentally induced attitude change. In L. Berkowitz (Ed.), *Advances in experimental social psychology* (Vol. 11). New York: Academic Press.

Danaher, B., Berkanovic, E., & Gerber, B. (1982). Media-based quit smoking program. In *Final report: Community cancer control of Los Angeles.* Report to National Cancer Institute, Washington, D.C.

Deal, T. E., & Kennedy, A. A. (1982). *Corporate cultures: The rites and rituals of corporate life.* Reading, MA: Addison-Wesley.

Dewey, J. (1910). *How we think.* Lexington, MA: Heath.

Drescher, S., Burlingame, G., & Fuhriman, A. (1985). Cohesion: An odyssey in empirical understanding. *Small Group Behavior, 16,* 3–30.

Evans, N. J., & Jarvis, P. A. (1980). Group cohesion: A review and reevaluation. *Small Group Behavior, 11,* 359–370.

Fairhurst, G. T. (1985). Male-female communication on the job: Literature review and commentary. In M. McLaughlin (Ed.), *Communication yearbook 9.* Beverly Hills: Sage.

Falcione, R. L., McCroskey, J., & Daley, J. A. (1977). Job satisfaction as a function of employees' communication apprehension, self-esteem and perception of their immediate supervisors. In B. D. Ruben (Ed.), *Communication yearbook 1.* New Brunswick, NJ: Transaction.

Farace, R. V., Monge, P. R., & Russell, H. M. (1977). *Communicating and organizing.* Reading, MA: Addison-Wesley.

Farace, R. V., Taylor, J. A., & Stewart, J. P. (1978). Criteria for evaluation of organizational communication effectiveness: Review and synthesis. In B. D. Ruben (Ed.), *Communication yearbook 2.* New Brunswick, NJ: Transaction.

Fisher, B. A. (1970). Decision emergence: Phases in group decision making. *Speech Monographs, 37,* 53–66.

Fisher, B. A. (1985). Leadership as medium: Treating complexity in group communication research. *Small Group Behavior, 16,* 167–196.

Flay, B. R., & Sobel, J. L. (1983). The role of mass media in preventing adolescent substance abuse. In T. J. Glynn, C. G. Leukefeld, & J. P. Ludford (Eds.), *Preventing adolescent drug abuse.* Rockville, MD: National Institute on Drug Abuse. (Research monograph 47).

Gibb, C. A. (1969). Leadership. In G. Lindsey & E. Aronson (Eds.), *Handbook of social psychology* (Vol. 4, pp. 205–282). Reading, MA: Addison-Wesley.

Gudykunst, W. B., & Kim, Y. Y. (1984). *Communicating with strangers.* Beverly Hills: Sage.

Guetzkow, H. (1965). Communication in organizations. In J. G. March (Ed.), *Handbook of organizations* (pp. 534–573). Chicago: Rand McNally.

Haccoun, D. M., Haccoun, R. R., & Sallay, G. (1978). Sex differences in the appropriateness of supervising styles: A nonmanagement view. *Journal of Applied Psychology, 63,* 124–127.

Heise, D. R. (1975). *Causal analysis.* New York: Wiley.

Hirokawa, R. Y. (1981). Group communication and problem-solving effectiveness III: An investigation of group phases. Paper presented at the Speech Communication Association Convention, Anaheim, CA.

Hirokawa, R. Y., & Pace, R. (1983). A descriptive investigation of the possible communication-based reasons for effective and ineffective group decision making. *Communication Monographs, 50,* 363–379.

Horn, P. D., & Horn, J. C. (1982). *Sex in the office: Power and passion in the workplace.* Reading, MA: Addison-Wesley.

House, J. S. (1981). *Work stress and social support.* Reading, MA: Addison-Wesley.

Hudson-Jones, A. (1986). Dialogues with cancer patients: Leon Schwartzenberg's *Requiem pour la vie.* Paper presented at the University of South Florida Conference "Communicating with Patients" Tampa.

Jablin, F. M. (1978). Message-response and "openness" in superior-subordinate communication. In B. D. Ruben (Ed.), *Communication yearbook 2* (pp. 293–310). New Brunswick, NJ: Transaction.

Jablin, F. M. (1980a). Subordinate's sex and superior-subordinate status differentiation as moderators of the Pelz effect. In J. Nimmo (Ed.), *Communication yearbook 4* (pp. 349–356). New Brunswick, NJ: Transaction.

Jablin, F. M. (1980b). Superior's upward influence, satisfaction, and openness in superior-subordinate communication: A reexamination of the "Pelz Effect." *Human Communication Research, 6,* 210–220.

Jablin, F. M. (1982). Organizational communication: An assimilation approach. In M. E. Roloff & C. F. Berger (Eds.), *Social cognition and communication* (pp. 255–286). Beverly Hills: Sage.

Jones, S. E., Barnlund, D. C., & Haiman, F. S. (1980). *The dynamics of discussion: Communication in small groups.* New York: Harper & Row.

Kanter, R. M. (1977). *Men and women of the corporation.* New York: Basic Books.

Krueger, D. L. (1979). A stochastic analysis of communication development in self-analytic groups. *Human Communication Research, 5,* 314–324.

Maccoby, N., & Farquhar, J. W. (1975). Communication for health: Unselling heart disease. *Journal of Communication, 25,* 114–126.

Martin, J. (1981). Stories and scripts in organizational settings. In A. Hastorf & A. Isen (Eds.), *Cognitive social psychology* (pp. 225–305). New York: Elsevier-North Holland.

Martin, J., & Powers, M. (1979). If case examples provide no proof, why underutilize statistical information? Paper presented at meeting of the American Psychological Association, Honolulu.

Mayton, S. M., & Andersen, J. F. (1985). Help me if you can: Communicator characteristics of acceptable peer helpers. Paper presented at the International Communication Association Convention, Honolulu.

Miller, V. D., & Knapp, M. L. (1985). The post nuntio dilemma: Approaches to communicating with the dying. In M. L. McLaughlin (Ed.), *Communication yearbook 9* (pp. 723–738). Beverly Hills: Sage.

Monge, P. R., Edwards, J. A., & Kirste, K. K. (1978). The determination of communication and communication structure in large organizations: A review of research. In B. Ruben (Ed.), *Communication yearbook 2* (pp. 311–331). New Brunswick, NJ: Transaction.

Monge, P. R. (1982). Systems theory and research in the study of organizational communication: The correspondence problem. *Human Communication Research, 8,* 245–261.

Moreno, J. L. (1956). Sociometry and the science of man. Beacon, NY: Beacon House.

Nagel, E. (1961). *The structure of science.* New York: Harcourt Brace Jovanovich.

Nieva, V. F., & Gutek, B. A. (1981). *Women and work: A psychological perspective.* New York: Praeger.

Northouse, P. G. (1986). Communication and cancer: Issues confronting patients, health professionals and family members. Paper presented at the University of South Florida Conference "Communicating with Patients," Tampa.

Patel, C. (1984). A relaxation-centered behavioral package for reducing hypertension. In J. D. Matarazzo, S. M. Weiss, J. A. Herd, N. E. Miller & S. M. Weiss (Eds.), *Behavioral health* (pp. 846–861). New York: Wiley.

Pelz, D. (1952). Influence: A key to effective leadership in the first line supervisor. *Personnel, 29*, 209–217.

Peters-Golden, H. (1982). Breast cancer: Varied perceptions of social support in the illness experience. *Social Issues Medicine, 16*, 483–491.

Pettigrew, L. S., & Thomas, R. C. (1978). Communicator style differences in formal vs. informal therapeutic relationships. In B. D. Ruben (Ed.), *Communication yearbook 2* (pp. 523–538). New Brunswick, NJ: Transaction.

Poole, M. S. (1981). Decision development in small groups I: A comparison of two models. *Communication Monographs, 48*, 1–24.

Poole, M. S. (1983a). Decision development in small groups II: A study of multiple sequences in decision making. *Communication Monographs, 50*, 206–232.

Poole, M. S. (1983b). Decision development in small groups III: A multiple sequence model of group decision development. *Communication Monographs, 50*, 321–341.

Quinn, R. E. (1977). Coping with cupid: The formation of romantic relationships in organizations. *Administrative Science Quarterly, 22*, 30–45.

Reardon, K. K. (1985). Gift giving around the world. Palo Alto, CA: Passepartout Travel Publishers.

Reardon, K. K., & Buck, R. (1984). Emotion, reason and communication in coping with breast cancer. Paper presented at the International Communication Association Convention, San Francisco.

Reardon, K. K., & Fairhurst, G. T. (1981). Specification of the concept "rule": A case study with the military. Unpublished manuscript, University of Connecticut and University of Cincinnati.

Rice, R. (1979). Investigations into validity and reliability of NEGOPY, a computer program for communication network analysis. Paper presented at the International Communication Association Convention, Philadelphia.

Richardson, J. L., Anderson, J., Selser, J., Evans, L. A., Kishbaugh, E., & Lavine, A. M. (1983). Compliance with chemotherapy: Theoretical basis and intervention design. In C. Mettlin (Ed.), *Progress in cancer control IV: Research in the cancer center* (pp. 379–390). New York: Alan R. Liss.

Richmond, V. P., McCroskey, J. C., & Davis, L. M. (1982). Individual differences among employees, management communication styles, and employee satisfaction: Replication and extension. *Human Communication Research, 8*, 170–188.

Roberts, K., & O'Reilly, C. (1978). Organizations as communication structures: An empirical approach. *Human Communication Research, 4*, 283–293.

Rodgers, W. (1969). Think: A biography of the Watsons and IBM. New York: Stein & Day.

Rogers, E. M., & Kincaid, D. C. (1981). *Communication networks: Toward a new paradigm for research*. New York: Free Press.

Sharf, B. F. (1986). Communication skills development as patient education. Paper presented at the University of South Florida Conference "Communicating with Patients," Tampa.

Schunk, D. H., & Carbonari, J. P. (1984). Self-efficacy models. In J. D. Matarazzo, S. M. Weiss, J. A. Herd, N. E. Miller, & S. M. Weiss (Eds.), *Behavioral health* (pp. 230–247). New York: Wiley.

Segal, D. (1985). Interpersonal relationships in the context of cancer: A communication perspective. Paper presented at the International Communication Association Convention, Honolulu.

Simkin, P. (1983). The birth plan: Vehicle for trust and communication. *Birth, 10,* 184–185.

Stohl, C. (1986). Quality circles and changing patterns of communication. In M. L. McLaughlin (Ed.), *Communication yearbook, 9* (pp. 511–532). Beverly Hills: Sage.

Thompson, T. L. (1982a). "You can't play marbles—you have a wooden hand": Communication with the handicapped. *Communication Quarterly, 30,* 108–115.

Thompson, T. L. (1982b). The development of listener-adapted communication in physically handicapped children: A cross-stiuational study. *Western Journal of Speech Communication, 46,* 32–44.

Tuckman, B. W. (1965). Developmental sequences in small groups. *Psychological Bulletin, 63,* 384–399.

Wilkins, A. (1978). Organizational stories as an expression of management philosophy: Implications for social control in organizations. Unpublished doctoral dissertation, Stanford University, Stanford, CA.

Williams, M. L., & Meredith, V. (1984). Physician-expectant mother communication: An analysis of information uncertainty. *Communication Research Reports, 1,* 110–116.

Name Index

Subject Index